MY INFANT

Other Books in the Minirth Meier New Life Clinic Series

For general information about Minirth Meier New Life Clinic branch offices, counseling services, educational resources, and hospital programs, call toll-free 1–800-NEW-LIFE.

MY INFANT

OFF TO
A GOOD
START

Dr. Paul Warren

A
JANET
THOMA
BOOK

THOMAS NELSON PUBLISHERS
Nashville • Atlanta • London • Vancouver

Published in Nashville, Tennessee, by Thomas Nelson, Inc., Publishers, and distributed in Canada by Word Communications, Ltd., Richmond, British Columbia.

The Bible version used in this publication is THE NEW KING JAMES VERSION. Copyright © 1979, 1980, 1982, 1990 Thomas Nelson, Inc., Publishers.

Anecdotes and case histories included in this volume are either hypothetical examples or composites of actual cases with names and details changed to protect identities.

Library of Congress Cataloging-in-Publication Data

Warren, Paul, 1949–
    My infant : off to a good start / Paul Warren.
        p.   cm. — (The stepping-stones series for Christian parents)
    ISBN 0-7852-8349-8
    1. Infants. 2. Child rearing. 3. Parenting—Religious aspects—
Christianity. I. Title. II. Series.
HQ774.W37 1994
649′.122—dc20   94–33806
                                                                    CIP

Printed in the United States of America.
1 2 3 4 5 6 — 99 98 97 96 95 94

For my wife, Vicky,
whose love of children
reminds me of God's love for children,
and to my son, Matthew,
whose love teaches and encourages me.

CONTENTS

When the first baby laughed for the first time,
the laugh broke into a thousand pieces
and they all went skipping about,
and that was the beginning of fairies.

SIR JAMES MATTHEW BARRIE, *Peter Pan*

ACKNOWLEDGMENTS

The author acknowledges the vision and direction of Janet Thoma, vice president of Thomas Nelson Publishers. Sandy Dengler's creativity made the manuscript come alive. Amy Glass's and Sue Ann Jones's careful editing kept the manuscript crisp and clear.

1. WINDOWS OF OPPORTUNITY

THE CRUCIAL EARLY YEARS

Bye Baby Bunting,
Daddy's gone a-hunting,
To fetch a little rabbit skin,
To wrap our Baby Bunting in.

TRADITIONAL ENGLISH NURSERY RHYME

Linda Mayron scowled when she stooped to peer into her mailbox and saw the letter. From the Lakeridge School District, it was addressed "To the parents of Daniel Mayron." She leaned against the mailbox and closed her eyes. *When will this all go away? When will it stop?* She sighed, fished out the letter, and tore open the envelope. Inside, she read:

> Dear Mr. and Mrs. Mayron:
> I regret to inform you that I have seen Daniel in my office three times this week. I would like to meet with you at your earliest convenience to discuss his behavior and academic standing.
> Please call my office for an appointment.
>
> Sincerely,
> Gerald Williams, assistant principal
> Lakeridge Middle School

What's wrong with Daniel? He's always in some sort of trouble. Daniel had been a challenge from the moment he was born. No, make that from before he was born. Linda still remembered the indigestion and the kicks he gave her during her last trimester more than twelve years ago.

Where did we go wrong? Jessica, the Mayrons' other, older child, was never this difficult. Jessica met life with sturdy resolution. Daniel defied it. Jessica really, truly tried to cooperate. But Daniel? Get real!

Linda stuffed the letter back in the envelope and collected the rest of the mail. *Summoned to the principal's office? Ridiculous! And this is only the second week of school! Alan isn't going to like this. He warned Daniel just last week.* Linda remembered the conversation . . .

"Daniel, it's make-or-break time now. You're not a kid anymore; you're a young man. We aren't going to take any more of this slacking off. This year you've got to buckle down, or we start looking into military schools."

Linda shuddered at the very thought of military school. Farming Daniel off to some rigid institution was downright cruel, not to mention what it said about their parenting skills. *There has to be another way. There has to!*

How to Stop Trouble Twelve Years Before It Starts

There *was* another way for the Mayron family, but it would take a great deal of time and effort. Much of that effort could have been minimized or possibly avoided outright had Daniel's parents possessed better knowledge about Daniel when he first came into their family. Daniel's problems grew out of a long history rooted in the time he was born some twelve years ago.

Most child psychologists agree that what children learn in their first three years of life profoundly affects their behavior and development patterns for the rest of their lives. I personally feel the first three years constitute the most critical period of a person's entire life. The misty pre-form of later positive attributes—staying power, love and affection, generosity, flexibility—hovers in the play of the tiniest child. Similarly, many of my patients' difficulties, like Daniel Mayron's, can be traced back to this time period.

And it is in this period, the first three years of life, that a child's developmental needs are met primarily through an informal education system—the family unit—over which we, as child-development professionals, have very little influence. You are your child's first and by far most influential teacher. Your home is your child's first and by far most influential learning environment. What you do now with your babies will profoundly shape what they will be able to learn and do through most of the rest of their lives. In a sentence: This is the time when the most benefit can be gained and the most damage can be done.

Youngsters who enter counseling in their early teens are not exactly set in cement, but close to it. Furthermore, they have been greatly altered, for better or worse, by the formal education system—the public or private schools. High school—even grade school—is long past the time when children's attitudes about themselves and about the world have become firmly established.

Gerald Williams, Daniel Mayron's school principal, discussed that very thing with Linda Mayron as their meeting began.

"Daniel isn't weird or terrible," Mr. Williams explained. "In fact, he's all too typical of the children our schools are called upon to educate today. I'd go so far as to say our schools are inundated with what we call 'special-needs' children. These are the kids, like Daniel, who have no identifiable genetic problem—"

"You mean like Down syndrome or something?"

"Exactly. Special-needs kids require extra help in certain subjects. Often, they need help learning acceptable, positive behaviors. The problem is, our formal education system doesn't have the resources to meet these needs—not enough personnel, not enough money, and in many cases, not enough understanding of how the child's needs specifically can be met."

But there is another problem, and that is the problem neither the schools nor I, as a pediatric counselor, can address at its source. During this most crucial period in a child's development, the child's informal education system enjoys very little outside intervention and virtually no support.

You see, until very recently, society almost totally discounted this period of a child's development. Since very small children do not achieve measurable results, such as grades, in an easily identifiable skill—learning to read or write or participate in formal sports, for example—the prevailing wisdom claimed that they were accomplishing little of significance. Kids, they figured, pretty much vegetated until they started school.

Nothing could be farther from the truth. In those first three years, the seemingly random play and interaction between an infant or toddler and the primary caregiver and others—the halo of older people around that little person's head—will establish whether the child trusts any other human being or ultimately, God. The child will figure out how to cope with adversity, how to react emotionally, how to solve a problem, and how to work through feelings in order to understand life. The child will not master all these things, but he or she will learn how to begin the process. The child will learn what the body does and, to an extent, what he or she can and cannot manipulate about the world.

What crucial lessons these are! They form the foundation upon which every other developmental experience in a child's entire life will be built.

If its foundation is weak, a building eventually crumples. If it's strong, the building stands for years. The foundation you lay for your child at ages zero to three, if solid, will allay many of the problems that otherwise will irritate and separate you eight to twelve years later. And that is exactly what this book is all about. In this book I want to help you by providing the strategies you need to build a strong foundation for your child so he or she can learn from the very beginning to cope and to love well in the world.

Taking Advantage of the Windows of Opportunity

"Coping and loving . . . ," Gerald Williams said as he sat back in his overstuffed chair. "Your Daniel, Mrs. Mayron, has developed some interesting coping mechanisms."

Linda wrinkled her nose. "And what is that a euphemism for?"

The principal grinned. "You're right; it *is* a euphemism. Daniel can't think well in a linear manner, and he can't memorize well in the same ways most children do. So he compensates for his lack of these skills by drawing attention away from them with disruptive behavior."

"Sounds pretty sneaky and sophisticated." Linda wasn't sure she wanted to be sitting here listening to all this. As much as she dreaded this conference, though, she had to admit she felt comfortable with the school principal. He reminded her vaguely of her Uncle Don, a jolly, overweight, avuncular fellow with a balding head and graying moustache.

"Not at all, at least not at a conscious level. This has all been going on deep down inside Daniel, below his conscious thought, for many years. It's how, when he was very, very young, Daniel figured out he could get through life. He needed attention and affection—every child does—and he developed this way of obtaining it."

"Affection? He gets just the opposite! His father is fed up with his bad behavior."

"Negative attention and positive attention are both

attention. Again, I emphasize that none of this occurred at a conscious, reasoning level. Kids don't develop good abstract thinking until school age or later. I might add, the way they build good abstract thinking depends in large part on the way they learn to think concretely, and that happens from birth on."

"Abstract . . . concrete . . . ?"

Mr. Williams pursed his lips a moment in thought. Linda noticed that his rather large lips seemed to drag his pudgy cheeks around with them as they moved. "With abstract thinking, I watch Big Bird move around a TV sound stage, and I know there's a human actor inside that big yellow costume making the bird walk and talk. With concrete thinking, I see a big yellow bird there flopping around, and nothing else. A twelve-year-old understands the abstraction that it's a puppet. A three-year-old can watch a human actor climb into the suit, but the moment the suit is zipped up and the head goes on, the child cannot grasp that it's really a person inside, even though the child saw the person get in. Small children believe only what they see as they are seeing it."

"I think I understand. And all that starts at birth? So how do you remedy what's missing?"

"In some ways you can. In other ways you cannot. I'd compare the beginning of a child's life to the brief window of time that occurs during a trapeze performance. There's the flyer and the catcher. The catcher swings from one trapeze and the flyer from the other. The flyer has to wait until both trapezes are swinging exactly right before he turns loose of his bar and takes off through the air. If his timing is the least bit off, the catcher misses him."

"Oh, my yes!" Linda smiled. "You know, I never really appreciated how exact their timing is until I watched a video of an old, old movie. Gina Lollabrigida and Burt Lancaster and Tony Curtis—I forget the name of the movie. It was about the first person to do a quadruple somersault between the trapezes; you know, four complete revolutions before the other fellow caught him. There's no second chance. Either he's caught or he falls."

"Exactly. There are certain developmental tasks a child must complete at a particular time or those tasks will be much more difficult. If these tasks aren't mastered we can compensate in part but not totally."

Windows of opportunity. Only a brief window of time exists during which the trapeze flyer releases his bar, performs his daring tricks in midair, and grabs his catcher. Likewise, a brief window of time exists in which a tiny child learns to love and trust without reservation. How do you make certain your child takes advantage of those limited opportunities as thoroughly as possible?

Part of your parenting prowess comes from instinct, programmed into you by God at birth. That instinct, the skeleton of your skills, must be given flesh and breath through learning. You learn in two ways: by example and observation, and from teachers, of which this book is one.

For instance, showing your child the depth of your love is an instinctive yearning. How well you accomplish that demonstration of love depends on what you learned from your parents' example about demonstrating love. Yet, if your parents were woefully deficient in this regard, you can still learn during adulthood in time to pass that gift on to your children. You can learn to be a better, more effective parent by watching and listening to other parents and to child-development professionals.

Because these windows of opportunity are narrow, I want to focus my advice on parents who are just starting out, who are best positioned to exploit the earliest windows. These books, called the Stepping-Stones Series, are organized to coincide with the specific years of development:

- *My Infant: Off to a Good Start*
- *My Toddler: The Beginning of Independence*
- *My Preschooler: Ready for New Adventures*

On the way to work the other day I passed a billboard with a profound message:

PARENTING BEGINS FROM THE MOMENT YOU DISCOVER YOU'RE PREGNANT.

You have two crucial opportunities in this first year. First, you must help your child learn to trust well and fully, and second, the child must learn not to fear abandonment. All the little day-to-day hassles and joys of parenthood should be focused on those two opportunities.

I believe the first window of opportunity opens, not at birth, but when you first learn you're about to have or adopt a baby. We'll talk about that opportunity first.

2. THE WINDOW OPENS

PREBIRTH AND PLANNING

You are the bows from which
your children as living
arrows are sent forth.

KAHLIL GIBRAN, *On Children*

T om Jasper almost whispered, so nervous was he. "Hon, I've got it ready." He felt like a chemist about to discover a cure for the common cold . . . like a scientist preparing to unleash an atom. He'd bought this in-home pregnancy test the moment his wife Marsha mentioned she quite possibly might be pregnant. They had both yearned for a child for more than five years. That yearning had translated into an uphill battle all the way. Fertility tests, scheduled intimacy, the whole bit. It was getting more than a tad too clinical for Tom's preference. Just when they almost gave up, Marsha missed a period. Maybe . . .

She shuffled into the bathroom with her raven hair all tousled, her fleece bathrobe slightly agape. To Tom's eye, she looked too delicate and slight of build to be a mother. And, oh, how he loved her. He wrapped an arm across her shoulder. They watched together.

The dot turned telltale red.

Yes!

"We're pregnant!" Tom whooped gleefully. He paused to look into Marsha's chocolate-brown doe eyes, and he saw what must have been mirrored in his own: joy . . . and fear.

What now?

Cracking the Window of Opportunity

What now, indeed? A small number of words, a big question. There was no turning back for Tom and Marsha now. With God's will, they would soon have a new family member. From this day forward, nothing would ever be the same. Change had begun for the Jaspers. And the window had already opened for this new life.

Their parenthood already begun, there is much they might do in advance of the child's arrival to make parenting smoother and easier a decade down the road. These are lessons that, had the Mayrons learned them, might have saved Daniel and his folks considerable grief. From the first indication of pregnancy to the moment the child draws that first breath, a lot goes on that will shape him or her for life. One of the earliest factors is attitude.

Attitude

Someone's always taking surveys. A few of the worthier surveys are written up in reputable journals; most end up in section D of the Sunday paper. This one fell somewhere in between. Surveyors interviewed the parents of a number of happy kids and a number of kids in difficulty. They concentrated on prenatal attitudes: What did Mom and Dad think about the baby before it arrived? Predictably, the parents of the well-positioned kids loved them and wanted them *before* they were born. Most critical was the father's attitude. Did he want the child and look forward to being Daddy? The second most critical factor was the mother's attitude toward her unborn child. A healthy, positive, eager attitude before the child's birth did much for making the child feel loved from the very start.

Everyone assumes that prenatal attitudes are a strong indicator of what postnatal parenting skills will be like. Parents who don't want their children or who resent them are not going to tackle the difficult, long-term job of good parenting with much initiative. But it goes far, far deeper than that.

Can the unborn baby sense being loved and wanted? Do children still in the womb know whether they are loved and desired? A variety of interesting studies and experiments indicate that they do indeed.

Your child knows before birth how you feel about him or her. From conception on, your attitude counts. This is not to say that a child who is unwanted, feared, or resented before birth is doomed to a miserable life. Hardly. Children can persevere in the face of such rejection and come out pretty good, but it's the exceptional child who can do well. The child's best situation is when poor parental attitudes change for the better, salvaging the day. And change they can. These factors, then, help a child get a vibrant, healthy start in life.

Desire

When birth control and family planning became a practical reality in the United States, the Planned Parenthood groups' motto was "Every child a wanted child." It was a lovely thought. Unfortunately, we have arrived nowhere near that point. Much storm and furor churns around the way a family ought to be planned, if at all. I leave those arguments to others.

When the Planned Parenthood groups coined their motto, they meant to say that only those parents who want children ought to have children. But that motto can be read two ways. Let's read its other meaning: Help every child who has been conceived be wanted. In contrast to all the energy poured into family-planning methods, almost no effort is being put into the other half of the equation: helping reluctant parents shift their attitudes. And that's where a strong, positive difference can be made.

Consider the case of Jenny Lawton. Jenny was six when her parents divorced. Her mother remarried when Jenny entered third grade. By the time she reached fifth grade, Jenny's nickname was "Fatsy." In the seventh grade, though, Jenny began to turn her life around. She developed poise, better study habits, and a healthier attitude toward herself. She lost thirty pounds over the next three years. Suddenly, for the first time ever, Jenny Lawton found herself popular.

When Jenny became sexually active in the ninth grade, she was on her own, left hanging out in the breeze without support. Her father had pretty much ceased contact years ago. Her stepfather never thought to discuss sexuality with her because he didn't believe it was his responsibility. That, he pointed out, was the mother's job. Her mother didn't talk about it in part because she didn't know what to say and in part because she was embarrassed to say it. Besides, Jenny was still a little girl. There was plenty of time, the mother assured herself.

In her sophomore year, Jenny learned in school about condoms and the danger of pregnancy and disease. That was all very good, but it didn't really apply to her at the moment.

Jenny entered her junior year pregnant.

Jenny was now faced with decisions mature women find difficult, and she was still essentially a child. Adults she respected urged her to give up the baby for adoption. Other adults, equally respected, counseled abortion. Her girlfriends, most of them not sexually active, offered all sorts of advice.

She sat her boyfriend down and forced him to talk about what he wanted and how he felt. She did not tell him what she wanted. Once he opened up (and that took some doing), revealing his inner needs and feelings, she saw the picture clearly, and she made her decision.

She would bear her baby and raise it. She would do this without any guarantee that her boyfriend would ever take an active fathering role.

Jenny's unborn baby posed severe restrictions on her education, her social life, her adolescence, her relationship with her parents and stepfather—all aspects of her being. She had every reason in the world to not desire the child. Yet she actively chose to want her baby. She even wrote it down as a pledge, signed, and dated it. Days of fear, resentment, dislike, annoyance, perhaps even hatred loomed in her future. Knowing those days were coming was part of her defense against them. That signed pledge was part of it too. Her desire for her child was the most important part. From that moment on, her child was a wanted child.

Expectations

Linda Mayron had no such moral and emotional baggage to deal with. She looked forward eagerly to the birth of Daniel. Her first baby, Jessica, had been a breeze— no major problems, no major frictions. Linda and Alan, obviously, were well suited to raising good babies. This next one was sure to be a snap. After all, besides being naturally good at parenting, Linda and Alan had all that excellent experience their first baby had provided them.

Uh-huh.

Basing expectations on children that came before leads nowhere but down. No two children in a family are ever alike. They share similarities, certainly. But they'll not grow up the same or respond in the same ways to life. They fulfill different roles in the family structure, and they are not genetically identical by any means. In fact, even identical twins differ in some regards.

For example, I know of a set of triplets, genetically identical boys, who look exactly alike. But they act differently. One is very good at left-brain stuff—math, science, logic, linear thinking. The second shines in right-brain ways—creativity, global thinking, emotional understanding, empathy. Where did that leave the third? He developed an intriguing mix of his brothers' attributes that was his alone. Combining creativity and warmth with cold logic, he writes understandable technical manuals for a computer firm. They're actually fun to read. He teaches shop and special-ed courses at a vocational school. He also creates sculptures, beautiful pieces designed and made with welding rods.

The fact that all children differ comes as a blessing to parents whose first child is delicate or difficult. It holds out the tantalizing hope that the next one will be easier.

However, the best attitude, I believe, is to muffle expectations altogether. There is no way of knowing in advance what a child will be like. The only guarantee is that your child will differ from every other.

Jenny had no expectations. That put her way ahead of Linda. Linda would find herself repeatedly frustrated when Daniel failed to meet the pre-formed expectations that came from her experience with Jessica. Linda's husband, Alan, had adjusted to fathering a compliant little girl; he was nowhere near prepared to love and discipline a child who was opposite Jessica in many regards. Expectations are just as hard on a father as on a mother.

Enthusiasm

Linda developed a dandy head of enthusiasm as birthing neared. Alan approached the baby's arrival with a sort of blasé attitude. He was the money-earner, not the overeager doter. He didn't intend to change diapers; he certainly had not done so with Jessica. This illustrates another aspect of expectations to be avoided: "What I did with the first kid is what I should be doing with the next."

In contrast, Jenny dreaded the birth. Even when she was as big as a hippo, she was still able to get out and around. She knew as soon as the baby came, she'd be staked down like a tent. Her enthusiasm for motherhood was tempered by the cold reality that she would struggle long and hard.

Parents who are enthusiastic about parenthood, by and large, will have the most fun with their kids throughout the years to come. But that's only half of the equation. Parents who are enthusiastic about parenthood will have happier, better-attached kids right from the very first moment.

As important as attitude is, it's only one aspect of approaching parenthood. Preparation goes hand in hand with attitude.

Preparing for the Birth

"Childbirth classes? Are you kidding?" Jenny's boyfriend, Darren, looked unconvinced when she approached him after school. "I'm not sure I want anything to do with this."

"You already have everything to do with this. Come on, Dare. It'll be fun, and you might even learn something."

Education these days is a crucial part of preparation for parenthood. I've always been a strong advocate of fathers as well as mothers participating fully throughout the prenatal and birthing period. That means joint attendance at doctor's appointments and birthing classes.

Doctor's Appointments

"Oh, come on! Not the doctor's appointments too!" Tom Jasper had always thought mommies did that on their own.

Yes, doctor's appointments. Two reasons: One is that the more active the father's role from the very beginning, the easier and more pleasant it will be for him to take on the daddy's role. The other is that he and his wife are supporting each other in this project. This is one of the facets of that support. He should know firsthand how the project is coming along. The doctor does not just thump on the melon and declare how close it is to being ripe. Doctor's appointments are also a time of parental education when the physician discusses the medical and physical needs of Mommy and the preborn.

Jenny had a good idea when she invited Darren along to the childbirth classes. They, too, are powerful educational tools for good parenting.

Birthing Classes

It's encouraging to see the number of health insurance companies and birthing clinics that now make such classes mandatory for both parents, although some parents-to-be still resist the idea. I know I did when my wife, Vicky, was pregnant with our son, Matthew. I was a doctor. I knew all about this sort of thing. I was *trained*.

What I was trained for, however, was to be a technician.

Nurses, doctors, and paramedical practitioners all know about the physiological process of becoming a parent. Birthing classes cover that to an extent, yes. Far more importantly, though, they serve as a foundational course for the practical, emotional aspects of parenting. No amount of medical training prepares a person for that. And in the long run, that is far more important than technical skill.

Birthing classes have evolved greatly over the years. At first they consisted of little more than "the baby comes out here." Parents, the professionals figured, didn't have to know much more than that. Doctors and nurses did the work of delivering the baby aided by all manner of drugs and accoutrements. The mother was pretty much an intrusion and inconvenience. In fact, goes the standard adage, if the doctors could have dispensed with the mother altogether, they would have.

As natural childbirth regained the ground it lost in the twenties, thirties, and forties, classes prepared mothers (just the mothers, by and large) for the various natural childbirth methods. These days, instead of focusing primarily on the birth process itself, many curricula have added practical parenting advice for both new mommies and new daddies.

Birthing classes serve another extremely important function. They are the best arena for new parents to enjoy the mutual support of others in the same situation. This is especially valuable for fathers-to-be, the parents who actually were dispensed with during the first half of the century. You're certainly familiar with the hackneyed stereotype of the expectant father pacing the waiting room and perusing outdated *Field and Stream* magazines while the mother does the actual deed elsewhere. (Once the baby arrived, the hospital generously allowed Daddy to look at his child through a layer of plate glass while they prepared the bill. He wouldn't get to see or touch the infant for the next three days. Thank heaven those days are behind us.)

I recommend that fathers attend the birthing classes even on those occasions when their wives can't. Parenthood in some regards is even more wrenching for Dad than for Mom, and Dad generally lacks support from the system. Until recently, he was the one on the outside looking in; society gave him a vital role to fill and nary a clue as to how to fill it. Today's classes, to an extent at least, redress that error.

The birthing class Jenny dragged Darren to proved to be a lot more interesting—and certainly a lot more fun—than what he'd expected. He felt pretty uncomfortable at first, a seventeen-year-old in a sea of fully mature males. Then the joking and the exercises loosened everyone up and he grew more at ease. He learned to his surprise that although he was not as sophisticated as these other men (not even as sophisticated as he thought he was), they were every bit as nervous as he was. These other guys knew no more about their approaching parenthood than he did. That, too, was a benefit of birthing classes; Darren no longer felt like the only stupid dimbulb in the parenting universe. The baby's arrival didn't scare him nearly as much anymore when he learned that Tom Jasper, age twenty-nine, was just as ignorant.

Birthing classes are not the whole of parental preparation; they are but the beginning. There are a lot of just plain mundane logistics to take care of in advance of the baby's arrival.

Physical Preparation

I can't think of any better way to let a fetus feel wanted than by taking care of his or her needs through a healthy body. That task does not fall solely on the shoulders of the expectant mother.

As soon as Tom and Marsha had confirmed their news with a doctor's appointment, Marsha was inundated with nutritional advice. Tom and Marsha always thought they ate fairly sensibly, but soon they began to rethink some of their eating patterns.

For example, there are breakfast persons and there are forget-breakfast persons. Marsha was not a breakfast person; she preferred to sleep the extra half hour rather than fix a meal for herself. Two hours later, at her desk, she could stomach a breakfast bar.

Three months into Marsha's pregnancy, that stopped. She woke up extremely nauseated—a horrible way to start any day. "Low blood sugar," warned her obstetrician. "Eat small bits of protein through the night and first thing in the morning," he advised.

Soon, Marsha was heeding that nutritional advice and feeling better. Tom, her built-in support group, helped her find an eating regimen that worked, even if he was a bit too fanatical. Eggs Benedict at 7 A.M. on a Monday morning was too much for Marsha, but a banana at seven and a cup of yogurt at nine went down all right. Tom did the food shopping (the thought of it was nauseating to her sometimes) and even learned to temper his zealousness with compassion. He became her silent supporter when he learned that his nagging upset her.

(Note to daddies: Encourage her, coach her, support her, but never, *never* nag or bully. And above all, no patronizing.)

I do want to reinforce the idea, however, that if you physically prepare for your upcoming birth, you will make the most of this initial window of opportunity to serve psychological and emotional purposes in two ways. A body that nourishes a fetus helps it develop into a healthy and happy child. Also, well-nourished parents enter into the joy of parenthood with greater élan.

Figure 1.1 on the next page lists some ways expectant parents can physically prepare for birth. I haven't gone into much detail because there are scads of detailed advice on the bookshelves that already do an excellent job of this.

What Dads Can Do

Tom Jasper was an active participant. He took over the cooking when the smell of anything turned Marsha's stomach. And he started doing more around the house—actual preparation for what would follow when the baby was born. From the neighbor down the street, Tom learned something he would never have thought of himself.

WAYS TO PHYSICALLY PREPARE
FOR GIVING BIRTH

- Avoid smoking, drinking alcohol, and taking over-the-counter drugs (except under the direction of your physician). Also, stay away from smokers and secondhand smoke. Just one little drink? Not even one little drink is recommended. There is no minimal safe amount of alcohol or drugs.

- Avoid hazardous conditions, especially chemical fumes (fresh paint is one example). Recent studies indicate that when a mother breathes airborne particles containing lead paint while in the last trimester of pregnancy, the child may experience learning disabilities later. In the first trimester, certain paint fumes and paint-remover fumes can trigger miscarriage.

- Eat well-balanced, nutritional foods. Avoid foods that are high in fat or sugar. Fill up on low-fat protein snacks.

- Drink lots of water, a minimum of eight glasses a day.

- Exercise regularly under the advice of your doctor. A consistent walking regimen is perfect.

- Get plenty of rest. It's natural for you to feel tired. Making a baby is hard work.

- Make plans for what will happen after the baby arrives. Buy the needed layette items, outfit the nursery, pick out names. Now's the time to think of something fun. For instance, friends of mine, both fisheries biologists, gave their unborn baby's room a fish theme.

- Enroll in birthing classes and consider taking a first aid class on infant CPR and choking, so you'll feel better prepared in case of an emergency.

- Expectant fathers should participate just as actively as mothers. *The Father Book,* which I co-authored with Dr. Frank Minirth and Dr. Brian Newman (Thomas Nelson, 1992), offers some ideas for a father's active involvement.

FIGURE 1.1

"You'll be shocked at how tired your wife is," the neighbor, Roy, told him. "This is our third, so I know. Amy gets completely drained from the lack of sleep and the nursing. Totally worn out. I have to do everything I can to help her with the work—otherwise she'd drop from exhaustion."

An added bonus to your helping your wife now while she is pregnant, as well as after the baby arrives, is that you are giving your child a healthy and happy mother (another boost to your child's three-year window of opportunity). As a result Mom is more emotionally able to look forward to this birth and to accept this baby when it arrives because she is not overtired and stressed out.

Tom did notice how much Marsha changed during the first three months of pregnancy. She hadn't gained much weight—that would come later—but dark circles appeared under her lovely brown eyes. She came home from work and parked herself on the living-room couch, there to stay until bedtime.

Since he wanted this baby as much as she did, Tom pushed up his sleeves and got to work. He slowed down at his job so he could do more around the house as well as accompany Marsha to her doctor's appointments. It was at one of these appointments in Marsha's last trimester that Dr. Olson asked them if they were prepared for the changes about to create havoc on their life as a couple.

Expect the Unexpected

"Prepared? You bet we're prepared." Tom grinned. "Got the carseat, the crib, the changing table, the diaper service, extra help when the baby arrives, and we picked out a name—Tanya if it's a girl and Brian if it's a boy."

Dr. Olson nodded. "Good. Good. But what I'm asking is, are you emotionally and mentally prepared for this little addition?"

Marsha looked confused. "We've been waiting for this moment for more than five years. I think we're ready." She readjusted her stomach in the chair. "I know I can't wait to get rid of this bowling ball."

"I'm impressed with how much you've both been preparing for this arrival. I've no doubt this baby will be loved and cared for. However, I always reserve this appointment for my 'Let's talk reality' lecture," Dr. Olson said.

Reality is that your house, your car, and your life will never be orderly again. Babies are great at what they do, and what they do best is make messes! I wish all first-time expectant parents could attend a mess class. Part of that class would be to visit a house with two or three children, one a newborn and the other of toddler age. If that had happened to Vicky and me, we might have been better prepared for the changes tiny Matthew wrought in our lives.

I'll never forget one plane trip to Cape Cod. Matthew was just under two. He was clean and tidy, dressed up in a tiny business suit like my own. I bounced him on my knee and played games with him. Suddenly he had this explosive bowel movement. (Actually, *explosive* is putting it mildly. It ended up all over Matthew and all over me.) The stewardess was very helpful. I know they're prepared for emergencies, but this was beyond the call of duty. Matthew rode the rest of the way in just a diaper, and you can't imagine my suit. When Matthew looked at me, he seemed to say, "Welcome to fatherhood, Dad."

It amazes me that I remember incidents like this far more clearly than the hundreds of things that went neatly as planned. I look at this period of childhood as an opportunity to celebrate the stains, the messes.

Celebrate? Oh, my, yes!

As he learned to feed himself, baby Matthew saw nothing mundane about meals. They were adventures. After an adventure, then, I would clean up the scattered peas beneath his high chair, the blobs of macaroni and cheese, the cracker bits and hot dog pieces. This was hands-on fathering, down and dirty, and the sheer intimacy of clearing up for my baby, who was not too good yet at being neat, pleased me immensely. I doubt Matthew fully appreciated my service, but for me it was, to use the weary phrase, a powerful bonding experience.

And as I enjoyed this doing, this helping, I reflected that my Father God does just the same with me. I—we—all of us—make messes in our lives, messes in our environment, messes in our relationships. Does God, in whose image we are made, enjoy the experience of bonding with an inappreciative child the way I did with Matthew? I would like to think so.

So what can you expect, in addition to this child? First and foremost, expect the unexpected. The parent-to-be knows in a general, clinical way that most everything will go against best-laid plans. But almost no parent-to-be realizes in advance how utterly profound and penetrating that truth is. Just when you've got the baby all dressed and ready to leave for church, she'll fill her pants. When you've finally fallen asleep, he'll start screaming. Life will never be quite so hectic again. Figure 1.2 lists just a smidgen of what we experienced with Matthew and what my patients have told me they experienced once their little bundle of joy arrived.

Be ready for a bumpy, jolty, and exciting ride during this period of your life. And be willing to roll with the punches. You will not only be doing yourselves a favor by minimizing stressful reactions to the impromptu problems, but you will also be maximizing the chance you have to build a strong foundation for this little bundle of joy. Babies are phenomenal reactors. Even in utero they react to stress in other people. Minimizing your own tensions reduces tensions in the infant, before and after birth.

Besides, programmed right into a baby's makeup is dependency. Your baby trusts you for daily survival simply because he or she must. Babies have no choice. The way you respond both to the baby and to the problems babies generate—with acceptance, tolerance, or intolerance—will comprise the first lessons your child learns about trust. If you're braced for these changes, you'll have a greater chance of being tolerant and accepting of them.

How well did the Mayron family do this when Daniel was in utero? I explored this with them at their first counseling session.

"Tell me about your pregnancy," I asked Linda.

WAYS YOUR LIFE
WILL CHANGE

- Your car and house will not be orderly and clean for a long time to come. It will be years before you regain the passenger and storage space to which you've been accustomed, what with carseats, strollers, and diaper bags taking up room.

- The laundry will never be caught up. Never.

- There will be endless messes beyond definition.

- You (both of you) will not get nearly enough sleep.

- You will be ignorant of the daily news and may forget who's president and whether you voted for him.

- You'll look in the mirror and shudder at your bedraggled reflection.

- You'll become intimately familiar with bodily functions.

- You'll never cry or laugh so much as you will during this time.

- You'll never have enough time in the day, for yourself, for each other, and for the baby.

FIGURE 1.2

"You've got to be kidding," she said. "That was more than twelve years ago. Water under the bridge."

"Tell me what first comes to mind."

"Well, let's see. Jessica was my first, and she was such an easy baby. The whole pregnancy was, too, for that matter. I felt great. Hardly could tell I was pregnant. I was active clear up until the day she was born. And she was such a good baby. I could never understand why some of my friends were having such trouble. Jessica was—is—a joy." Linda stopped. Her eyes took on a faraway look.

"What about Daniel?" I prodded.

"Daniel . . . now that's another story entirely," she said. "We were so happy with Jessica. It seemed so easy, so we wanted another one right away. I got pregnant when Jessica was two. Right from the start, this pregnancy was different. I had horrible morning sickness. Instead of gaining weight like I did with Jessica, I had actually lost weight by my fourth month. My doctor put me on medication to control the nausea.

"The last trimester was the worst. I was tired, worn out from taking care of Jessica and feeling bad. Daniel gave me terrible indigestion—why, even a banana would give me heartburn. He was an active baby at night. Rolling around and kicking. I was so glad when he was finally born. I was sure things would go easier then, like they did with Jessica."

"And did they?" I asked.

"No way!" Linda and Alan answered in unison.

Do you see what I mean about expectations? And rolling with the punches? Minimizing expectations before birth and accepting Daniel for what he was following birth would have eased a lot of tension at the very outset. Daniel simply did not fit into Jessica's mold, though heaven knows the Mayrons tried to shoehorn him in.

I do not, in this case or in any other instance, suggest that the Mayrons were wrong. Casting blame does nothing to ease a situation. More to the point, there was no blame in the sense we usually associate with blame. Even at Daniel's birth, the Mayrons had slipped into a trap anyone can slip into (and many do). Tom and Marsha, and Jenny Lawton as well, could avoid that trap the way all traps are best avoided: by knowing it is there. Preparation, then, is the trap release.

One other aspect of preparation is best done before the baby arrives: planning. Although it can be taken care of at any point in a child's life, the earlier you handle it, the better. Children are most responsive when they are very young. A little planning in infancy and pre-infancy will go a long, long way.

Planning for Opportunity

Linda Mayron was ten the year she rolled the tractor into Lower Hadlock Pond. It was a green-and-yellow John Deere, a classic, circa 1930, and the pride of her Uncle Bert's life. Uncle Bert operated a tiny farm on Mount Desert Island in Maine, just a few acres. He didn't make a living from it. He played with it. He took off a couple hundred bales of salt hay every summer and raised twenty acres of oats or barley. In short, he accomplished little more than to provide feed for a couple of steers, a few pigs, and his ponies. *Ah, his ponies!* How Linda loved visiting Uncle Bert!

Linda especially loved helping with the haying. She was allowed to operate the ancient tedding machine, sitting on a steel seat and working levers as Uncle Bert pulled the machine across the bottoms with his sturdy old tractor. So she knew a little something about tractors the day her seven-year-old brother, Robby, climbed up on the John Deere's seat and kicked it out of gear. Slowly, majestically, it began rolling down the pasture slope, right toward the pond. It picked up speed with inexorable certainty, lurching down the lumpy pasture. Terrified, Robby jumped off the back and ran for the house. Linda caught up to it, clambered up the back over the power takeoff, and dragged herself up into the seat. But her legs were too short and too weak to depress the big iron brake pedal. She rode it into the pond, still trying to stop it.

Her Uncle Bert yelled and howled. He would have disowned her if he had owned her. Her mother wailed and wrung her hands and denounced her. Her father took his belt to her with far greater vigor than usual.

No one paused from chastising her long enough to believe her version of what really happened. Cute, wide-eyed little Robby got off scot-free.

Nearly two decades later, every detail still burned vivid in Linda's memory. As she described the event in my office during a scheduled session, she hugged herself and gently rocked back and forth. Beside her on the sofa, her husband, Alan, stared at the floor, looking uncomfortable. In the other corner of the office, twelve-year-old Daniel gaped at her. Clearly, her son had never heard the story before.

"Would you say, then," I suggested, "that you grew up under a strict, autocratic father?"

Linda murmured simply, "My father used the belt."

Discipline

Discipline is one of the touchiest of a parent's responsibilities, and one of the most difficult to handle well. Linda and Alan Mayron weren't doing too well with Daniel. Although they didn't realize it yet, they weren't doing all that well with Jessica, either. We explored the question of discipline during that counseling session.

"Under what circumstances did your father use corporal punishment—the belt?" I asked.

"All of them. Anytime one of us would get out of line . . . Mom's favorite saying was, 'Wait 'til your father gets home and gets the belt.' My brothers and I'd worry all afternoon until our father got home from work."

"Have you ever spanked your own children with a belt?"

"I don't spank them at all." She grimaced, sad-eyed. "I have to have Alan do it. I can't. I just can't."

"Mmmmm. What form of discipline do you routinely use?"

"Well, uh, I talk to them. Explain what they did wrong. And threaten them with the loss of a privilege." She shrugged helplessly. "It works fine on Jessica."

"But not with Daniel, right?"

"Right. He won't do a thing I say. He just plain ignores me, Dr. Warren."

Over in his corner, Daniel glanced guiltily at his parents and began picking at the piping on the chair arm.

"When you threaten the loss of a privilege," I asked, "do you follow through?"

"Well, sure." Linda laughed nervously, but there was no mirth in her voice. "Sometimes."

Linda Mayron simultaneously illustrates two of the three patterns parents commonly follow when disciplining their children. Family secrets of success lurk in the patterns, and so do traps. One of the best ways to promote success and avoid the traps is to plan discipline before it's needed. Had the Mayrons mapped out their strategies from the beginning, life would be flowing a lot more smoothly for them now.

Most parental discipline patterns seem to fall into one of three categories: discipline as the parents were disciplined, discipline in the opposite ways the parents were disciplined, and making discipline a mix of different styles. Let's look briefly at these three patterns.

Discipline As the Parents Were Disciplined. Linda expected Alan to fill the role her father filled in her own childhood. When I asked her if that were true, she denied it. But that's what she was doing, as she eventually realized. Her mother did a lot of accusing and hand-wringing, but no disciplining. Most parents who give discipline little thought fall automatically into the pattern of repeating their own past.

Discipline in the Opposite Way the Parents Were Disciplined. If Linda, who was raised under a combination of harsh discipline from her dad and essentially none at all from her mom, were to encourage permissiveness, that would be the opposite of what she knew growing up. Many new parents, recalling their childhood, vow, "I'll never do that to *my* kids." Past experience also includes the patterns that occurred within the families of extended-family members, neighbors, and others. "My uncle [aunt] [cousin] [whatever] let the kids run wild. I'm never going to let that happen with my kids."

Frequently, parents overcompensate for what they felt they missed out on while they were growing up. I frequently see this played out in overly permissive households. Parents who grew up under strict, authoritarian rule sometimes resent this type of discipline. Because of that resentment they let their own children run rampant with little or no boundaries or rules. They may even reward their children's misbehaviors with gifts and money.

A Mixture of Discipline Styles. In Linda Mayron's case, this pattern would mean balancing the two extremes of her own childhood. She, as the mother, would take a firmer lead, and she would expect Alan to lighten up.

In all of this we have not considered Alan's childhood. There are, of course, two patterns coming into a marriage: his and hers. His is just as influential as hers.

Alan had never thought much about how his parents handled discipline. He slouched in his chair and propped his fingertips together in an A as he talked about his childhood. "Dad wasn't home much. He worked a twelve-hour shift. We kids grew up knowing that if you disturbed him, you paid. You never talked to him while he was watching the news or his football games. You could talk to him during baseball games, but if someone got a hit and Dad didn't see it because you were distracting him, it was your fault. So we didn't talk to him during baseball games, either."

"So your mother handled the routine discipline."

"Yeah. She'd yell a lot. Explain to us why we were bad. And we could tell when she was getting to the end of her patience. She usually had a pretty long tether, except during her time of the month. I knew all about 'time of the month' when I was ten."

Alan's pattern, although not like Linda's, fit into Linda's well: an authoritarian father and a mother who explained transgressions. The styles were sufficiently similar that they mixed well in the Mayron family.

But—and here's the rub—they never thought about it. Dangerous traps lurk in the Mayrons' patterns. If similar traps exist in your family, they will snap shut on your family's happiness and accord if you don't see them and avoid them. Injurious disciplining patterns emerged more or less by default in the Mayrons' household because the Mayrons had done absolutely no strategy planning before the fact.

The best time to come to grips with what kind of parents you will be is right now, during the prenatal stage before the baby arrives. It is the only good way to spot traps and avoid them. To begin the planning process, assess your own background. The form on the following pages, "Assessing Your Discipline Background," will guide you.

Parenting Traps

Unfortunately, traps lurk in these three discipline patterns. Let's look at some of those pitfalls.

Blindly Following the Past. Linda unconsciously allowed the past to control her. She administered discipline ineffectively or even wrongly because she was reacting, not to her children's unique needs, but to her own past. The background assessment form was designed to help you identify your own past. Knowing your background helps you know what to avoid, if necessary.

Disciplining Inconsistently. Yes, this one ensnared the Mayrons as well, and on two levels. In this trap either one parent is permissive and the other authoritarian—in other words, inconsistent with each other's styles—or both of them swing from one extreme to the other depending on the situation—behaving inconsistently within their own individual style.

These were the traps that undercut the Mayrons' disciplining. Without a healthy parental model growing up, neither Alan nor Linda was sure which way to treat their own children. Linda didn't want to be too authoritarian because she remembered her painful and strict childhood. But, having a strong religious upbringing, she also didn't want to let her children misbehave without punishment. So she tended to waffle, unable to act when an immediate

ASSESSING YOUR
DISCIPLINE BACKGROUND

Consider the following questions and fill in the answers. Then keep them handy for future reference throughout your children's developmental years. I highly recommend that both expectant parents do this exercise and then go back and update it periodically as you see yourselves in certain parenting patterns that remind you of your past.

What kind of disciplining did you receive as a child? Close your eyes and think back to your earliest memories. Try to think of the earliest incident you remember when you really got in trouble.

Linda's recollection: "I must have been about five. My brothers and I had gotten hold of my dad's new portable transistor radio. We were fighting over it. I tried to tug it out of my brother's hand, and the antenna snapped off."

Write your recollection here:

_____

_____

_____

_____

How did your mother and/or father react—what did they say or do?

Linda said, "My mom was furious. She grabbed it out of our hands and sent us to our rooms. She said, 'Just wait 'til your father sees this.' We waited a long time in our bedrooms. When Dad came home, he blew up and hit me on the cheek."

Describe how your parents reacted.

_____

_____

_____

_____

How did you feel then?

Linda's response was, "I felt shocked and terribly hurt. Of course my jaw hurt for a while. I think I had a small bruise. Mainly it was just shock."

Write what your feelings were.

_____

_____

_____

_____

How do you feel about it now?

"Funny you should ask," Linda said. "When I think about it now, it still brings tears to my eyes. I guess I never really thought about it much up until now. But if I can remember it so vividly now, thirty years later, it must have affected me. I feel really sad. I loved my dad so much, and I can't understand why he hurt me like that, even today after I've been a parent myself."

Write your answer here:

_____

_____

_____

_____

Now use the following guidelines to analyze that incident and other discipline situations you can think of:

A. What would have been the best response?

_____

_____

_____

_____

B. How could your parents have better hit upon the best response?

_____

_____

_____

_____

Quite possibly in the incident you recall, your parents did indeed make a near-perfect response. Make note of that as an example to emulate. Linda's case was not so. Her parents should certainly have voiced displeasure, but the mother should have made an immediate response, particularly to children who were so small. The father should have mitigated his response with the sure knowledge that these were preschoolers behaving as preschoolers do, without the maturity to guide themselves from within.

C. Assume the same situation occurred in your generation; you are the parent and your kids made the misstep. What should be your response?

_____

_____

_____

_____

D. Based on this analysis, do you see any resolutions or promises you should make for yourself in advance of parenthood?

_____

_____

_____

_____

response was required and not consistent in carrying through with threats of even the mild disciplines she imposed.

Alan, on the other hand, believed in strong discipline when he was home. He believed fathers, like his own, should be authoritarian. He took no interest in Linda's situation or in the children's discipline when he was absent. Like a judge sitting in circuit court, he heard cases when he was in session. The world revolved without him when he was not there. When Daniel didn't respond appropriately, Alan threatened military school.

Inconsistency from Alan and Linda had created a weak foundation for their children, particularly for Daniel because he was the most difficult of the two (their words, not mine).

Jenny Lawton, the teenager whose child had not yet arrived, faced yet another trap.

Abrogating the Parenting Role. Far too frequently, when a couple divorces one parent backs out of the picture completely or nearly so. Rarely does the noncustodial parent assume any role at all in the children's day-to-day discipline.

In Jenny's situation, there was no husband to assume the father's role, and her situation was complicated greatly by the fact that she lived at home. She was a parent, but she was also a child of parents. They would assume disciplinary control over Jenny herself more or less by habit. This almost always happens when the adult child remains or returns home, no matter how old he or she may be. Jenny would be considered subject to her parents' discipline by them and quite probably by herself as well.

Who, then, would discipline the youngster? When conflicts about style or degree arose, and they absolutely, certainly would, whose will would prevail?

As Jenny finished school and went to work or college, her parents would probably be the baby's primary caregivers. They were also still Jenny's caregivers. Jenny could safely assume that this sort of exchange would frequently take place:

"Mom, I don't want the baby [doing] [eating] that."

"Oh, Honey, that's all right. Don't be so strict. Let it go," or, "Oh, it's just this once."

The roles could reverse, of course, with Jenny being more permissive than her parents. Either situation is extremely distressing to the baby.

Who would be right in the conflicts Jenny would encounter, herself or her parents? That is not the question at issue. Instead, the question will be, "Whose will will prevail?" and that does not have to do with who is "right" or "wrong." It's a control issue, and Jenny will face it with any caregiver, whether it be parents or some other person. In an extreme conflict of wills, other caregivers can be replaced. Parents cannot.

This problem is not necessarily spawned by Jenny's situation alone. Frequently I see problems where grandparents have crossed the line from *helpful* to *meddling* or even *undermining*. Again, planning is the key.

Planning in Advance to Avoid Discipline Problems

"Oh, sure," Jenny might say, taking exception to my suggestion to plan ahead. "How can I know what my baby's going to do before it even gets here? You have to wait, and when the kid does something bad, then you correct him. Isn't that right? And then you deal with your parents."

That's reactive parenting, and there is a place for it. Much more effective, though, is *proactive* parenting: having the guidelines for both teaching and discipline already in place so you and your children all know exactly where the limits lie.

Tom and Marsha Jasper, anticipating their first baby after so many years of trying, enjoyed the perfect opportunity to iron out problems before they arose. Any effort expended on this is effort well spent.

To plan in advance, thereby springing the traps harmlessly, you must first *determine what your parenting predilections are now.* You did this when you filled out the form assessing your discipline background. I suggest you frequently review the questions and responses, then add to them as you can in order to gain a clear overall view of your own style and preferences.

Having done that, *build a tentative plan.* Discuss the following points with each other. Make your respective positions clear. Whether you agree or not (you won't), know exactly what you both feel strongly about and where agreement and disagreement lie. Here are some issues to discuss as you build your plan.

Corporal Punishment. Is striking, slapping, or spanking ever justified, and to what degree? This is a volatile subject that requires prayerful and informed discussion by both parents.

Tom and Marsha Jasper disagreed heatedly in regard to corporal punishment. He was all for it while Marsha eschewed it. Their preliminary compromise: Immediate corporal punishment only for infractions involving the child's safety, running into the street, for example. No corporal punishment after age nine at all. They chose age nine because it was half of eighteen, the child's usual leaving-home age. Also, they knew corporal punishment is not a particularly effective deterrent after eight or nine anyway. They also promised never to tell the kids that spanking would end at age nine.

Alternative Discipline Measures. These measures include grounding, loss of privileges, monetary payments, standing in a corner (yes, that's still done), a cooling-off time—time-outs, as they are often called—and others. Considerations must include who will determine whether these measures are used and to what degree and whether the child will be able to appeal a parent's verdict before the other parent.

Expectations. What will be expected in the way of behavior once the child is crawling? Walking? Once the child can play in the yard?

Restitution. Should a child be required to render restitution or recompense for errors and disobedience? If so, how and to whom?

Rewards and Bribes. Will rewards and bribes be offered, and, if so, for what behaviors? Who will offer them?

Proscriptions. What will the child *not* be allowed to do and play with? Some parents feel strongly about guns, junk food, video games, certain television programs, types of music, Barbie dolls and G. I. Joe, certain books and stories, and other toys and forms of recreation. You won't cover all the bases in advance, by any means, but starting with a consensus in this area will help immensely in reaching agreement on similar issues down the road. As your child grows, modern technology will invent other bases and topics you don't even dream of now.

Dress and Grooming. Will there be a family dress code? If so, delineate it now, but be prepared to compromise later.

Other Points. Discuss other things that are relevant to your lifestyle and any values that are not covered in the topics discussed here.

Now, *build a working plan.* This involves compromise on some issues and giving in completely on others. Go over each point above and decide exactly what you will do *as a team* in that situation. When you're done, neither parent will have scored a complete victory, but you will have a strong guideline for how you want to discipline your child.

I'd like to suggest, as a final step in this planning, that

you *pledge each other your cooperation*. Addressing each other, repeat after me:

> I, _____, do pledge to maintain an atmosphere of teamwork in the raising and disciplining of our children. To that end, I pledge never to deliberately undercut your authority. I pledge to support your wishes as actively as I support my own. When conflicts arise, as they surely will, I pledge to enter into good-faith give-and-take to reach consensus on our approach.

Jenny Lawton would do well to sit down with her parents and carefully go through the list of topics presented in this section. By doing so she could achieve three objectives. It would bring home to her mom and dad the important fact that she is a concerned parent, not just their little girl, Jenny, anymore. It would clear the air about disagreements before they happen. And it would serve its primary purpose of laying the foundation for actual discipline once the child arrives.

But what about the Mayrons? Their children poise on the verge of adulthood. Is it too late for them? Not at all. Because their children are old enough to deal well with abstraction and theory, the Mayrons might include Daniel and Jessica at some stage of their deliberations, inviting the children's opinions perhaps, but *not* allowing them a say in the final working plan.

Guidelines, particularly on the issues above, are of inestimable help in maintaining firm, even discipline.

Planning to Build Parenting Skills

How do we learn to be parents? After all, our children do not come with an operating manual, and the Bible doesn't provide much specific information. I believe this is in God's plan.

If He had provided an eleventh commandment on parenting, it's likely that we would take it literally and use it with no exceptions on each and every child. But children, by their very nature, are exceptions. Each is an individual human being with an individual temperament. Thus, I believe God, in His infinite wisdom, left the door open on parenting techniques.

Seek Help. So if we don't have written directions from God, how do we learn to parent? Educators tell us that humans learn best by example. However, you can now see that how your parents parented may or may not be the right way for you, to be followed blindly as you parent your own children. Parenting books, like this one, can help fill in the gaps, offering a perspective other than the one you grew up in. That simple change of perspective can in itself be immensely helpful. Observe. What do you see in others? How do people whose kids you admire handle problems? Ask them. Build a foundation of knowledge and tips even before the beginning.

Plan for Error. One cautionary note. It's very, very hard to change patterns that have been programmed into us since birth. Parents are people. They make mistakes, especially under stress. When you become a parent, you will make mistakes, too, guaranteed. Your own parents made mistakes. Although we are human and imperfect, we can lift ourselves and our children free of the error or at least minimize its consequences. The first step in escaping is to recognize that you can err, and the second is to learn a better way.

Keep Learning. I, for one, am never done learning. That is the key to being an effective parent: Never stop learning. Plan to make your children a lifelong occupation, one for which you will constantly train. Take advantage of new parenting techniques and seize any opportunity for free parenting classes.

Does it make a difference? Absolutely.

Several recent studies have proven that parental education is an effective deterrent to child abuse. Not only have we, the experts, seen a marked decline in abuse cases where such education is offered, but we also see the added benefit of mutual support from other parents. Through this education, parents are taught to rear their children with understanding rather than frightening threats and brutal responses.

Mutual support groups and parental education are especially helpful in cases where difficult-to-manage kids are involved (such as those with attention deficit disorder or hyperactivity or some other behavior problem).

Allow for Special Needs. Every child has special needs. The differences are primarily a matter of degree. Children with visible birth defects, physical damage or impairment, or behavior problems are easily diagnosed. Be on the lookout for children who appear like any other child but possess hidden needs not easily pinpointed.

Adoptive Parents

Adoptive parents are in special need of support because they come into an adoption with such high expectations and good intentions. Unfortunately, many of these adoptive children have problems genetically determined or prenatally determined over which there is little control. Adoptive parents usually are not so fortunate as to be involved in their adoptive child's prenatal and birth period. They may well have missed out on most, if not all, of their child's three-year windows of opportunity. And, as we'll see with the Mayron family, going back later to repair damage done at this stage is much harder than repairing it as it happens or avoiding it altogether.

I'm so convinced of the benefits of having parents with similar problems use each other as sounding boards and support that I'd like to see adoptive agencies provide such group support long after children have been adopted.

The Arrival

To quote an old-line navy admiral, "The brass polishing stops when the shooting starts." The day comes when planning becomes moot. The action starts. We're on our way!

3. HOW DOES MY BABY GROW?

PHYSICAL DEVELOPMENT

Mary, Mary, quite contrary,
How does your garden grow?
With silver bells and cockle shells
And pretty maids all in a row.

EIGHTEENTH-CENTURY NURSERY RHYME

T om Jasper peered into Marsha's eyes, his attention completely focused on her face. Well, almost completely. An awful lot was going on down at the other end.

"Here comes another one, Tom! How'd you get me into this?!" Marsh screamed.

Tom swallowed. He'd never seen Marsha like this. No matter what their birthing instructor said, he wasn't prepared to see his wife go through this much suffering.

"Breathe! Breathe with me, Marsha," he pleaded.

"Okay, Marsha, give me a big push NOW!" the doctor instructed cheerily.

"Push, Honey! You can do it." Tom sat behind Marsha and supported her back. He honestly didn't know how much longer Marsha could keep it up. He looked at his watch. Seven P.M.—twelve hours since they had gotten to the hospital.

Marsha made a strangulated *glurping* sound Tom had never heard before. The doctor said, "I see the head. It's crowning. Good work, Marsha. Take a deep breath and relax."

Tom felt a little giddy and faint. The head? This wasn't a book or class anymore. This was the real thing! He stroked Marsha's sweaty forehead.

"Okay, on this one I want you to give it all you've got." The doctor sounded like Knute Rockne at the Rose Bowl. Easy for him to say, perched on his stool, all calm and comfortable.

In the next few seconds everything seemed to plod along like it does in one of those movies where they slow down the speed during the critical part. Tom didn't know how or when, but somehow he ended up catching the baby when Marsha made the last push. It was the slipperiest thing he'd ever held, like a greased pig in mayonnaise. He was afraid he'd drop it.

Not an "it." No. Never an "it."

His son.

Tom was the first person in the world to touch this newborn boy. He was greeter and receiver, safety net and protector. He held the future in his hands. Literally.

Distracted, he was fumbling the future. The nurse helped him wrap his boy in a blanket and put him on Marsha's chest. His son, his child . . . Tom felt hot, wet tears run down his face.

Congratulations!
It's a Baby!

Girl or boy, it's here, and you can't put it back. Most parents never forget the moment their children are born.

It's a full spectrum of feelings squashed into a moment—some good and some not so good.

It is also the opportunity for every relative, friend, stranger, and passing drifter to offer advice. Some is based on folklore (don't ever let a newborn lie under a hazel tree or sleep under a quilt pattern called turkey tracks), some comes from good, solid, empirical evidence (baby digestive enzymes can handle certain foods and not others), and some is just plain voodoo. One of the topics most subject to an outlandish array of opposing opinions is the concept of parent-child bonding.

Bonding: Myth or Fact?

Bonding is the act of attachment between you and your child. It is the basis upon which you will build a relationship with him or her. It transcends affection and is not quite the same as love.

We're finding that bonding doesn't have to be instantaneous to be effective. In famous studies conducted by researchers John Kennell and Marshall Klaus, the sensitive period for bonding in human babies—that is, the time when they attached best—was identified as months, even years, after birth.

The bonding concept—call it a fad—began as a way to force change in the sterile, harsh environment of the hospital's delivery-room procedures. It more or less evolved in ways its early proponents never intended: It can make parents feel guilty if they don't immediately fall in love with this slippery, wet creature.

While some parents experience instant bonding as soon as they first lay eyes on their newborn, others don't feel this same attachment for many months. Either way works. However, where bonding fails to occur at all because of some mental, emotional, or physical circumstance, a relationship problem usually develops between the child and the mother or father. Kennell and Klaus's studies even connect future abuse and neglect with nonbonding between a child and his or her parents.

The most important thing new parents should realize is that they have an entire lifetime to bond with their children. They need not expect it to happen seconds after delivery. As they faithfully nurture their children, bonding will come. It *will* come.

A lot of fathers complain that they were not given the opportunity to bond with their children as infants. And because of circumstances beyond their control (such as archaic hospital practices that prevented them from seeing a child until after delivery and recovery), some of this does happen—more so in the past than in the present. The advances in birthing practices have brought the father into a more active role throughout the entire process of creating a new citizen, from conception to teenager. A recent study done in Israel (and reported in the *Tacoma Morning News Tribune* on June 21, 1993) bears this out. Several fathers were blindfolded and asked to pick out their babies from a group of three-day-old infants by stroking the infants' hands. In over 60 percent of the cases, the fathers chose their own babies.

An infant will bond to the person who fulfills his or

her needs the most—the one who cleans up those messes, who talks, coos, holds, and cuddles, be the caregiver male or female. In families where a nanny does this, children seem to bond more vigorously to the nanny than to the parents. With the change in the employment picture today, more and more fathers are opting to stay home and take care of their infants while their wives go back to better-paying jobs. In these cases, the children may bond more to the father than the mother.

Keep in mind, too, that infants are quite literally wired to respond to touch. Tactile sensations mean far more to a small child than to an older child. Infants receive a great deal of information through their sense of touch—who is touching them, how that touch is administered, and the motivation behind it. Snuggling, holding, and stroking contribute richly to a bonding experience.

Little Brian Jasper was lucky to be starting out with both a mom and dad to welcome him with open arms. (Tom didn't drop him after all, slipperiness notwithstanding.)

Your First Opportunity to Help the Newborn Grow

Healthy and growing . . .

Although physical problems over which there is no control can assail a baby, normally speaking, parents are the key to whether a baby thrives. From the very beginning parents are also concerned with laying the foundation for the future. One of the opportunities for doing so, you'll recall, is to help the baby learn to trust. Right here is where that opportunity is best served, and it will be served easily as you learn to read your baby. Fortunately, even the neophyte parent can become attuned to the cues baby sends, and baby does indeed send them.

Everyone knows babies are born dependent. The question is, how much so? To what degree is your newborn a clean slate, and to what degree is the child already on his or her own, if at all?

The title of a popular syndicated television show, "What Every Baby Knows," tells you there is enough material in that infant brain and body to give the program sufficient material to fill a five-day week, year in and year out. Infants already know an incredible amount of things when they are born, and they blot up other things rapidly. They are an intriguing mix of wisdom and innocence, cunning and artlessness. To help your little one thrive, you will add to what the baby already understands instinctively as well as program in the artifacts of our culture—saying "please" and "thank you," refraining from punching others' noses . . . the list goes on. If you want to learn to read the complex little being, it helps immensely to realize how that brand-new brain thinks and views life. See that, and both your lives will flow much more smoothly now and in the future.

Physically, infants are more dependent upon nurturing than are most animals, and I am not talking about mobility and such, which goes without saying.

One thing not programmed in is patience. Infants' lives consist of this moment only. Needs already met are no longer of interest; needs a minute from now of no consequence yet. It's an important thing to keep in mind. A screaming, demanding baby is acting neither spoiled nor impertinent. The child is asking for what he or she needs.

"Oh yeah?" Jenny Lawton sniffs. "You haven't heard Sara squall."

"Does she just belt it out instantly?"

"No, she usually starts out fussing and leads up to it. But the lead-up time is really, really short. A minute or two."

"That's how long it takes her to realize she needs something."

Respond to a baby's cries immediately? Absolutely. I doubt a child younger than one can be spoiled by too much attention, and I say this for several reasons.

To begin with, here's that first opportunity, and it is the opportunity to instill trust as well as other important early lessons in social interaction. Remember always that the infant is learning with a brand-new brain devoid of maturity or prior experience. Our own lessons in trust will differ greatly from that infant's, for our life experiences have already changed our understanding of trust. You are forming that background for your baby with every need you meet.

The infant's trust lessons can be encapsulated in two sentences: "I need. I receive." Over and over. Those lessons lead to: "Even if my needs are not met immediately, I can trust my caregiver to meet them soon. I'm in good hands."

But there's a dividend here for the parents as well. This is Mom and Dad's one chance in life to completely serve another human being at this level of need-meeting. It is a service providing little in the way of an immediate return, but it is satisfying and gratifying beyond any reasonable measure.

The Infant's Needs

The baby's survival needs remain basically the same during the first year of life: he or she needs love and touch, nourishment, and protection. You're better able to fulfill these needs successfully if you have an idea what to expect during this first year.

Nourishment. Warmth and protection, yes. Everyone knows that. But love and touch? Nice, perhaps, but hardly a necessity, one would think. Yet study after study in many different countries have proven that infants deprived of cuddling and love fail to grow. Should those infants be placed in a hospital or other setting and provided with round-the-clock care and love, touching and gentle handling, they blossom. Returned to an environment that deprives them of cuddling, they no longer thrive. Soon they cease to grow at all. Handling and affection are just as necessary as milk.

Meeting needs teaches trust. A derivative rule therefore becomes:

TO TEACH TRUST, CUDDLE AND HANDLE YOUR BABY.

"Who wouldn't want to cuddle a baby?" Jenny snuggled her Sara in close with one arm as she arranged the blankets in a borrowed baby carriage with the other. "Oh, sure, there are sickos out there who hurt babies, but I mean regular people." She lay Sara in the pram and tucked in the blankets. "Did you see the baby carriage roll down the steps in . . . I forget the movie. Kevin Costner, I think."

"*The Untouchables?*"

"Yeah! Adults are shooting each other and dying, but what really grabbed you? That baby buggy." She paused, headed for the park. "Does bouncing along in a baby buggy count for holding and cuddling? I guess not, huh?"

Good question.

The very, very young do best when they're attached closely to parents. I've seen some excellent baby-carrier and sling designs (and some truly terrible ones). Typically, a frameless carrier allows your baby to ride on your chest either facing you or facing outward. Beware of carriers that are a maze of complex straps and attachments. You'll so dread using them you'll use them less, or not at all. Keep it simple. Another excellent model hangs from one shoulder, crossing the chest and back to sling the baby on the opposite hip. At the age of six or seven months, on the average, the baby has enough starch to ride in one of those baby backpacks.

"Oh, those!" Linda Mayron grinned. "Alan and I carried the kids in those for years. They're great. I would even put Daniel in a backpack to do the grocery shopping so I didn't have to worry about him climbing out of the baby seat in the grocery cart. I remember once taking a tour of the Hershey chocolate factory. We had Jessica in one of the baby backpacks on the market. We were looking through the glass and pointing to the candy workers, and they were looking out the glass and pointing to us."

Carriages and buggies, however, also offer movement, a change of scene, and recurring attention face to face by the caregiver. Baby needs all that. Should Jenny take her Sara out for a stroll in a buggy? By all means! Make it personal for baby with frequent smiles and touches, adjustments of the blankets, and such.

Strollers become more useful as children get heavier and grow to crawling and toddling age and beyond. As their world expands, the stroller provides new vistas, not to mention taking a weight off Mom or Dad. I recall a friend of mine, a zoo-oriented person, who took two children ages three and six to the zoo. She rented a stroller, ostensibly for the three-year-old. But kids lose interest in zoos quicker than some adults do. The kids had a great time pushing each other in the stroller, alternately riding, and using it to carry the bag of peanuts. It became a diversion as well as a convenience and contributed to everyone's pleasure and good spirits.

Infant Massage

Physical touch and attention—infant massage provides that in spades. We adults don't think much about tactile sensations because we have learned to rely primarily on other senses. Only when those senses are reduced do we turn to touch. Blind persons, for example, have finely attuned abilities—they can read Braille much faster than can sighted persons, including blindfolded ones.

For messages from the outside, babies rely primarily not on hearing and sight, but on touch. *Who is touching me, how is it happening, and why?* We adults know and dismiss impersonal touching, such as jostling in a crowded elevator. But babies take every touch personally.

Lately, proponents of baby massage suggest that a beneficial routine to set up when your infant is young is a regular massage. (Incidentally, cat fanciers recommend cat massage; it's not limited to infants!) Such massage serves both infant and parents well by promoting bonding and health.

Baby massage is a fairly new concept. It's a special way fathers can become more involved with their infants, especially if the infants are nursing and Dad feels somewhat left out. Numerous studies have shown that even children with developmental problems, such as Down syndrome, deafness, and blindness, as well as cerebral palsy victims, benefit from regular and frequent physical touch by developing at an accelerated rate.

There are other benefits of massage. It helps soothe colicky babies, and it's a good way to help your baby fall asleep. A regular routine of a massage before bedtime helps a baby settle down to a restful night.

Several good books and classes are available to instruct you in baby massage. Hands-on demonstration by an expert is even better. The following review describes the general techniques.

Goals to Keep in Mind

The primary purpose of infant massage is to communicate with the baby in a way the baby understands instinctively—through touch. There is no better way to relax a tiny child and to say, "I love you." Physically, massage improves the child's circulation, to a degree. Human beings possess two different fluid systems, blood and lymph. Blood is moved through the body by the heart; lymph has no such central pump. Clear and thin, lymph fluid circulates primarily in response to body movement as organs are squeezed and muscles flexed. Massage can contribute greatly to healthy lymph movement.

Principles to Keep in Mind

Your baby thinks from the head down. By that I mean that the child's major interest lies in his or her head and face, particularly at first. The exterior of the tummy is of passing interest to the infant, and legs and feet are good for nothing more than to wave in one's face, grab, and chew upon, if that. As you massage your infant, you will probably want to begin at the top, the site of primary interest, and work down.

About half of an adult is muscle, but infants are maybe one-fourth muscle. They don't have enough muscle mass in any one spot to develop tension knots, stress tightness, and other muscle difficulties to which some adults are prone; masseurs literally pound the tension out of adults. Vigorous kneading is also part of a grown-up's massage, but you'll want none of that for the baby. Keep it gentle, smooth, and very soft. As a general rule, the smaller the infant, the softer the touch.

Finally, remember that this is a communication device and an exercise in calming and relaxing the baby. If you are hurried or uptight, you will not achieve your objectives. You must also be relaxed and ready to spend the requisite time without hurrying, or else the baby will get a White Rabbit massage and corresponding message ("Oh dear, oh dear! I must hurry! I'm late!").

The Technique

To minimize friction, the masseur or masseuse—for convenience I will say *masseur* throughout, meaning a parent of either gender—uses a light oil film between the hands and the baby. What kind of oil? Most masseurs recommend against mineral oils for infants (for one thing, it will invariably reach the baby's mouth; do you want mineral oil entering his or her digestive system?), and that includes major commercial baby oils. Vegetable oils such as coconut oil or peanut oil work well and are digestible. The skin tends to blot up lotions (after all, that is their purpose), and the masseur must continually replenish his or her hands when they are used. Only if the baby's skin is very dry, and babies' skins hardly ever are, is lotion the substance of choice.

Massage your infant's head *before* you apply any lotion or oil. You don't want substances of that sort anywhere near the delicate eyes and mouth.

Lay your infant faceup on the floor, on a changing table, or in your lap with the head farthest from you. Smile and talk as part of your massage; your baby will blot up the happiness of your happy face. Consider the following suggestions as you begin the massage.

The Head. With your fingertips, massage the scalp in little circles. Now's a great time for eye contact and verbal strokes. Stroke the forehead softly from the center outward. Lay a hand on each side of the baby's head to work the face with your thumbs. Stroke the eyebrows outward. Stroke from the bridge of the nose between the eyes down to the cheeks. Work the cheeks gently. Stretch the skin around the upper lip by drawing your thumbs outward, then stretch below the mouth. Finally, massage around the jaws and ears, paying special attention behind the crook of the jaw, up by the hinge. There are important lymph nodes back there.

Now oil your hands. They needn't drip with the stuff. A light coating will work just fine.

The Torso. Smooth the chest skin from center outward, following those tiny ribs. Without lifting your hands, come back to center by sliding down the sides and around and up, following the lower line of the ribs. Cross the baby's chest repeatedly by starting your left hand at his or her lower right chest and stroking to the left shoulder, then running the right hand from the baby's lower left chest to upper right shoulder. Do this rhythmically several times.

Stroke first one hand and then the other down baby's tummy as if there were a pile of sand or sugar at the top of the tummy bulge and you were scooping it down to the legs. Make primary contact with the pinky edge of your open palm. Lay your open hands against the sides of baby's tummy and stroke with your thumbs from the center outward.

To massage the back, lay your baby tummy-down—across your legs, if possible. Place your flat hands next to each other. Now, starting at the shoulder blades and moving down, stroke back and forth with your palms in alternate motion, the left moving across baby's back, away from you, as the right moves toward you, back and forth, back and forth. Work down to the buttocks and back up a couple of times. Work little circles with your fingertips all over the baby's back. Stroke with the fingertips of one hand from the shoulder blades to the buttocks several times.

Many masseurs leave the back rub until last for two reasons: First, it means they only have to interrupt the massage once to flip the baby, and second, the back rub is the most relaxing and enjoyable part of the process, an excellent way to end the massage.

The Limbs. The basic movements work equally well on arms and legs. Not many of us have ever milked a cow or goat. If you have, you know the technique. You can "milk" the infant's limb either upward from torso to end or downward from end to torso. Most masseurs do both. To milk downward, grip the ankle or wrist gently in one hand, wrap the other hand around the limb, and stroke downward several times. To milk upward, wrap one hand around the limb at its base and the other just above, then stroke upward with each in turn.

In a variation, wrap one hand around the limb near the base and wrap the other just above it. Gently, gently, twist your hands opposite each other as they slide up the limb. Remember how you used to make snakes out of modeling clay by rolling the clay between your flat palms? Do that in a gentle manner with each limb, sliding your hands upward by degrees.

Treat each little hand and foot by massaging it with your thumb tips, supporting it firmly with the other four fingers. Stroke the instep and palm with your thumbs. Softly stroke the tops of the hands and feet.

Mini-Massages

Small children with short attention spans sometimes grow impatient with lengthy massages. Don't wear out your welcome. Limit the massage to brief stroking of the jaw, tummy, arms and legs, and back. A short massage, performed gently and without oil, also works well after a bath to calm an active baby and prepare him or her for sleep.

Bombarded with advice about such previously unknown things as infant massage, parents sometimes feel inundated. Add to that the fear of making some innocent mistake that will warp the child into a gnome that Wagner would write operas about, and it's understandable that new parents worry. So what can you do to keep from doing wrong?

Minimizing Error

"I don't know what I'm doing." Jenny sounded just plain scared during Sara's first neonate checkup.

So did Marsha. "I read all the baby books, and I still don't know what I'm doing," she said during Brian's first neonate checkup. At her side, Tom Jasper didn't look the least bit confident either.

Relax.

The parents of a firstborn anticipate some mystical secret to raising a perfect baby. It won't happen. No one is perfect. Mary raised the only perfect child, and that was not all her doing.

In a Doonesbury comic strip sequence some time ago, the surfer named Zonker was acting as nanny to a baby girl. He told the baby's mom about the great day he and the baby had enjoyed adventuring together at the park and elsewhere. Mom asked acidly, "What about the nap and bath and doctor's appointment and . . . ?" She was centered on the practical business of baby-raising. Zonker was keyed to the fun of a personal relationship. Frankly, Zonker had the better idea. Not unlike the Mary-versus-Martha argument in Jesus's presence (Luke 10:38–42), parents can get so worried about serving, they neglect the human connection.

Of course I do not suggest skipping a doctor's appointment or neglecting absolute necessities. But please never forget the precious one-to-one relationship that forges trust in a newborn. Feed it. Build upon it. Above all, enjoy it. That is your first priority. A personal relationship.

TO TEACH TRUST, BUILD A SOLID RELATIONSHIP.

For those who feel lost without definite guidelines, let me offer a few specific suggestions for avoiding error.

1. Never worry about spoiling a new baby.

There was a time when experts recommended letting a baby "cry it out." Feeding-on-demand proponents fought it out tooth and claw with those advocating "follow a rigid schedule." The arguments abated as the experts finally realized that a baby will pick its own tempo, and no two are alike. I seriously doubt that a child can be spoiled at this age. Neither can that child ever receive too much personal attention.

2. Guard against physically hurting the child.

Striking, hitting, spanking, and shaking an infant in any way is absolutely forbidden, both legally and morally. Your baby is not capable of right and wrong. The infant is not even in full control of his or her body parts.

Physical hurt goes beyond that, however. The baby's head is quite large and heavy in proportion to the body, and the neck is very thin. If the baby's body is jolted, the head whiplashes violently with no muscle resistance and no neck strength to temper the effect. Therefore *never ever shake an infant!* Shaking a baby can cause permanent brain damage or death.

Take care when other small children are about to keep them and the baby under a constant eye. A toddler trying to pick up an infant (and for the most benign of reasons, wanting to help) can cause severe injury by folding the baby wrongly or dropping the child. The next guideline is related to this one:

3. Watch your anger.

The pressures of parenthood can seem overwhelming, especially for first-time parents. Anger is a common reaction to their frustration.

"Oh, I know that!" Jenny grimaced. "It was two in the morning, and Sara wouldn't stop crying. My head said she was just being a baby and didn't know any better, but my heart was furious at her. I didn't know what to do."

"So what did you do?"

"Rocked her and cried myself."

Good response! Jenny safely let off steam and simultaneously nurtured her baby girl with positive physical contact.

There is a woman in my church, a lovely lady everyone regards as superhuman. She was unable to bear children, so they ended up adopting two girls.

"Lori and Mary are only nine months apart," she explained to me one day. "Right after we adopted Lori, they called about Mary. We couldn't say no. You might say I was saddled with twins nine months apart. People tell me it was more difficult than if I'd borne my own children.

"Anyway, one afternoon I absolutely couldn't take it anymore. They were both crying. I couldn't soothe either one of them. So I strapped them both in their carseats and set them in the middle of the nursery. Then I went out into the living room and had a good cry myself. It was only a few minutes, I think. I don't remember now if they stopped crying or fell asleep on their own. But you know what? For the longest time I felt so guilty about leaving them like that. I felt I should have been able to handle it. After all, it's what God would expect of me, right?"

I shook my head. "No."

"I know that now," she said. "And during a Bible

study a few days later, I admitted to doing this and asked for forgiveness. Instead of judgment, the rest of the women looked at me and said, 'Congratulations, Jeannette, you've finally admitted to being a mother and being human. We were wondering when you were going to do that. It's okay to feel that way.'"

Jeannette looked at me with eyes filled with tears. "It felt wonderful knowing that others understood," she said. "I did the best thing I could at the time. I assured my babies' safety, and then I got away from them until I had my emotions under control. But I still feel so guilty."

Jeannette is a wise woman. Her guilt is secondary to her babies' safety. How infinitely more would her guilt burden her had she injured either child or let a child suffer injury!

An alternative Jeannette might have employed would have been to call up a friend or relative and ask him or her to give her a break. Her first instinct, however, was good: Safety first. And that leads to one final guideline:

4. Don't be too hard on yourself.

If you're reading this now and you recall a time when you might have taken out your emotions physically on your baby, don't worry and fret. The past is the past. Mistakes are made by imperfect people such as we are. Learn from them and move on.

Sometimes the so-called mistakes are not mistakes at all. A lot of what goes on in a baby is not influenced at all by the parents. For example, parents are occasionally faced with what is euphemistically labeled a "colicky baby."

Why Are You Crying?

There is no other noise that carries more impact than a baby's cry. Perhaps you saw the old *M*A*S*H* television episode that illustrated this. In the opening, we see Hawkeye (Alan Alda) under psychiatric treatment. The root of his problems are eventually traced back to an occasion when he was trapped in a disabled bus with several Korean villagers. The enemy lurked nearby; any noise would alert them to the stranded bus and its occupants. In the back of the bus, a baby started crying. Hawkeye hissed at the mother, "Can't you shut that kid up? We may all die here." The child ceased crying; tears streamed down the mother's cheeks. She had smothered her infant to save the rest of them. It drove Hawkeye crazy. Literally.

The show was fiction, of course. A dramatization. But a part of the lasting appeal and power of that old *M*A*S*H* series is the fact that it was based so solidly upon human nature and motivation. We are indeed profoundly affected by an infant's cry. To sacrifice a crying baby, even one whose wails endanger a score of people, could tip us over the edge.

Usually there's a good reason for your baby's crying; the mystery is finding out what that reason is. The following order sometimes helps when all else fails:

1. *Check my diaper. I'm wet and/or dirty, or I'm discomfited by a pin or an ill fit.*
2. *Feed me; I'm hungry.*

3. *Cover/uncover me, I'm cold/hot.*
4. *Hold me. I'm lonely.*

So many people try the first three and fail to recognize the fourth. It is as valid as the other possibilities. Serving that fourth option does not—let me repeat, *does not*—spoil a small baby. For children younger than a year old, the fourth is as pressing a need as the other three.

How do you know the child is lonely? Pick the child up; the crying stops. Lay the child down; the crying starts again.

There are instances, however, when none of the four is "it." In the medical profession we call this *colic* because we don't have any other word or explanation for it.

Colic

"Colic—let me tell you about colic." Linda Mayron assumed the attitude of a world-weary survivor. "Daniel had colic. No matter what I did, he wailed. Nothing worked. Nothing. It was a horrible first few months."

That defines colic in graphic terms.

Colic is usually, but not always, the result of an underdeveloped digestive system. In very crude, simple terms, the baby has gas and cannot pass it. A part of a newborn system's underdevelopment includes the very tight anal sphincter, which has not developed to the point that it can relax enough to release the gas. A bloated baby suffers real pain.

By the time the six-week milestone rolls around, the anus has usually developed enough that the baby can release the gas. At the same time, the rest of the system does a better job of digesting milk without forming gas. Maturity, then, eases the problem spontaneously. Very often, parents of colicky babies report with intense relief an entirely different baby at that age.

All healthy babies have a big, round tummy (incidentally, a lot of what's in there is liver; babies have a proportionally large liver because it performs so many important chemical functions). But a normal tummy is soft and giving. Push on it gently and it shifts and squooshes. A bloated baby's tummy will feel drum-hard, and the skin may even appear almost glossy, it is stretched so firmly.

There are several ways you can help a very young baby suffering from gas:

- Sometimes infant massage does the trick, relaxing the whole baby.
- Nursing moms can also help reduce colic by watching what they eat. Foods that produce gas (spicy foods, vegetables from the cabbage family, and milk products) should be avoided. The La Leche League, an organization dedicated to assisting nursing mothers, has some excellent information to help a mother determine a more suitable diet if her baby suffers from colic.
- Open the anal sphincter by inserting a rectal thermometer. Have a diaper poised beyond the baby's upturned bottom as you do so, to serve as an absorbent wall for whatever comes out.

  "Oh, that's gross!" a young mother protested. "I know it has to be done, but . . . and the explosive gas . . . and . . . yuck!"

Parents of very small babies do a host of gross things they never thought they'd be able to tolerate. The thermometer ploy works. That's what counts.

• Try the football hold.

As a friend explained it, "When Britney Sue would start crying, my husband held her like a football, facedown over his forearm with her head above his elbow and her crotch cradled in his hand. He'd walk around and gently pat her back. He acted as proud as a pig in a hat; he was the only one of us who could quiet her and get her to sleep."

The pressure on the infant's stomach in this hold helps release pent-up gas from one end or the other. And of course there is the comfort of being held, always soothing to a fussy baby.

Colic can also result from overstimulation. For some babies, a specific time of day (usually the busiest for the family—early evening) spurs a crying jag that nothing or no one can soothe. Try rocking the baby in a darkened room with little or no noise. On rare occasions, letting the infant cry may be the only answer.

A family with tension generated by causes other than the new baby—economic troubles, medical problems, problems with older siblings, losses and reversals—may inadvertently produce a colicky infant. Below conscious level, the child picks up the family's uneasiness and tension and communicates it as restlessness and crying.

Maturity produces amazingly rapid alterations at times. During this first year, your baby will grow and change more profoundly than at any other period in his or her entire life. It is also during this first year, usually right around the time of that first smile, that most parents fall deeply and desperately in love with their babies.

What If There's Only One Parent?

Marsha Jasper was in the hospital recovery from giving birth at the same time as teenager Jenny Lawton, the high school junior. At Jenny's bedside were her mom, dad, and boyfriend Darren.

Single parents. They come in all flavors, from very young kids who made a very old mistake to divorced men and women to widows and widowers. Some receive a modicum of support. Some do not. Almost none receive enough.

In these family situations, I am deeply concerned for both the child and the parent. Single parenthood is an exceedingly fragile relationship between an infant with intense needs and a parent with intense emotional and economic distractions. A number of severe dysfunctions can result, and almost never do parent and child emerge from the experience with the assets and advantages two-parent families provide.

That gloomy caveat aside, let me add an encouraging word: Single and dual parents share basically the same windows of opportunity for their children, and both can exploit those windows to prepare their children for adulthood in effective, wholesome ways. The major difference is that this process will be more difficult for single parents, as is just about every other aspect of parenting.

I suggest these overreaching rules of thumb that single parents might keep in mind:

1. A single parent must be willing to *ask for help*.

Probably because the opportunities are more obvious—school-age kids go to sports events, stay overnight at a friend's, and such—we are far more apt to help a single parent with school-age children. But the single parent of an infant or toddler needs our support even more than does the parent whose child is well down the road. And it's probably because we're uncomfortable helping out with such intimate duties as caring for a baby that we tend to be reluctant to offer that help. This is, therefore, all the more reason a single parent must be assertive enough to ask for help.

But who should be asked? Generally a single parent will go most often to his or her parents. They're usually more than willing to help. And in certain limited areas, they may be the best choice. However, parents should not always be the first choice for support (even financially). When the single parent moves home, he or she becomes a child again, and the mother/father-daughter/son roles are too ingrained to change.

A colleague of mine visited his folks on the East Coast one summer. He called his best friend in New York and arranged to meet him for dinner in New Jersey. Before he left, his mother asked what time he'd be home and warned him against being too late.

"I couldn't believe it, Paul," he told me. "Here I was a forty-five-year-old man, telling my mother when I'd be home. It was ridiculous, but I fell into that same old pattern. What's worse, she expected me to be home early! I was hearing that in junior high."

The nuances of that interchange demonstrate that the parent-child relationship flares up whenever one is in the physical presence of the other (sometimes it will manifest itself in letters and phone calls as well). My colleague could laugh it off and go home to reality. The adult child living with the parents cannot. Add to that the responsibilities of raising a child alone, and observe how easy it is to transfer those responsibilities onto the ready and (usually) willing grandparent. The one who suffers the most is the child.

Another very common difficulty is labeled by psychologists as "emotional incest." Rather than nurturing the child, the single parent calls upon the child to meet various needs of the parent—emotional satisfaction, perhaps even an economic contribution. The energies the child should be spending upon growing up are instead spent helping the parent meet life. I cannot overemphasize the damaging drain this places upon a child; we'll discuss it in more detail in the next chapter.

The single parent who is able to ask for and receive help from a variety of sources will not be as likely to look to the child to fulfill emotional needs. Thus, I feel it is absolutely imperative that every single parent have at least one other close same-sex friend for support. And that's just for starters.

2. Single parents must come to grips with the fact that they are *partnerless*.

This involves going through the grieving process to resolve and finalize the bitter reality that they most likely will go the distance parenting alone. This grief is in addition to grieving an actual death that has left the parent alone. Coming to grips includes also committing to forging ahead, to accepting life the way it is—as one instead of two.

Jenny Lawton probably did not consciously go through this step at first. Soon after her baby's birth, though, she visited a cousin who lived in a rural area of Texas. With her new baby on her arm, Jenny walked out among the scrub mesquite and peppergrass and the lazy, buzzing flies. She listened to sparrows chirp monosyllable warnings to each other as she approached. She watched a hawk trace invisible circles through the wide blue sky.

She stopped by an outcrop and sat down on a boulder made warm by the sun, pressed her knees together, and settled her baby Sara in the cradle of her legs, Sara's head on her knees and her tiny bottom tucked tightly against her lap. Unimpressed by nature, Sara squinched her face together and drew her legs up into a little baby-knot. She stretched and dozed off.

Jenny pictured that tiny mite at a year of age, bouncing around and getting into things. She pictured Sara at three and at five and on the first day of school. Jenny would have next to no social life and next to no money to call her own, no prospects for a good job, no education beyond high school. She would be totally giving up at least ten years of her life, the ones that ought to be the most exciting and fun.

It is claimed that children of single parents have more trouble in school, more trouble forming relationships, more trouble relating to the opposite sex and developing social skills. Jenny might be able to minimize those problems for Sara, but she couldn't completely save her daughter from them.

Was it worth it? An adoption agency was ready to place week-old Sara the moment Jenny released her. On that rock in the Texas sun, Jenny decided she would not look back. She would do whatever it took to raise Sara, with or without a partner, the best she could. Sara didn't belong to a stranger. Sara was part of her. Jenny would accept her responsibility.

Then the high school junior scooped her brand-new baby up against her breast, and for the next twenty minutes rocked back and forth, weeping uncontrollably.

Commitment and grieving. They are necessary components of single parenting.

3. Single parents must *resolve the guilt of not having a parenting partner.*

Frequently, problems I see with single parents stem directly from this guilt. With an intense need to somehow make it up to the child, single parents tend to overcompensate in two ways. For one, they foster a lot of self-pity, a "poor-me" attitude. "It's so hard. That's why Johnny is so difficult to handle." Too often, this leads to the second result—an entitled child. That's a fancy word for *spoiled*.

Single parents burdened with this guilt will bend over backward to gratify their children, often at the expense of their own needs and the true needs of the child.

To resolve this guilt before it becomes destructive, single parents must seek out other singles who have coped successfully with the problem. I say "successfully" because it's too easy for single parents to get together with others for a mutual complaint party—the old misery-loves-company tendency. Instead, it's absolutely essential to find a support network of adults who have been there and *made it*.

4. Single parents shouldn't try to change facts.

Johnny's mom must not try to whitewash Dad by telling Johnny or anyone else what a splendid sport he is. Likewise, Mom mustn't tell Johnny that his father is a despised so-and-so! Let Johnny make his own perceptions and judgments. As hard as it may be, Mom must tell Johnny the fair and honest truth, nothing more.

Jenny had a different problem, in a way; she didn't know what the facts were. Darren was a kid. So was she. They acted stupidly. And yet, at the time, it seemed so right. What would Jenny tell Sara when the questions started coming? Did Jenny love Darren? She wasn't sure. Did Darren love her? He didn't seem at all eager to jump on the daddy bandwagon. Their passionate affair had dissolved into a murky morass of question marks. How do you explain that to a tiny inquiring mind?

Time would alter Jenny's perspectives immensely, just as it alters any parent's. The divorced or deceased spouse will somehow freeze in time eventually and become an artifact of the past. Life will roll on. Jenny would be wise to put aside concerns about what to tell Sara for at least two years (and she probably won't have much to say about Darren for several years thereafter, until Sara begins to become aware of family units in the greater world outside of home). By then her own perspectives will have changed dramatically. She will have new truths to explain to her little girl, cloaked in new and more mature insights.

Another fact singles must face is that Mom can't change her sex at will, nor can Dad. Facts are facts—Mom is a mom; she can't be a father also. Dad can't be Mother and Father simultaneously. The single parents who can honestly accept this blatant reality will feel less pressure to perform perfectly, knowing they don't have to be something they are not.

5. God loves and takes care of single parents too.

The reason I mention this one is because it's so easy for us to see the Bible as speaking only of the two-parent family. In Scripture, God ordained three institutions: the church, the government, and the family. Division in any of them causes deep, disruptive, and painful feelings. Those of you who have been involved in the splitting of a church certainly know what I'm talking about.

A divorce, even though more common than the splitting of a church, awakens the same disruptive feelings in those of us who are bystanders as well as those involved in the split. It is, in fact, the death of a tiny church. What results is a lot of perceived and actual judgment. Too often, we feel a tendency to avoid a divorced single parent for fear of being over-spiritual or over-judgmental.

In various references (1 Kings 17:8–24, Acts 12:12–17, and 2 Timothy 1:5, to cite just a few), a mother, grandmother, or widow is mentioned, making the inference that it *is* possible in God's eyes to do it alone. There will be problems, but as Paul said, "the genuine faith that is in you, . . . dwelt first in your grandmother . . . and your mother" (implying an absent father) (2 Tim. 1:5).

6. Single parents must see themselves as having something to *give back to society.*

I had the fortune to visit a church recently that boasts the most varied and triumphant cross section of society I've ever seen. I saw all races, all sorts of disabilities, starting with the wheelchairs in the front row, all types of families—step, single, traditional, extended—and every level of economic status. I thought to myself as I sat in the congregation, *Boy, if Jesus visited Earth, this is where He'd come.*

The entire congregation is united in one purpose: they love the Lord. And in so doing, they love and support each other. They truly walk the talk that Jesus gave.

It was this congregation that gave me important insights into single parenting. One of the most useful was the realization that the single parents of this congregation were not only accepted just like any other family but also empowered with the ability to *give as well as receive* assistance.

From those people I saw that wise single parents move

beyond the mind-set of being the needy ones, and in addition to receiving, they give back—to their churches, schools, and communities. We've all heard the adage, "You can't out-give God." Give support and love, and it returns tenfold.

Seventeen-year-old Jenny Lawton faced heavy, heavy challenges for one so young. Still, she would experience joys, too, in equal share. Her range of emotions would match in magnitude those of Marsha and Tom Jasper and every other parent setting out. She was challenged; she was not unique.

Marsha Jasper looked over at Jenny one afternoon as they sat in their wheelchairs in the hospital entryway. They were holding their babies, waiting to be picked up and driven away into reality.

Marsha shifted baby Brian in her lap as she broke the nervous silence. "I sure hope I know what to do now."

"It's kind of scary, isn't it?" Jenny peeked at the tiny bundle that was Sara. "I just hope she stays healthy and growing."

Marsha nodded. "Me too."

Healthy and growing . . . although this book deals primarily with the child's emotional and psychological development, that growth is not divorced from physical growth. Also, parents tend to wonder, "Is my child ahead? Behind?"

Please remember that within very broad parameters, there is no "ahead" and "behind" at this age. Each child marches to a drummer unheard by any other child. In the following chart I've shown the approximate times when certain physical developments will take place. Use this information as a guide to watch your own child's development, but take it with a grain of salt. It can give you some clues of what's to come, but remember that every child is different.

Growth and Development Landmarks

Age
Newborn

Landmark
Rooting and sucking behavior—anything placed near the baby's mouth will make the baby seek and suck as if looking for a nipple. Baby will also automatically grasp objects when placed in his or her palm. Newborns exhibit a startle reflex, called the Moro reflex. The mouth pops open as the hands and arms fly out.

Age
Two to four weeks

Landmark
Your newborn will gradually fixate on your face or those of other human beings. This fascination with the human face will grow. It is the predecessor to the first true smile.

Age
Four weeks

Landmark
When laid on the back, your baby will exhibit the tonic reflex, striking a pose similar to a fencer about ready to thrust a sword, but with both fists clenched.

Age
Six weeks

Landmark
Your infant may start to follow objects with his or her eyes as you move them across the baby's line of sight. Use brightly colored or black-and-white objects with lots of contrast.

Age
Six to eight weeks

Landmark
Usually the first true social smile appears around this period. Although some infants start smiling earlier, doctors believe smiles before six weeks are not true social smiles spurred by a specific person but are instead a baby's automatic response to various stimuli, including the human face. Parents disagree.

Age
Two to three months

Landmark
Your baby may start to bat at objects that interest him or her instead of just looking at them.

Age
Fourteen weeks

Landmark
Your baby has better head control now. When laid on his tummy, the infant will raise his head and flex his body up on his arms at this age. Also, he will become well attuned to his primary caretaker's voice and face. His legs will grow stronger. An infant at this stage will kick out his legs in thrusting motions.

Age
Four months

Landmark
The infant has nearly adult vision capabilities at this age and can focus on near and far objects of interest. The first teeth may start to appear at this stage, making some infants fussier than others.

Age
Four to five months

Landmark
A baby at this age will be thoroughly interested in exercising his or her arms, legs, and torso. Somewhere in this period, the baby will learn to turn over. His or her hand and eye coordination improve. The baby will grasp at what he or she is interested in. Babies also tend to hold their hands together at their midsection during this period. From this period on, babies regularly smile and turns their heads toward their caretaker. This is the period, parents say, when they become truly enamored of their babies. At this age, babies are generally content and delightful to be around.

Age
Six months

Landmark
Babies will actually reach for and retrieve objects at this age. Anything they grasp will immediately go into their mouths for exploration. They will be able to turn over and sit up without being supported. In a way, this is the most frustrating period of an infant's life. He or she is intensely curious about the surrounding world yet unable to move about and explore it at will. The baby may vent this frustration by raging.

Age
Eight to nine months

Landmark
Watch out! The first signs of movement usually appear at this age. Your baby will start to scoot or roll or crawl around. Your house should be childproofed by now (see Chapter 6). Your baby will begin to understand and perhaps even say his or her first words. And the baby will recognize and associate certain words with his or her primary caretaker(s). Before this period, babies are generally friendly to all human beings—a necessary trait for survival. But around this age, they will recognize and prefer their circle of family members. Your baby may cry and cling when someone outside this circle approaches her. This phenomenon is called stranger anxiety. It is perfectly normal, although not all babies experience it.

Age
Eight to twelve months

Landmark
Your baby will be mastering crawling as well as a new motor skill, climbing. He or she will pull up to a standing position while holding on to something for support. Constantly curious, he or she may do seemingly boring activities for endless minutes. This curiosity is critical for your baby's future development. If it isn't noticeable by this age, contact your pediatrician.

Age
Eleven to twelve months

Landmark
Sometime in the next three months, the baby will accomplish the last of his or her crucial motor skills—standing alone and taking those first few steps without help. Soon the child will be walking, and in a few short weeks, running and able to climb

to new heights, literally as well as figuratively, moving upward as much as a foot at a time. (I remember a friend of mine who was picking apples from the top of his tree one fall afternoon. His wife came shrieking out the back door when she saw that their one-year-old had climbed to the top of the ladder and was reaching for Daddy's pants leg.) Stairs and hinged doors will have particular fascination for children of this age. Allow them to explore, but supervise carefully!

Please note that these developmental landmarks vary somewhat depending upon the individual child. Don't be concerned if you haven't noticed some of these changes at a specific age. I'm merely giving this general framework to show how fast a child changes and grows within his or her first year of life. If you have any serious worries, please see your pediatrician.

Creating a "Perfect Child"

Tom and Marsha Jasper, parents at last after all those years of trying, had observed everyone else's children carefully. They knew exactly how they wanted their own little one to behave.

"Brian will be perfect, of course." Only the twinkle in Marsha's eye betrayed her teasing. But down at the deepest level of her longing, it wasn't teasing at all. Way down inside her, she meant it.

Tom, too, envisioned a perfect child.

The problem? They weren't envisioning the same child. The child will certainly pick up on this dichotomy below conscious level, and it will probably translate as confusion. *Who am I? Who do you want me to be?* The child will be getting two separate answers at a time when individuation and personality are just beginning.

The Jaspers did not share with each other their individual visions of how to create perfection. Certainly they planned in advance how they would respond to such issues as degree of permissiveness and range of discipline, and that planning helped immensely in minimizing problems. However, now that they felt they had solved all their potential problems, they quit communicating at a level of fine detail.

When a baby starts crawling, and more so when he or she begins to walk, discipline commences. For with that heady mobility a window of opportunity swings wide open. Remember that our two goals for an infant are to teach trust and to help the child deal with the threat, or fear, of abandonment. When the little legs start into motion, so do those two opportunities.

Here is where parenting begins in earnest. The premobile infant offers no need for discipline. Personal interaction has little or nothing to do with will, or more particularly, conflict of will. With mobility, all that changes.

When Parenting Styles Differ

In creating their perfect child, what Tom and Marsha Jasper wanted to avoid (and Jenny and her parents also, for that matter) was a clash of style that would give the baby mixed signals.

To see what I mean, consider Linda and Alan Mayron's experience with Daniel when he started crawling. I broached this subject with them at one of their early sessions.

"Do you remember when Daniel started crawling?" I asked.

Alan Mayron answered, "Not really. Do you, Linda?"

Linda frowned and pursed her lips. "Let's see," she said. "Jessica had just turned three, so Daniel would have been close to nine months."

"What do you remember about this time period?" I asked.

Alan snorted. "The kid was into everything. I remember that part of it clearly enough. I'd come home from work, and the house would look like a bomb had exploded."

Linda, instantly defensive, interrupted. Her tone of voice suggested that this was a bone of contention that had never been buried. "It's just that Daniel was fascinated with everything. I mean everything. Like whatever Jessica was playing with. He broke a lot of her toys. And he stuck everything into his mouth. I had to keep my floors clean enough to eat off of."

I nodded. "I remember my own Matthew being the same way at that age. He had a rare knack for finding things in all kinds of out-of-the-way places. Then, pop! into the mouth it went. He found my cufflink that had been missing for years. So how did you cope with this hectic time?"

"Well, the first thing we did was buy a playpen. We never needed one with Jessica because she'd stay out of things we told her to. But Daniel . . ." Alan blew a raspberry.

"How much time did Daniel spend in his playpen?" I asked.

Linda gave her husband a quick glance as she said,

"When Alan was home at night, I had to keep Daniel in the playpen most of the time because Daniel got into everything and it annoyed Alan. But during the day, I let him explore. So I guess maybe no more than three to four hours a day."

And her surreptitious glance at Alan? I could read that now. *It's your fault your little boy was penned up like that.*

Linda's last statement was one of many clues that suggested Daniel had received mixed messages from his parents even at this early age. As we discussed and examined this period at greater depth, we identified the trend.

When Alan Mayron was around, Daniel's explorations were strictly controlled. As early as eight months, Daniel was spanked if he got into something he wasn't supposed to; but only when his dad was home. When Linda supervised him during the rest of the day, Daniel was allowed free rein of most of the house and was rarely admonished.

Opposing messages. From Alan: Don't annoy me. Stay quiet, stay to yourself, do not tear things apart. Don't be curious; it's disruptive. From Linda: Explore, examine, dig in, roam free. Feed your curiosity.

This pattern, as you would guess, continued throughout Daniel's growth and development.

New parents Tom and Marsha could avoid that push-pull opposition in two ways. They could keep communication open, discussing not just the cute little things Brian did each day but what they thought of them, sounding each other out. Also, they would both watch for those opposing messages and ask themselves what Brian would be hearing and sensing from each of them. They would all benefit as the parents took the time to examine the day's events from Brian's point of view.

When opposing messages surface, one of the parents is going to have to give way. I suggest that, had Linda and Alan Mayron seen their conflict of preference, it should be Alan who should let Linda's view prevail. The criterion? Daniel needed freedom to reach out, to explore. His need would (within reason) supersede Alan's preference for a quiet, uncluttered home.

Alan might take solace in the fact that this is a brief phase of a few years. Daniel would eventually learn to pick up after himself, would cease finding the pans in the cupboards so fascinating, would enjoy a longer attention span as he grew.

Ideally, Alan could join Daniel in play and exploration, to the immense and eternal benefit of them both.

Below are a few parenting tips and strategies I would recommend, based upon the child's age.

Recommended Parenting Strategies for the First Year of Life

Age
Newborn

Strategies
Respond to cries promptly. Cuddle and hold your baby often. A simple mobile placed where your baby (not you) can see it while lying in the crib or on the changing table can be beneficial. I recommend using black-and-white patterns at this age. Also, expose your baby to a variety of different environments and experiences. Take him or her with you to a variety of places (it

might be the last time you'll be able to do this without an interruption). Use a carrier that holds the baby close to your chest as you go about your daily routine. In other cultures, babies are kept with their mothers in a sling the entire day.

Age
Two to three months

Strategies
To facilitate head control, place your baby on his or her tummy for a few minutes each day. (Some babies don't like being on their tummies. It's a great impetus for them to learn to roll to their backs.) The act of lifting the head helps develop the muscles for head control. Use a carrier or sling liberally. An infant seat set up in the kitchen as you go about preparing the evening meal allows baby to participate by watching. Babies start to swipe at things at this stage, so provide some safe, dangling objects to swing at. From about two months on, your child will be intensely interested in his or her own reflection in an unbreakable mirror. Change your baby's scenery frequently to provoke a sense of curiosity. Continue to respond to crying needs and cuddle, cuddle, cuddle.

Age
Three to five months

Strategies
Play with and enjoy your baby. Talk to him or her regularly and don't be afraid to use "baby talk"; researchers have found that babies respond more to this high-pitched tone. This is a good time to begin reading aloud to your child. Some of the new board books for the very young, such as those by Susan Boynton, are charming. You will probably not hold the child's interest for more than a few minutes at a time. Change the scenery often, and don't leave the child in a crib or playpen for extended periods (a couple of hours a day should be the maximum).

Avoid curtailing movement by wrapping your baby tightly in blankets or clothes as you did when he or she was a newborn. The child will appreciate the freedom to move around now. Crib toys should be sturdy and able to take plenty of abuse. Crib gyms and kicking toys are especially useful.

Age
Six to eight months

Strategies
Play and talk to your baby with plenty of face-to-face time. Help the baby develop the back muscles by aiding him or her to pull to a sitting position. The game of "peek-a-boo" is a real hit now (for baby; you'll probably play it until you're bored spitless). Allow your child the freedom to move about. Put a blanket on the floor and allow him or her to develop the coordination needed to squirm, creep, and crawl. I don't recommend long periods in playpens, infant seats, or other contraptions that restrict the child's movement. Keep on responding to cries and, you guessed it, cuddle, cuddle, cuddle.

Age
Nine to twelve months

Strategies
First and foremost, childproof your home if you haven't already! (See Chapter 6 for specific suggestions.) I recommend leaving at least one or two cupboards accessible with some harmless plastic containers and pans so your baby can explore at will. Supervise your child more during this time period, but allow him or her to explore. For instance, let the baby climb the stairs and then assist him or her in coming back down. When you can't guard the stairs, block them off with a gate. Don't force certain activities on the child if he or she isn't interested. Reading is fine, but be aware that a child of this age has a very limited attention span. At about ten to twelve months of age, you can

begin to set rudimentary limits on acceptable behavior. Continue to show your baby love, do lots of cuddling, and respond to crying promptly.

Freedom to Reach Out

Baby curiosity is the most wonderful thing!

Jenny Lawton demurred. "In two minutes flat, Sara had toilet paper strung from one end of the house to the other!"

Martha Jasper also demurred. "Brian learned to crawl one day, and the next day he pulled the magazine rack down on his head."

Linda Mayron joined in. "Daniel was ten months old the day he flushed Jessica's stuffed kitty down the toilet. Do you know how much a plumber charges for that kind of thing?"

Freedom to explore means three things:

1. Your baby is growing in all the right ways.
2. You will be so exasperated for the next year that you could scream.
3. Your house had better be babyproofed by now!

I Am Me!
The Gloat of Independence

All of these first sorties of exploration and discovery are extremely healthy. They are the baby's first efforts at individuation and separation. He or she is becoming an individual person, as opposed to a mere adjunct of Mommy and Daddy.

Marsha and Tom Jasper learned that the way most parents do. Peering over the bassinet like two spies, they could hear little Brian's soft, rapid breathing.

"Is he finally asleep?" Tom whispered.

Marsha nodded. "Finally."

They had been waiting for this moment for a couple of hours. Marsha had planned a romantic candlelight dinner for just the two of them. But Brian had demonstrated that he was now an entity in his own right as well as a force to be reckoned with—and he had different plans. In fact, it had seemed that he somehow sensed Marsha and Tom's plans excluded him. For the last two hours he had screamed lustily and constantly.

Nothing they'd tried had worked. Finally, Tom put Brian into the carseat and drove him around the neighborhood. After about the three-hundredth loop, Brian fell asleep. Tom sneaked him back inside and gingerly put him in his bassinet.

Together they tiptoed back to the kitchen where Marsha's lasagna had been warming in the oven for nearly three hours. It was slightly dry, but who cared at this point? Peace and quiet. Just the two of them. *Heaven.*

Tom popped the cork and, with a flourish, poured their sparkling cider. Ah, the festivity of it! They touched their glasses together in a merry toast.

Clink!

From the back bedroom came the response, "WAAAAAAAAH!"

4. HUSH LITTLE BABY, DON'T YOU CRY

SEPARATION AND INDIVIDUATION

Trust begins at the beginning.
It cannot be added on later.

It was one of those afternoon lawn parties where everyone stands around talking but nobody really wants to say anything significant. The Dallas Cowboys, the weather, the antics of Calvin and Hobbes as depicted in that morning's paper—that's usually about as heavy as the conversation gets. At this particular party, however, I ended up in a conversation of vital importance.

The young woman, a very poised, articulate person, asked me, "You're the father of a son, right?"

"That's right."

"And I hear a friend of yours recently adopted a three-year-old."

"That's correct."

She lost a bit of her poise, biting her lip a moment. "So did my husband and I. Adopted a three-year-old, I mean. What advice did you give your friend that would help him offer his adopted child the same advantages your biological son has?" She puckered her delicate brow. "Do you know what I mean?"

Yes, I knew what she meant, and the honest answer to her question would have been, "None. He didn't ask for any advice." But that, of course, was not what she was seeking. Curiously, at that time she did not know my occupation. She was not asking my professional opinion; she was asking a father's advice on fathering.

Adoption inserts some pretty volatile issues in an already-complex situation—parenting. But whether a child be biological or adopted, certain precepts of separation and individuation apply right at the very beginning.

We sat down to talk apart from the crowd, this young woman and I, and I began the discussion by telling her about the Lines.

The Fruit of a Bad Beginning

If the sport was "Picking Lousy, Rotten Bosses," Michael Line was batting a thousand percent. At twenty-six, he'd already held down seven different jobs under seven really nasty employers. He is currently unemployed.

His first boss browbeat him and never gave him credit for getting anything right. His second, a woman, came on to him sexually, and when he responded she fired him for sexually harassing her! Enraged by the injustice, he tried to sue her, but no lawyer would take his case. The next two employers thought he ought to put in a sixty-hour week for thirty-five hours of pay. He quit them in a hurry. The fifth was an alcoholic, the sixth a nut, the seventh extremely abusive.

Meanwhile, Michael's brother, Trent, lucked into a

dream of a job with a boss who believed in giving raises every six months. In three years Trent had built up sufficient savings to buy a house in suburban Dallas. It didn't surprise Michael. Trent always got the breaks.

Now Trent was not only married, the bride was so nice that it looked like his marriage ought to last. Michael? He could count off more breakups than jobs.

Trent and Michael, the lucky brother and the hard-luck kid, were reared nearly identically in the same household. So why were they so different? Or was it just the luck of the employment draw?

As you may well surmise, luck was not at issue. Individuation and separation were. Although they grew up under the same parents, they actually were playing with two very different decks of cards, stacked right at the beginning of life. They were treated alike—and that was the first problem. They were *not* alike, not by any stretch of the imagination. That's one aspect of individuation; literally, each child is a unique individual, dealing with life in unique ways. The other aspect of individuation also comes into play: one learned trust before the age of three, and the other did not.

Individuation and separation, the processes by which a baby gains a personal identity and independence, begin about crawling time. Amazing changes take place inside that little head and body as the infant begins to crawl. He or she can suddenly make decisions about where to go; that never happened before. The infant rapidly develops spatial skills that were not there before. For example, he or she can crawl from the hall into the kitchen and know how to get back out into the hall. The child's world not only turns three-dimensional, but the child has some small amount of say about where to go within it. This new mobility is accompanied by spatial awareness and rudimentary navigational skills.

For the first time, this major change goes on inside the baby without parental contact. Crawling brings the first occasion when the baby is truly on his or her own. It's a major milestone.

Steps of separation and individuation will continue through the next several years, incremental lesson by incremental lesson. Then, in the early teens, the child will wrench free of the family's immediate grasp and forge the last important parts of an individual identity. It's a long, long road, but at its very beginning it depends utterly upon the infant's primal lessons of trust.

Trust

What is trust?

When a salesman croons, "Trust me," you stuff your wallet deeper in your pocket.

The teenage driver hops behind the wheel and says, "Trust me," and you check your change to see if you have bus money.

You sign a contract and trust that the other party will also honor it. That trust, of course, is backed up by the weight of law, which helps.

God says, "Trust Me," and you do your level best to do so, knowing that He, above all, is totally trustworthy.

Trust takes many forms. The kind I'm talking about can be defined as, "being confident the other person will come through for you." Add to that, if you wish, "being confident you will come through for yourself." This kind of trust will affect how capably a person can form intimate relationships, if at all. It is the basis of nearly all casual relationships. This is the kind of trust you must engender in your little one. Without it—well, let's look again at Michael and Trent Line.

When Trust Is Absent

Barbara Line, the boys' mother, has three grown children. She and her husband, Frank, adopted their oldest, Michael, when he was three-and-a-half. As sometimes happens, a year after the adoption she gave birth to Trent. Three years following that, Frank and Barbara had a third child of their own, Amy, now in college. Even though both boys received virtually the same care, they now function very differently as adults.

Michael's biological mother died in childbirth, leaving behind a large family. Utterly devastated, the father gave up and buried himself in his own grief. First Michael's grandmother tried to raise the kids. When it became too much for her, an aunt tried. Finally, the family was broken apart, with social services placing the children in various foster homes. Charmed by Michael's cute appearance, the Lines adopted him from one of those foster homes.

Michael, the Lines learned, had been a difficult baby, but they thought nothing of it. Many babies get a rocky start and do just fine. According to the aunt, Michael was so hard to raise that he was a major factor in the decision to separate the siblings. The aunt further stated that she felt resentful toward Michael because his birth killed her closest sister. She admitted that at a logical level her feelings were unfair and ridiculous, but that was how she felt anyway. Democratically, she bore equal animosity toward the father who could not handle his own loss "like a man."

"It's such a very sad story," Barbara Line said softly. "It's why I bent over backward to try and let Michael know how much I love him. I still do. But he never accepted my love."

"Did you tell him you love him?"

"A million times. This is strange; he literally won't believe me. He'll say something like, 'You don't really mean that. You're just trying to be nice.' As soon as he could, Michael left our house to live on his own. We still keep contact, but it's sporadic. It's certainly not the same as Trent."

Michael, the hard-luck kid. Michael, who cannot develop or sustain an intimate relationship.

"It's in the genes, right?" Barbara suggested. "Something he inherited from his father or something?"

Possibly. We're learning that a lot of the details about our makeup are inherited rather than taught. But Michael's home life during his crucial three-year window of opportunity never permitted him the lessons of trust in either others or himself. In fact, because of his turbulent first three years, his personal identity lies in shambles.

Trust 101, the Basic Lessons

I am not assigning fault by any means. Michael's father was stricken by grief and lacked support to help him overcome the blow. No doubt Michael's grandmother did what she could to take care of this bawling infant, but she had a whole parcel of children with needs to care for. The aunt also did her best despite her prejudices, but she had her own family to tend. Michael was not deliberately damaged. It just happened. The lessons he needed never came. No one realized he needed them.

Trust Lesson Number 1: Michael could not count on human beings to meet his needs.

Michael, a sad, hurting, little baby, was shuffled to three homes within his first year of life. Although he was almost totally helpless, circumstances placed him in competition with five siblings. Each time, his primary caregiver gave up when the going got tough.

Trust Lesson Number 2: Michael's family gave him conditional love—he was loved on the condition that he be a good little boy. If he wasn't, he was abandoned.

Abandonment. What an intense fear for any human being this is! For most children, this fear is forced into abeyance as they learn trust. It still looms large in Michael's adult life because he learned, by experience apart from words, that this worst fear is a reality. It came true three times during his first year, long before his rational mind developed.

Now, remember when separation and individuation begin—not before six to nine months of age, most generally, and then only in the most primitive, preliminary ways. Until that time the baby has little sense of personal identity. You and I cannot really empathize with a total lack of personal identity because we've possessed ours, for better or worse, for such a very long time. With the loss of Michael's mother, the giving up of his father, and the loss of a sequence of caregivers, Michael was not just abandoned but, at the deepest level, annihilated—a feeling that not only was he left alone but because he was left alone, his existence was in jeopardy. His existence did not merely depend upon those others; it *was* those others.

Three years down the pike, Jim and Barbara Line could shower all the love in the world upon that devastated little boy, but it wouldn't "take" well because Michael had no way to absorb it.

Trent, the lucky one, followed the usual path to separation, individuation, and the trust behind it. He had one major caregiver, his mother, and a father who, while not taking a particularly vigorous part in Trent's infancy, was there for him. Trent could step out farther and farther as he grew up, knowing the adults around him would do their best to help and protect him. In a word, he had good backup, and below conscious level, he knew it. In adulthood he could trust others to do what they were supposed to do. On those occasions when they did not— and every adult betrays a trust now and then—his core knowledge from infancy remained secure. He might grow wiser and warier, perhaps even cynical, but he wouldn't lose that basic ability to depend upon another.

Over and over, Trent's feelings would be hurt, his pride

wounded. No matter. He knew who he was, secure in his personal identity. The wounds would hurt, but they weren't fatal at a deep level. Michael's were. He had no strong identity or foundation of trust to protect him from criticism. Because he did not know himself, he could not read others well.

Do you see how this profound difference between the two men affects their ability to form deep and lasting relationships? Frankly, Michael is pretty much doomed to a life of what he has now. Intensive psychiatric help may make some difference, perhaps even a great difference. But it will never totally undo the damage inflicted in those first three years.

Damage Control. How might Barbara and Frank Line have minimized the damage that had previously occurred? Obviously they didn't know or understand the full importance attached to Michael's early abandonment experiences; probably they wouldn't, from their adult perspective, call them abandonment at all. But let's say they did realize that Michael was going to need very special help and attention in order to develop trust—that they could not simply raise Michael as they would have reared another child, such as Trent.

If they adopted Michael in infancy, the problem would still be there but not so severe. By providing the baby Michael with plenty of tactile contact, hugging and cuddling, plenty of verbal attention and eye contact, plenty of attention of the sort that your grandmother would warn you spoils the baby, Michael could restore a large measure of the ability to love and trust.

In his second year, Michael would be taking his first steps in real individuation, literally and figuratively. He'd be walking, and the new mobility would add to his independence. Also, he'd be starting to separate himself from his caregivers in his own mind. But that's scary. To illustrate, picture yourself walking across a chasm on a six-inch-wide board. If the board were lying flat on the ground, you would walk on it with complete comfort and ease, knowing if you tipped off, you'd fall less than an inch. But walking over a chasm, if you tip off the board, you're gone. Now picture yourself performing the feat with the aid of a dependable handrail beside you. That handrail is the adult caregiver in a one-year-old's life.

Michael's handrail was not dependable. People came and went. Worst of all, they did not understand his pain, for so many adults assume tiny children cannot feel loss. They misread his fear and hurt as naughty behavior. Frank and Barbara, had they entered his picture at this time, could probably have developed into a fairly trustworthy handrail by loving him in spite of his acting out, applying the extra attention and contact I described above.

At the age of two, and certainly at the age of three, Michael was talking and understanding fairly complex verbal messages. The Lines could reach him perhaps, if he was reachable at all (children vary widely in their receptivity to the ministrations of others), with the physical contact, patience, sweet firmness rather than arbitrary firmness, and a constant barrage of positive verbal messages.

Although positive verbal messages, drummed home over and over, would not have been able to negate the sense of abandonment, the feelings that no one in the world can be trusted, they would have minimized them. They would have helped. What messages?

"I love you," Barbara and Frank said over and over, but they voiced their love mostly in Michael's later years, as he was growing. They didn't think to verbalize it strongly when he was little and, it seemed, simply babbling.

"You are special." The Gaithers gave us a wonderful song, "You're Something Special," that says this beautifully: "You're the only one of your kind." Michael needed to hear that from the very beginning so he could get the message through more than one avenue to his heart. Music uses different brain pathways than do spoken words.

"You can trust us to do what is best for you." Children often interpret that promise much differently than do the adults, but the message, delivered simply and constantly, still would make some effect.

And there would be loving touch . . . always loving touch.

When Jenny Lawton heard the story of Michael and Trent Line, she nearly wept—not so much in sympathy for them as in sorrow for herself. "That means to give Sara a strong identity and trust and all that, I'm going to have to stick to her side for the next eighteen years! I'll never have a life of my own!"

"Good news, Jenny! That's not what that means at all. For separation and individuation also depend upon what we call *object constancy.*"

"Constancy! See? I told you!"

"As opposed to *object permanence*."

Does that mean Jenny should become chained to Sara, never to leave her side in case she might wound the little tyke for life? On the contrary. Jenny's job is to show Sara that when a trusted person leaves, that person will come back. Object constancy does not mean the object is there constantly. It means the object is constant (faithful) to a promise to return. Here's how the lesson works.

Object Constancy

"I hate peek-a-boo. It's *soooo* boring!" Jenny held up the diaper in front of Sara's face again. "Where's Sara? There's Sara! Peek-a-boo!" Jenny sat up straight. "Mom can do this a lot longer at a time than I can."

To little Sara, if you don't see it, it's not there. You don't see Mommy? Sara is hidden by a diaper? They're gone. An infant of Sara's age equates physical presence only with what she can see. Perhaps babies love the game so inordinately because of its mystical quality—whoever plays it always comes back. The diaper whips away and we're together again.

"Yeah," Jenny would be quick to point out, "but I already do that. I go to school; I'm gone. I come home; here I am. Isn't that it?"

That's it exactly! But Sara's primary caregiver is Grandma, not Jenny. Fortunately, when Jenny gets home from school, Grandma steps back out of the picture. An important person leaves. That important person returns with constancy and consistency. Sara receives crucial lessons in trust and separation.

Another separation lesson comes when the caregiver disappears while the infant is sleeping, as when a baby is put down for a nap, and returns when needed. The infant learns at a nonverbal level that caregivers can be counted upon.

Forcing the Lesson. Tom and Marsha Jasper had never heard of object constancy. They practiced object permanence, though they certainly didn't know that either. When the object caregiver never physically leaves, that's permanence.

With peek-a-boo, Marsha became bored even quicker than Jenny did. *Who needs it? Let's read a book instead. Reading a book is important anyway.* Marsha was right in that, and the presence or absence of peek-a-boo wasn't going to make a big dent in little Brian's life. But Marsha never, ever parted from Brian, and that *would* cause problems.

Marsha was teaching object permanence, for Brian went along with her everywhere. He traveled with his proud parents to the Jaspers' extended-family get-togethers to be shown to all the relatives. That's nice. He went with Marsha to the grocery store, the park, the mall, the gas station, the dry cleaners. That's good; a change of scene stimulates development. He watched Mommy get her hair cut and pick out rental videos. From wake-up to beddy-bye, Mommy was there.

Tom and Marsha did try once to go out together alone. Brian screamed as they left. Miserable, Marsha insisted upon returning early, unable to enjoy the anniversary date.

More forces were at work here than just object permanence, however. Without realizing it, Tom and Marsha Jasper were moving away from each other.

As a submarine navigator said, "You don't worry about major navigational errors. They quickly become obvious and you correct them. What you have to watch for are the tiny errors of half a degree. The error isn't noticeable, but by the end of the run it will put you hundreds of miles away from your intended destination."

Similarly, subtle change upon subtle change wrought a serious rift in their union, which neither recognized as it was happening. And the big loser? Little Brian, for Marsha was attaching to him in unhealthy ways. That attachment is the opposite of separation and individuation—and prevents it. We call it *emotional incest*.

Emotional Incest

Picture a waterfall plunging over a steep cliff into a pool below. As long as water keeps coming over the falls, the pool remains full. If the flow stops, the pool will eventually dry up. As a parent, you are the waterfall. Your job is to flow over and fill up your child's pool. In order to do that, your waterfall must keep flowing; the water cannot come from the pool, surging back up the cliff.

At first, Tom and Marsha Jasper poured ample water over the side to fill Brian's pool. But the flow unintentionally slowed until Marsha was trying to siphon water back uphill. That is emotional incest, and it works like this:

Tom did his best to be a modern daddy. He bathed Brian now and then, changed him occasionally (assiduously avoiding the really grody ones), and entertained his son while Marsha cooked or cleaned. But face it; Tom was nothing more than a baby-sitter. Way down deep, he considered himself so, and so did Marsha.

Raising a baby takes lots of money, so Tom worked hard. In fact, he worked harder, spending more and more time with his accounting firm, racking up overtime, and taking outside projects such as tax preparation.

Marsha took to motherhood with the cheerful determination of a winning demolition-derby driver. Nothing stood in her way, and she reveled in her role. As the months passed, Marsha became more and more involved with little Brian and less and less involved with big Tom. The man was hardly ever home anyway.

Tom sensed the change before she did. He felt vaguely jealous of his own son. Honestly! He kissed it off as a phase all fathers must go through and took on another tax account. His paycheck increased 22 percent.

You can see what was happening. Marsha needed to be the sun in somebody's sky. Everyone has that yearning. Tom came home for meals and sex and sometimes not for the meals. A fulfilling relationship must be far more than that. For attention, affection, and need, Marsha turned to her other man, Brian.

Certainly the relationship between Marsha and Brian was not developing as a relationship between two adults. I'm not suggesting that sort of incest. This was an emotional drain. Rather than pouring love and comfort into

Brian, Marsha was unconsciously trying to draw love and comfort out of him.

Selfish as they are, most babies are awfully good at returning love. Baby hugs, baby giggles, baby fists bopping you in the nose (and all the while that happy baby grin says, "Isn't this fun?"), and grabbing your hair—infants are programmed to charm. That's how they endear themselves and thereby get their needs met. Marsha was charmed. In a sly, subtle way, when no one was looking, her primary affection shifted from Tom to Brian. She had a new center in her life from whence would come the answers to all her needs.

How can such an insidious shift be reversed, especially when no one realizes it has happened? Once it's seen, there are definite steps both Tom and Marsha must take, but until it's recognized it will not be reversed. Let's look at the symptoms first and then possible solutions.

Symptoms of Emotional Incest

- Marsha feared to let Brian out of her sight. She was afraid to distress him by her absence. She was afraid no one could take care of him (especially in an emergency) the way she could. Down deep inside her, she needed his feedback, his presence. Object permanence replaced object constancy.
- Marsha and Tom didn't communicate as often or as well as they used to. That's a big red flag. In an ideal situation, Mom and Dad should be closer than ever at this point.

- One parent or the other—in this case Marsha—becomes intensely possessive of the child.
- The child exhibits severe separation anxiety. Brian cried when Marcia left and never settled down until she returned.

Either parent can become embroiled in emotional incest with a child of any age. It need not be the mother of an infant or even the primary caregiver.

Finding a Solution

Once the problem is recognized, how might the parenting partners successfully reverse the trend and swing back to a stable relationship?

- First and foremost, Tom and Marsha had to focus on their marriage. "A happy marriage ensures a happy child." That might involve counseling, books, or tapes, or simply sitting down and discussing problems and solutions *in love*. If they choose the latter, they will have to be careful about bringing in peripheral small and not-so-small gripes. These will not be sessions for airing grievances but for mending fences.
- Practice forgiveness. This is the heart and soul of reconciliation.
- Begin the healthy lessons of object constancy. Marsha should separate from Brian (ideally, leaving Brian in his father's exclusive care) for short periods, then longer periods. This is amazingly beneficial to the mother.

Just to get away awhile is invigorating once she can overcome her reluctance to let go.
- Engage the secondary caregiver to the extent that there are, in essence, two primary caregivers.
- Pay careful attention to each other as man and wife. This includes not only communicating frequently and at a deeper level (and not just about the baby, either), but actively giving each other more time.
- Nurture the self as well as each other.

All this is much easier said than done, the last two items in particular. But for the baby's sake and for the sake of the marriage, it must be accomplished.

If you see signs in your situation that one parent is becoming overly dependent upon the child, by all means sit down and discuss it immediately. Difficulties multiply as long as the problem goes unchecked. The enmeshed parent will resist, of course. Enmeshment is self-satisfying and hard to give up. Seek outside observation and counsel if necessary.

In Tom and Marsha's case, a counselor might recommend they take the following specific steps to bring their relationship back to its normal intimacy.

1. Plan a night to be together, just the two of them, at least once a month and preferably more often.
2. Together, the two must arrange for Marsha to get away by herself in a regular and constant basis to run errands, meet friends for lunch, whatever.
3. Make more opportunities for Tom to be alone with

Brian while Marsha is physically absent. Think "bonding" here.

4. Marsha ought to make contact with other moms of babies Brian's age. The people in her birthing class could be a good starting point. Share experiences and discuss problems (including over-attachment). Besides the cross-fertilization of ideas, Marsha should be seeking attention and personal interactions from an adult peer group.

The other cure and preventative, the nurturing of self, is extremely difficult for parents of infants. There simply isn't enough time in the day, particularly if older siblings are part of the picture. Marsha would be wise to broaden her interests, or renew them, by taking up hobbies or outside interests—anything to remind herself that there is more to life than a baby.

Mutual Support. By mutual support, I mean a peer group of parents at about the same stage of life. Mutual support benefits more than just the parents. It also does much toward helping babies during this time period. And it is never more needed than in the case of the single parent.

Mutual support for Jennifer Lawton was difficult. Many people who would leap right in to assist a struggling married mother ignore a teen mother. In such cases the subconscious feeling seems to be, "She had her fun. Now it's payback time. Let's not encourage this sort of thing by helping." Finding other moms in the same situation was not easy for Jennifer either. Juggling school and motherhood left her no time to seek out support apart from her parents.

Are parents a good choice for support? Not usually. They are not peers, and that poses an immense problem. They are too closely enmeshed emotionally in both baby and mother to provide objective support.

A single mom doesn't have the option that Marsha had—using her husband to give her a breather. Thus, stresses are more unrelenting. Curiously, so are the expectations. For some illogical reason (at the deepest level it's guilt, I suspect), single parents, much more than dual parents, believe they can—indeed, they *must*—do it all. "Succeed," they scream to themselves, "and succeed brilliantly!" Of all parents they most need outside help, and they tend to be the most reluctant to ask for it.

Jennifer Lawton wanted to do it perfectly, and she did not even have the advantage of maturity. But she had herself, and she could learn to give herself excellent support. When the world turns its back, there is still you.

Personal Support from Oneself. You are the only human who is close to you every second of every day. Since parents, particularly single parents, need support from every quarter they can muster, here's your chance to gain support from still another avenue. There are ways they can help themselves, but first they must know themselves—and that's not easy.

People have a difficult time seeing themselves. "O wad

some pow'r the giftie gi'e us to see oursels as others see us," wrote the Scottish poet Robert Burns. If you can't see what you really need, how can you meet that need?

The principle is this: Take inventory of yourself, not just once but every now and then. Then treat yourself not like you but like some near-stranger you are observing from afar. What advice would you offer that person?

Good. Now take it.

A personal inventory should include your responses to the following questions:

1. What makes you angry?

When's the last time you got angry? What was the external cause?

What might be a couple of underlying causes?

Did the expression of that anger immediately impact the baby in any way?

How could you avoid that sort of thing next time?

2. Are you holding in your anger?

Anger repressed—that is, turned inward—becomes depression. In addition, as hormonal balance shifts following birthing, mothers often experience a temporary condition called postpartum depression, or the "baby blues." At one extreme, the women may require drug therapy to get their hormones back on track. Hear me: Needing a drug regimen to reestablish a good hormone balance is not a sign of weakness. If hormones get far enough off kilter, no amount of self-talk or pep talks will bring them into line.

Your body is chemically out of balance and will *not* rebalance itself without outside chemical help.

Symptoms of depression include listlessness, increased appetite or loss of appetite, mood swings, volatility, reduced interest in activities (including activities that formerly brought pleasure), emotional unavailability, the blahs, reduced sexual interest, boredom, and an inability to get things done (never consider this inability a symptom as it stands alone; new parents *never* get things done).

Do you demonstrate more than a couple of the above symptoms? If you saw your present mental state in a friend or acquaintance, would you diagnose the problem as depression?

If any of your answers are yes, get a medical evaluation immediately.

3. When's your best time of day? When do you feel perkiest, get the most done, enjoy the day most?

Reserve your favorite activities for those times. You can do laundry when you're feeling lousy. If your best time coincides with your baby's good time, you're in special luck. Make the most of it by spending the time with your baby in stimulating fun things—reading books, taking a walk, visiting somewhere, going shopping.

4. If you were a person being observed from afar, what would you spot as your most immediate needs?

Try to meet them or arrange to have them met.

5. You have interests and needs that are uniquely yours. What are they?

How can you best meet them?

Almost anything you do within reason to nourish your selfhood, to differentiate yourself and keep yourself separate from the baby, will aid in the baby's individuation. The dividends, in other words, extend far beyond yourself. Children cannot become their own persons if they are tightly enmeshed in Mommy or Daddy. And the time to draw the line between parent and child is right now, at the beginning.

Understandably, Jennifer Lawton could not feel much of herself as a person. During Sara's neonate month, Jenny suffered hormonal depression exacerbated by sadness about her situation. Her friends were preparing for the junior-senior prom, and the volleyball team was headed for state finals. While her classmates and teammates enjoyed these rituals of spring, she sat in a dark room, rocking a cranky baby tormented by gas.

Jenny's needs? All she wanted was for things to be different, to be a kid again and have some one pick her up and cuddle her back to sleep.

5. BABIES ARE MADE TO BE CUDDLED

SOCIAL DEVELOPMENT

And Jesus called a little child to
Him, set him in the midst of them,
and said, "Assuredly, I say to you,
unless you are converted and
become as little children, you
will by no means enter the
kingdom of heaven."

MATTHEW 18:2–3

Age one month: Brain Jasper's grandmother picked him up, and he couldn't care less.

Age three months: Brian Jasper's grandmother picked him up, and he smiled at her. She immediately rewrote her will to leave him the family fortune.

Age five months: Brian Jasper's grandmother picked him up, and he cooed and smiled at her. She instantly commenced plans to groom him for the presidency.

Age nine months: Brian took one look at his grandmother and clung to his mother's neck, howling. Grandma promptly decided that her daughter-in-law didn't know beans about raising a child to respect his elders, let alone to care about them. Maybe Speaker of the House was the best she could hope for him.

Children's attitudes toward all the other human beings in the world change dramatically during babies' first year. Overnight, an open, laughing, go-to-anyone baby becomes a shy, woodland creature afraid of everyone. And vice versa.

This is all very natural. In fact, emotional and psychological growth *require* that children go through specific stages of social skill. Those stages reflect the children's changing awareness of the people in the world around them.

The First Step in Relationships: Family

The first step for an infant consists of recognizing that there are other people out there. Family members, naturally enough, are the first people noticed. In the beginning, the child's universe consists of Mommy. Then Mommy and Daddy. The parents create a solid three-way social relationship with their child. Once that relationship is comfortably in place, infants will have the handrail to steady themselves as they venture out into a scary odyssey to adulthood. They will feel much more confident about reaching out beyond the threesome.

Picture your newborn as a deflated beach ball, essentially two-dimensional. To transform the beach ball into three solid dimensions, you'll really have to huff and puff. One series of breaths you are already administering—the steps of individuation and separation we've just discussed. This separates your baby as a person apart from all other persons, a person who now must *deal* with all other persons.

The first breath, then, is: A healthy sense of being. Through separation and individuation, you are giving your child an understanding of who you are, who the child is, and how God made him or her. You strive to give your baby a sense of identity separate from you.

The second breath is similar: A healthy sense of what makes relationships work.

You are already on the road to teaching your child about trust, interdependence, communication, and interaction with another human being.

The third breath is painful but necessary: as gently as practical, help your child down off that pedestal. You must help the kid find out he or she is not the center of the universe after all. You can do that by what some call narcissistic wounding, and it is absolutely necessary. This is gently done in the first year of life. Each infant must experience that Mom and Dad are vigilant to meet the child's every need but that some limits to immediate gratification do exist.

Narcissistic wounding is the other great opportunity that must be first met during this first year and mastered during the next two years.

Sounds terrible. Abusive, even. Perhaps I can best define it by describing the children who are devoid of it. We label as "spoiled" those children who have never been blessed with narcissistic wounding, with removal from the pedestal. The fancy psychological term is "entitled." That is, these children think of themselves as entitled to anything they want. They demand their own way—and get it.

Spoilage does not remain spoilage. It festers into "exemption." Exempt children consider themselves exempt from the rules that govern all other people. They come to believe that laws, guidelines, moral standards—all those sorts of things—are for people not smart enough or aggressive enough or worthy enough to operate independently of them. Rules are for the "little" people. Exempt children or adults are extremely manipulative, routinely using duplicity and deception to gain whatever end is desired at the moment. Truth becomes relative, meaning "Whatever I want you to believe."

You know such people. You know the havoc they can cause. I am not suggesting that if you spoil your newborn he or she will become the next great serial murderer, but I will point out that within the psychological makeup of all serial killers lurks that exempt child.

Egocentrism and the Pleasure Principle

The terms *ego* and *egocentric*—that is, self-centered—are given a bad rap they don't deserve. Ego, a sense of self, is very necessary. Just because some people suffer from an inflated ego does not make a sense of self a bad thing. Controlled, self produces sturdiness and greatness.

Egocentrism is programmed into infants by God Himself and for the best of reasons: It contributes materially to a baby's very survival by making the baby so aware of personal needs that the infant immediately lets the rest of the world know, in no uncertain terms. How else could we know to faithfully meet an infant's needs unless we are reminded that they exist?

Along with this feeling that he or she is the center of the universe, a baby receives from God the desire to seek pleasure and to be satisfied, what Sigmund Freud called the "pleasure principle." This principle also gets a bad rap in Christian circles (so does Freud, for that matter, but that's another issue). Somehow it becomes vaguely sinful to satisfy one's own pleasures. In some cases, it *is* sinful, but when it is, other laws are being violated. Again, misuse does not negate the God-given pleasure principle.

For a baby, pleasure consists of food, warmth, cuddling—the very stuff growth is made of. So let us celebrate these two ingrained factors as seen in their utter purity—in a newborn child.

Managing the Principles

"Celebrate? In a pig's eye!" Linda Mayron, the beleaguered mother of twelve-year-old Daniel, sniffed disdainfully. "Daniel has altogether too much ego, too much egocentrism. He's selfish and always out to have a good time. Daydreaming. I don't care who programmed them in. How do you get them out?"

What Linda was asking, essentially, was, "How do you shape children, newborn or twelve, so they fit into the rest of society?"

You do so by managing the principles of egocentrism and pleasure-seeking, and that management begins even before the child leaves infancy. The goal is to teach the child to control both from within, and the first step toward that goal is to manage them from without.

Linda looked unconvinced. "Do you suppose that would work on a boy Daniel's age?"

The basic principles are valid for any age. How they are applied and to what extent they are applied are age dependent. The first step in the Mayrons' situation would be to decide which parental desires would be negotiable and which would be chiseled in stone. You do about the same thing with an infant.

First, differentiate between critical and noncritical.

"Critical is feeding and burping, right? Noncritical is picking up the toy Sara just threw across the room." Jenny Lawton hungered to raise a perfect child. She was ready for this discussion.

At five or six months, Sara probably forgot instantly about a toy that was cast out of sight, but Jenny's instincts were good. The bare necessities of babyhood are not to be manipulated. Attend to critical concerns immediately. Other things and factors in the infant's life can be worked with.

Sara was an easy baby to raise, early to fall into a routine that was comfortable for everyone. Brian, though, the Jaspers' little one, ate every hour and a half during his first two months. "That gets pretty old in a hurry," Marsha grumbled. "But what are we going to do?"

Feed him. At age two months, that's not negotiable.

Second, help Baby grasp a sense of time.

For a six-month-old, "In a minute, Dear," is synonymous with, "Tomorrow, maybe, if I feel like it." To a person without a sense of time they are identical concepts. Without a sense of time, patience is not possible, and patience is a necessity for anyone dethroned from that comfortable pedestal.

An infant cannot grasp the differences between an hour and two hours, between an hour and half an hour. An hour is a lifetime when you're tiny. But the baby should know that time exists.

Even tiny babies who are still unable to sit alone can be taught anticipation, which is a precursor to the time concept. You do it, of course, with games rather than lectures. For example:

Holding baby on your knee, *gently* bounce your leg up and down to: "Trot, trot to Boston. Trot, trot to Lynn. Be careful, Baby [name] that you don't fall in." As you draw out the word *in,* tip the baby backward, supporting the wobbly little head with your fingertips. Bring the baby upright again quickly. The trot-trot game elicits wonderful baby giggles as the infant learns to anticipate the dip. Pause briefly after the word *fall* and watch the eyes get big.

Another exercise is the time-honored, "This Little Piggy." (Complete text, for persons from the planet Mars: This little piggy went to market. This little piggy stayed home. This little piggy had roast beef. This little piggy had none. This little piggy went "Wee-wee-wee!" all the way home. With each "little piggy" you count off a toe or finger. Give the wee-wee-wee at the end a high pitch and tickle the baby's tummy gently. Time the wee-wee-wee to promote anticipation.)

Babies of all ages love games like these. As they grow, they can develop a more sophisticated anticipation until by age one or so, they can actually wait a minute.

Picture Brian at age nine months, sitting in his high chair. He has scattered his Cheerios and eaten his applesauce. Now he wants his cookie.

But Marsha can't produce a cookie instantly. "In a minute, Brian. I have to turn the potatoes or they'll burn."

That, of course, is not good enough.

Marsha might personalize her "In a minute, Brian" by giving him a quick smooch on the head (assuming his hair isn't full of applesauce, not an unreasonable possibility). Thereby he knows he's not forgotten or ignored. She might also make eye contact when she can, similarly to assure him he's not being neglected.

Within the promised minute or so, she frees up her hands long enough to dig out a cookie.

Brian has just received an excellent lesson. His are not the only needs and activities requiring attention. Other people's needs may come first, but they delay, rather than replace, his desires. And he receives a nonverbal, rudimentary idea of time.

Marsha didn't see that at first. "It seems too rudimentary to actually be a lesson."

To adults, certainly. We know what time and patience are. To the baby, patience is an alien concept. You are literally starting from scratch to develop in the baby the ability to move beyond egocentrism and immediate gratification. These are hallmarks of socialization, but they do not come naturally.

Third, be consistent.

Not only does consistency promote patience, it builds trust. Consistency has two parts. To make it effective, keep both parts in mind:

1. Follow through with what you say you're going to do. There is such a thing as delaying baby's gratification and such a thing as putting something off and hoping the little tyke will forget about it. "Later," and "in a minute" become "eventually, if you keep yelling." That teaches none of the right lessons. If you promise, with some form of *wait* as a contingency, deliver.

2. Maintain consistency between caregivers. Any and all caregivers should be on the same wavelength when it comes to delaying or granting an infant's gratification. And here is where Jenny Lawton ran into big trouble. As much as she wanted Sara to be perfect, she also wanted Sara to be happy. She hated seeing Sara cry for something she ought not to have to cry for. If Sara wanted a cookie, there were certainly enough people around that Sara should have one. *Now.*

Jenny's mom went too far in the other direction. She had a tendency to make little Sara wait for everything until such time as granting the favor fit her own convenience. "Sara can wait. She just has to learn patience."

"But Mom, she's too young to be that patient."

"You're never too young to learn to wait."

In this situation, Jenny was the kid and her mom the mother. Not only did Jenny's will not prevail, it wasn't even seriously considered.

Jenny's dad stayed out of it altogether.

Who was right, Jenny or her mom?

Neither and both. That's not the issue. Consistency is the issue, and they lacked it. This is an area where they should have reached a consensus. Because they did not, they should sit down immediately and discuss it, coming to some kind of agreement to which both will adhere.

Finally, know when to blow the whistle.

In some arenas, enough is enough, and it becomes appropriate, even necessary, that adult needs totally supersede the baby's needs and desires. This, too, is a lesson in socialization, and teaching it can be exceedingly difficult on parent and child alike. The Jaspers provided an excellent illustration of the concept.

Little Brian developed sleeping problems toward the middle of his first year. He'd wake up several times during the night and wail. He wasn't particularly hungry, although he'd often take some milk; Brian hardly ever turned down food. He was mostly just lonesome. He wanted to be held.

That's a need, but so is sleep. Brian could catch up on sleep anytime during the day (to Marsha's undying gratitude), but Tom and Marsha could not. To them, lost sleep was lost sleep, and too much lost sleep was detrimental. Someone's needs had to take a backseat, and the logical someone was Brian.

Exhausted, Marsha and Tom discussed the problem together and laid out a mutually acceptable plan to solve it. They followed these guidelines:

1. Have a plan. You can simply cut baby off from whatever the gratification may be, but that teaches no lessons. Tom and Marsha could each apply his or her own solution independently, but they might well work at cross-purposes to one another. Setting up a plan and following it (even if some aspects don't work at first or don't work at all) makes the path as smooth as possible.

2. Keep baby's preferences and thought processes in mind. Children are extremely conservative little creatures. They love routine and thrive on it. A bedtime routine at about the same time each night does much toward alleviating sleep problems. Tom agreed not to rough-house with Brian just before bedtime. Tom did, however, try to wear the kid out early in the evening. (He discovered soon enough, however, that babies that age don't wear out.)

Marsha decided to give Brian a warm bath, not because he particularly needed daily bathing, but because a bath is a relaxer. Then Tom provided his son with a baby massage, they each read a brief bedtime story to him, Marsha gave him one last little feeding, and they lay him in his crib in the darkened room. This, then, would be the unerring routine of each evening: bath, massage, story, feeding, good night.

3. Stick with it. Brian went to sleep right away, but three hours later, at ten-thirty, he woke up howling. Tom and Marsha steeled themselves. The agreement was, let Brian cry for five minutes, then pat him on the back without picking him up.

Brian had not been consulted in this, and he let them know his displeasure. He refused to settle down after a minute or two of contact and soft words. They let him go with another five minutes of howling, then Marsha went back in and rubbed Brian's back. After a long, *long* fifteen minutes of this, Brian finally fell asleep.

Three hours later (Did I say children have no sense of

time? They're born with a functional alarm clock.) Brian woke up. This time it was Tom's turn. Five minutes. Another five later. And another. It took a half hour before Brian calmed down.

At 4 A.M. when Brian set forth again, Marsha wanted to just bring the kid into bed with her. At least they'd all get some sleep. But no. They stuck with the plan for four long, long nights. Had it required seven, they probably would have hung in there, but four was all it took.

What, then, were the lessons? Tom and Marsha learned an important one: firmness and a plan produce results. Brian learned an initial, painful lesson that his identity and his parents' were different. This would be crucial as he entered his second year of life where separation and individuation are the giant tasks of growing.

In all such situations, where individual needs collide, nothing succeeds like common sense. Tom and Marsha figured out what they needed and how to achieve it. A little common sense and clear thinking go such a long way.

The Second Step in Relationships: Meeting the Outside World

At seven months, Brian loved the get-togethers that were a Jasper extended-family specialty. Aunts, uncles, cousins, and the grandparents all assembled once monthly for a potluck. As Uncle Les was fond of saying, "It's not a reunion. It's a big, happy gang war." While cousin fought playfully with cousin and plotted against siblings, the adult brothers and sisters caught up on the news and imparted bulletins of their own. Everyone dispensed advice, requested or not, and ate too much potato salad.

Normal Interaction with Strangers and Near-Strangers

Brian, being the youngest, received special attention at these gatherings. Marsha handed him off to some relative when she arrived and took him back when they left. Moving from lap to lap, Brian doted on all the loving and cooing. He learned from Uncle Les to blow raspberries (an important step toward speech, Les claimed). He enjoyed a different version of "patty-cake" from Great-aunt Edna. He gummed too much potato salad.

At eight months, Brian loved the gathering. At nine months, he arrived on his daddy's arm at the picnic site, took one look around, and wailed, terrified.

Brian would eventually come to understand about extended families, and one day he, too, would fight with his cousins. But as an infant, he regarded all those people as strangers because he only saw them once a month, and for a baby a month is an inordinately large percentage of the total lifetime. There is a period during a child's development (some arrive at it sooner, others much later) when strangers become scary.

The Jaspers were wise in introducing Brian to other faces and other people early on. They were also wise to remain at Brian's side or nearby during these meetings, associating themselves, the familiar, with the unfamiliar.

When Brian became frightened of strangers, they were wisest of all. They did not force him to socialize when he was afraid to. True, well-meaning aunts and uncles begged to take him and show him "it's all right." But Brian clung to Marsha, so, against the advice of the well-meaning aunts, Marsha kept him. She was right.

As the baby goes through a phase, and the baby will go through a good many, honor that phase and lead him or her gently out the other end of it. Socialization is not an event. It's a process. Good groundwork was laid early on, when Brian first came into contact with strangers in singles and in bunches. When the phase passed, he would become gregarious again.

More immediate to small children are situations in which the baby and both Mommy and Daddy part daily, sometimes for extended periods.

Day-care and Baby-sitting Situations

"Maybe that's where we went wrong," Barbara Line mused. "With two little children to support, we couldn't make it on one salary—Frank is a schoolteacher—and I had to go back to work. The boys spent nine or ten hours a day in day-care. So did Amy, from infancy on, but it didn't seem to hurt her or Trent too much." She sighed heavily. "It was only Michael. I just don't know."

Day-care is socialization with a vengeance. Forced socialization. It can be stimulating under certain circumstances. Too often, though, it is disastrous. Increasingly, it is becoming necessary. Many families can simply not meet expenses on one income.

Day-care was already a necessity for Jenny Lawton so that she might complete high school. Let's assume day-care has become a necessity also for a family like the Jaspers.

I suggest the following order of day-care options for children under age one, decreasing in preference:

1. In-home care by the mother and/or father
2. Part-time care by a baby-sitter (a family relative) at your home or her home (with no more than two other children)
3. Full-time care by a baby-sitter at your home or her home
4. Part-time care in a day-care center
5. Full-time care in a day-care center
6. Childcare providers who change every two or three months—inconsistent times and persons

The last option is obviously the least preferred, but it's what happened to Michael Line.

Option 6, unfortunately, is also the choice divorcing families usually end up with. During an emotion-charged split, the last thing parents think about is childcare for the kids. They're usually more concerned about the emotions of their children. Yet consistent childcare is one way they can help ease the emotional pain a divorce inflicts upon their children. Can a divorce be forged somehow without pain for the kids? Never.

Never.

Never.

Before Mom or Dad moves out, reliable childcare

should be arranged and in place. I recommend explaining to the children in the simplest, honest terms what will happen to them and reassuring them that they will not be abandoned. They are safe. Emphasize it. Reemphasize it. Say it over and over.

Option 1, no matter what, remains far and away the best.

Vary the Options. Increasingly, people are working at full-time jobs at least part of the time in their homes, communicating with their offices by telephone, modem, faxes, and computer networks. What a blessing that is for childcare! It makes option 1 possible. Even if Mommy or Daddy sits in a den closed off from immediate contact with baby, that parent is there. Available. Parents who have this option may, if the work requires it (and it often does), need to hire an in-house baby-sitter for the minute-by-minute baby-tending as Mom or Dad works.

Option 1 offers any number of other variations. Flexible work schedules allow moms and dads to jointly share childcare duties. Two of the psychotherapists at a Minirth Meier New Life Clinic, man and wife, arrange their schedules so that one or the other of them is home with their two small kids. An afternoon or two each week, when schedules don't permit one parent to remain at home, the children stay in a stable, unchanging day-care situation while Mom and Dad both work. That afternoon or two, a maximum of three or four hours per "dose," is good socialization. It's one of those situations, limited and brief, that can be considered beneficial. The arrangement provides an added bonus—Dad as well as Mom functions in an active caregiver role, not to be regarded as a mere baby-sitter.

Jenny's option was chosen for her. Her only way to finish school was to live at home while her mom and dad took care of their granddaughter. Because of inconsistencies between their childcare styles and Jenny's, and because of their own parent-child relationship with Jenny, this was not the best option. But Sara was enjoying the fruits of stability, and that was very important. Her world was solid. The opposite situation is what makes option 6 so poor; continuity and security are both lost.

Nannies. Mrs. Doubtfire and Mary Poppins—two more diverse nannies you'll never find. For a long time during America's egalitarian era, nannies fell into disuse except among the very wealthy. Now they're making a comeback. In a two-salary family with several kids, especially small children, a live-in nanny doesn't cost much more than extended day-care, and it offers several advantages.

Stability is a major advantage, of course. The children remain in their home; that's another plus—a variant on option 3. Childcare is consistent and manageable; Mom and Dad have the last word on the kinds of details Tom and Marsha agreed upon before Brian was born, details of discipline and lifestyle. A nanny can step in when a sick baby robs Mom and Dad of needed rest. The nanny can also take the baby for a stroll at any time of day as weather permits. The nanny has the time to sit and play.

There are disadvantages, however. Childcare can become sterile on the parents' part, even unemotional. The nanny takes care of the baby all day. Mom and Dad get home from work, spend an hour or two with the child, then it's bedtime. The baby has been tidied up and probably fed by the time the parents get home. Mom and Dad never get to celebrate the messes, and I reemphasize that tending to the messes, illnesses, and the problems bonds like nothing else can. By default, the child shapes the major bond, then, with the primary caregiver, the nanny.

These disadvantages can be minimized, but Mom and Dad must be aware of them and actively work to minimize them. They won't dissolve by themselves.

Theories of Socialization

Jean Piaget, the famous Swiss psychologist, divided childhood into four stages. According to Piaget, the first two years of life encompass the sensorimotor stage. During this stage children are preoccupied with the stimuli they receive from the world—the sights, sounds, touch, taste, and smell. They use these senses to develop their motor skills—rolling over, reaching, picking things up, sitting up, crawling, standing, and finally walking. These sensory details are also responsible for developing children's language skills as well as their visual capabilities.

Thus, the parents' responsibility during this stage is to provide an environment whereby children can develop these necessary skills. This does not have to be, by any means, a so-called "enriched environment" with lots of toys, educational flash cards, and sensory stimuli. To enrich any environment, Mom and Dad need only enter it and play with the baby.

Often this does not come easily and naturally. I am not saying this in a sexist framework, but differences of style do exist between most men and most women. For instance, men tend to be goal-oriented. That is, they need to see a tangible result at the end or the process of getting there will hold scant appeal for them. Finish that task! Complete that job! On to the next!

Playing with a baby is all process, with no easily discernible goal. That's tough for many daddies to handle.

Women, on the other hand, are generally more process-oriented. The act of doing something is itself sufficient fulfillment for most of them. They are more attuned to being with their babies and enjoying the process, messing around with no point, without a clear goal to guide them.

Both parents, therefore, should analyze where their focus lies. Fathers at first may have to force themselves to goof off, so to speak, in goal-less activity. Mothers, among other things, must learn to be patient with fathers. How often does a mother cry out, "Not that way!" and redirect her husband's efforts? Be tolerant, both of you, of varied parenting styles.

Play Groups

Aside from day-to-day interaction and care, there's little else an infant needs to learn socialization. Infants don't have to be in the company of other children their age. It is not until the age of three or later that most children can form any kind of actual relationships with their peers. At this age, socialization means relationship primarily with parents and secondarily with siblings and certain caregivers. It does not mean socializing with, let alone making friends with, other small children. Infants simply do not.

Play groups are loose associations of parents of children of a similar age. The parents bring themselves and the children together at regular times to play as a group. The play groups that form during this age are more for the parents' benefit than the children's, and viewed in that light, they are indeed an excellent benefit. Play groups provide a chance for parents to get together for companionship, mutual support, and cross-fertilization of ideas. They get the family out of the house and stimulate baby with a fresh environment. The other babies are mere window dressing.

Do all infants socialize in these ways according to these mileposts? Just about. In fact, Piaget and others have identified specific steps in the socialization process according to the following general guidelines:

Piaget's Schedule of Socialization Development

"Oh, good! I just love these lists and stuff," said Jenny Lawton, who read every magazine checklist and answered every slick-magazine questionnaire she came across. *Ten ways to see if you and your true love are compatible.* Jenny decided she and Darren were not. *Twenty questions to help you find your best career.* Jenny found out she was best suited to arc welding. Now here was a set of steps to tell her if Sara was normal or ahead of schedule. She loved that kind of thing.

Birth to two months
- Baby's only socialization is the direct relationship with one primary caregiver and, with time, a second. That social grouping provides all food, warmth, and comfort. Handling and tactile stimulation are as necessary as milk.
- Stimulate for growth and development by taking the baby along with you as much as possible; expose the child to the variety of sensory stimuli your world provides. These stimuli include the casual interaction of other people. The child will observe them but not relate to them significantly.
- Somewhere around six weeks of age, your child will begin to smile regularly at you. Smile back; respond to changes of expression.

"Yep. That was Sara," Jenny agreed. "I'd like to see the sucker who doesn't respond to a baby smile."

Two months to four months
- At this age, babies begin to develop into truly social human beings, recognizing family members and smiling regularly. It's a trait to be encouraged as much as possible by smiling responses and spontaneous, eye-to-eye "conversations."

- Certain actions and expressions invite the first giggles and laughter.
- The child begins to evince a strong sense of curiosity.
- Vision will be nearly fully developed through varying distances. The child will turn his or her head to see beyond the usual range of view.
- Babies make their first attempts at batting at objects.
- They start to gum objects of all kinds.
- Play with baby should be directed at reinforcing these skills.

"Oh, we did," said Jenny. "If my finger were rawhide, it'd be chewed into a shriveled little nubbin."

Four months to six months
- During this time, babies become fully responsive to other people in their lives.
- Babies begin to respond to tickling. You can keep a baby giggling uncontrollably by playing "cootchie-coo" at this age.
- At about this point, infants bond fully to the mother and father and vice versa. It's said that there is no other age where a human being is as high on life than he or she is at six months.
- Coos, gurgles, and laughter become the forerunners of verbal communication. Encourage them.
- Babies begin to see that certain behaviors on their part elicit favorable behaviors on the part of others. A smile brings a smile. A funny noise provokes cheerful laugh-

ter. The baby begins to deliberately perform these behaviors to garner the desired response.

- Expose your child to a variety of stimuli both inside and outside your home. Play, play, play with your baby.

"I wish I could play more," mused Jenny as she made faces at Sara in her lap. "I'd like to come home from school early, but they're making me complete my phys ed requirement. I hate phys ed."

Six months to eight months

- Anxiety about strangers and near-strangers may appear toward the end of this stage. Allow it.
- At this age, babies begin to play simple social games with siblings or adults such as peek-a-boo or cootchie-coo.
- Babies become interested in cause-and-effect relationships during this period. They explore, for example, what happens when they open a cupboard and the sound it makes when they slam it shut.
- They pick up small objects and put them in their mouths.
- Toward eight months, babies can sit in a high chair and feed themselves safe-sized bites of food.
- As the baby becomes mobile, create a safe and uncontaminated environment that can be explored at will.

"We're in that stage now." Jenny looked just plain tuckered out. "I can't begin to describe the clutter. Toys all over. If Mom didn't keep coming home from the store with toys, it wouldn't be this bad. You know, a few nice things for her to play with, that's all she needs. But not all this stuff. And that's not even mentioning the pots and pans out on the floor and those cottage-cheese cartons."

Eight months to twelve months

- Review the baby's environment for safety hazards. About 80 percent of all child accidental poisonings occur between the ages of eight months and two years. Choking is also a severe hazard.
- Expect nonstop activity. From this age on, a toddler can outperform a conditioned athlete. (In fact, a study proved professional football players who mimicked a two-year-old petered out long before the toddler did.)

"Oh, sure," Jenny said, grabbing Sara as the baby scooted off across the floor. "Thanks a lot!"

Socialization After the Fact

As Barbara Line read over the list detailing children's social development from birth through grade school, she thought about Michael. Physically, he developed right on schedule. Socially? Few smiles, no closeness. Heaven knows she tried to get close to him. It was as if he kept his elbows locked so no one could come near or hug him. Whatever his problems, they were psychological rather than physical.

Wasn't there some way to restore the years the locusts

had eaten? Poor Michael, condemned to loneliness and bitterness—there must be an answer. Surely God wouldn't doom an innocent child damaged by circumstance.

Suddenly furious, Barbara slapped her hand on the table and shouted loudly, "Hang it all, Michael-child, I love you! I do!"

She could perhaps pay for a psychological evaluation. There might be something, now that he was an adult, that he could learn about himself and perhaps turn himself around. Kids don't see the future well enough, but by this age Michael had a good look at it.

If psychological counseling would help, she and Frank could handle the cost. They'd already invested a lifetime in Michael; a few dollars more wasn't going to make much difference to them. That money just might make a world of difference to Michael.

On impulse, she picked up the phone and punched in his number. A passionless recorded voice informed her, "We're sorry. The number you have dialed has been disconnected."

Frustrated beyond words, she threw the whole phone across the room.

6. THE MANY MEANINGS OF GOO-GOO

LANGUAGE DEVELOPMENT

Do you hear the children weeping,
O my brothers,
Ere the sorrow comes with years?

ELIZABETH BARRETT BROWNING,
The Cry of the Children

So then Darren stopped by the locker and said, 'Why aren't you going Friday night?' And I told him . . ."

Jenny paused in midsentence and burst out laughing. She sat draped across the overstuffed chair in her knotted I'm-on-the-phone pose, talking to her best friend, Bev. "Dad just went into the bedroom to tell Sara to go to sleep. Sara's been in her crib for half an hour now. And she blew him a raspberry! You shoulda heard it! Dad's big old voice saying, 'Now go to sleep, Honey,' and this little baby goes *Bpbpbpbpbpbpb*."

Jenny stopped and frowned. "What do you mean, that's all I talk about? It was cute." She frowned harder. "Well, Miss Beverly Tired-of-Hearing-about-the-Kid, that happens to *be* my whole life. Sara is coming along great, and I'm glad my life is going this way, and it's a darned-sight richer than your life. Good-bye!"

The All-Importance of Language

Were Jenny to assess the importance of language in her life and Sara's, she would find that actual communication is only a part of it. Language also provides a pleasure of its own. Teenagers on the phone are not just communicating as such; they're enjoying language. And babies do the same thing with their babble.

When Sara blew that raspberry at her grandpa, she was by no means being disrespectful, of course. Babies have no concept of respect and disrespect, the ranking of humans that gives one person glory above another. Sara was taking pleasure in making noise. Sara did not know or care (neither did Jenny, for that matter) that the messy noises with which babies experiment are the second important step toward the exceedingly complex skill of language mastery. The first? Hearing.

Baby's First Contact with Language

Do babies hear while they're still in the womb? Observation and some experiments indicate they do. They apparently hear their mother's voice, certain ranges of music, perhaps their father's voice (in a birthing class I watched the patently intriguing sight of a young man yelling loudly at his wife's bulging belly), and sharp noises such as explosions.

From birth to about six months, the newborn will attune to the unique nuances, sounds, and rhythms of his or her birth language, be it inflection or a *diphthong*, a monosyllable comprised of two vowel sounds. By the age of one year, the baby's window will have closed to all except the sounds of its birth language.

All this takes place by ear, for the infant has yet to utter that first word. When the baby does at last begin to speak, the skill will not come by imitation of sounds but by reproduction of sounds carrying meaning. In other words, you need not speak baby talk to your child like a parrot, using short, stilted, simple words. Children who develop the best language skills seem to come from homes where they are spoken to like human beings right from birth.

This is not to say you ought to avoid the silly, repetitive baby-babble that adults apparently love to inflict upon wee ones. One of the very best exercises in controlling mouth and tongue a baby can perform is to simply trade happy noises with an adult.

The three-year-old speaking with the parents' accent is not just mimicking words. That child is already capable of hearing another accent or dialect and translating it mentally into the accent of birth.

To illustrate, New Englanders with a heavy Down East accent change the *ar* sound most Americans pronounce as *ahr* to a short a: *aa*. A *kahr* (car) becomes *kaa*. Now, in a small town in Maine, a friend of mine was transporting small children to and from Head Start. One four-year-old asked her, "What's your little girl's name?"

"Mary Margaret," said my friend, an Ohioan, pronouncing the second name *MAHR-gret*.

Instantly the child came back with, "Mary *Maa-gret*. That's a nice name." She had dropped the *ar* sound. The child did not spell yet or know her alphabet. She did not just mimic the adult's words. Her brain automatically transliterated the word she heard into the speech she knew.

And of course, crying is a nonverbal language all its own.

Cries and Whimpers

Jenny scowled, pouting, at her cereal bowl. "I can't get over that! Bev as much as said, 'Quit talking about the baby so much. It's boring.' She's such a spoiled snob! All she talks about is boys. And CDs. And which rich kids own how many clothes. And shopping at the mall." She spooned another glob of applesauce into Sara.

Across the table, her mother shrugged. "Bev's world and your world are different. No, she probably isn't interested. Babies don't mean that much to her yet. But just wait 'til she has a little one."

"Yeah. If she does, the placenta will be a Gucci bag." Jenny watched Sara gnaw on a chunk of toast for a moment. "Mom? I said my life was richer than Bev's. Do you think it is?"

"Look at how much you've learned. You know just about everything Bev does and a whole lot more." Mom poured milk on her cereal. "For instance, when the baby cries, what do you hear?"

"The baby crying. Oh. You mean, interpreting it. Telling what it means."

"You're very good at that. Didn't you ever notice?"

Jenny's ear, without training, could pick up many of the meanings in Sara's first attempt at communication, the nonverbal act of crying. Jenny recognized any cry of pain or real fear as something to respond to immediately—even faster than immediately. When he or she is in pain or intense fear, an infant usually sucks in great breaths, pauses, and wails, then repeats the pattern. This cry of true distress sends adrenaline boiling through the veins of any parent.

Discomfort cries, from low rumblings to periodic crying to loud wailing, elicit a somewhat more leisurely response.

A hunger cry can actually bring on the "let-down" reflex in a nursing mother.

True language development differs greatly from nonverbal communication such as crying or simply yelling. Breathing, tone of voice, and intricate maneuvering of tongue, lips, and mouth, together with incredibly exact control of the voice box, or larynx, all come together in a complex and utterly fascinating phenomenon, human speech. But that's only half of it. The brain must first organize the thought to be expressed, translate it into words that will mean something to another person, and then instruct the mouth and larynx step by step as it fashions those words coherently, emitting exactly the right sounds in precisely the correct sequence. The wonder is that children below the age of three master it so very well.

Language Development

We doubt that newborns comprehend the meaning of words, as such, but we know they are preparing themselves to communicate by developing two crucial skills. The first and probably most critical is listening. Although newborns don't have quite the acute hearing ability of adults, within a few months, babies' hearing matches ours. Soon it will exceed adults'.

Because neonates haven't yet developed the ability to look where sound comes from, most parents don't notice that their newborn is listening to their speech. Research suggests that newborns become attuned to their biological mother's voice before birth.

An infant begins from birth to recognize the specific sound of his or her primary caretaker's voice, and that primary caretaker may not be Mommy. Daddy, adoptive parents, or another—whoever is in charge—rings Baby's first bells. As the baby grows, he will become so attached to his caretaker's voice that, as the caretaker enters a room and speaks, he will voluntarily turn his head in her direction.

Loud noises will startle the newest infant. A baby who does not jump at loud noises may be suffering impaired hearing. If a child is slow to respond to sudden sharp and loud sounds, have the hearing evaluated immediately. Considering that an infant conveys almost nothing about what is going on inside that tiny head, you will be amazed at how much experts can learn about the baby's hearing. Partial losses, if corrected quickly, will not impede language development. Left to drift or worsen, these losses can cause serious harm, for it is during the first six months, remember, that Baby's language development flowers, and hearing is a very large part of that flowering.

The other skill newborns develop as a prerequisite to language development is understanding the concept of communication, both as pitcher and as catcher. Crying, though pretty basic and simple, is a pitching attempt. When babies' crying brings the desired result—food, warmth, dryness, cuddling—they learn that, by gum, they can indeed tell the world what they want with some hope of getting that desire met. This is an important and profound lesson that we, in our infinite adult wisdom, often overlook.

However rudimentary, the very act of communicating, the joining of what I am thinking with what you are thinking, is a giant victory for the spirit. It is a reaching out, absolutely necessary to the growth and happiness of the human soul.

How soon can babies discern meanings—that is, be on the catching end? On record is the observation that a normally hearing baby, the child of hearing-impaired parents, signed "milk" at the age of three months.

Hearing-impaired parents and children face special challenges when it comes to communicating through language. Signing, as it is done in America, is a language all its own, with its own syntax and structure. You can sign exact English, but that's not the same thing as American sign language per se. In fact, signers can identify regional accents and colloquialisms by communicating with others from across the country.

So complex is language processing, children who grow up fluent in American sign language may face special challenges learning to speak at all or even learning to read and write. If your child appears to be hearing-impaired, study up immediately on the latest in various alternatives to spoken communication. The earlier your child grasps this second fundamental—that communicative give-and-take is possible—the better he or she will be able to address all the rest of life's challenges.

Helping Baby Speak

Spit is a delightful fact of life when you're a baby. You can have so much fun with spit. Sneeze and watch your caregiver's face wrinkle up. Blow a raspberry and watch your caregiver smile, encouraging you to do it some more. Let the spit drool, and you'll receive wonderful things to chew on. Blow bubbles for a cheap laugh. Smear it all over Grandpa's glasses. Ah, spit!

The baby neither knows nor cares that making noises with saliva is a necessary precursor to mouthing and saying certain sounds (r's for instance). The saliva just happens to be handy as a lubricant and sound variant. Babies respond to the human voice even as they ignore other sounds. Researchers, who love to quantify and test everything, presented babies with a variety of sounds, including a disembodied human voice. The infants responded primarily to the voice sounds, answering with babble and other noises. But then, any mother, Jenny Lawton included, could tell you that.

It is Mom and Dad, and another caregiver if appropriate, who becomes Baby's first and best teacher, and the language school is the most informal school imaginable. Simply stated, it is *talking*. When Jenny takes Sara out for a stroll and talks about the squirrels and pigeons and trees, she's teaching language. As Jenny talks primarily to herself during a diaper change ("Oh, gross! What have we here?

Sara Sweet, did I ever tell you you're a little poop? Hey, who's still the cutest of them all? Sara Sweet!"), she's teaching language. When she invites Sara to accept one more bit of strained peas, she is teaching language.

If those nosy, quantifying researchers have proven anything in study after study, they have demonstrated that content, well-developed children come from environments where they are talked to and played with by adults on a frequent basis. Silent, withdrawn children—who, incidentally, are almost always slow in speaking—come from an atmosphere in which they've had little interaction with adults and have been left to themselves for long periods of time to find their own entertainment.

Not that babies don't entertain themselves. Wee ones manage to fascinate themselves with their hands, their feet (which always come as a surprise when they appear in front of the babies' face), and the sounds from their mouths. They may well converse with themselves, particularly when awakening.

Babies equate language with pleasure, and here is that pleasure principle in action again in a new dimension.

"Yeah, I'll believe that," Jenny would say. "Did you ever notice? Sara doesn't make sharp, angry sounds when she's babbling. You can yell at her but she doesn't yell back. She talks—you know—uh, conversational."

In addition to the hunger to communicate, pleasant feelings and comfort are a driving force behind a child's language development.

Wise parents choosing an alternate caretaker for their baby, therefore, will look for a chatty, cheery person who has no reticence about talking frequently and conversationally to infants.

This pleasure principle is another reason parents should affirm that their infant's hearing is normal. Deaf babies babble like anyone else until about six months of age, then they taper off. Some doctors believe that the babies, unable to hear their own sounds, take no pleasure in the act of verbalizing and for that reason lose interest.

I cannot overemphasize that the common denominator among all areas of your child's development is your physical presence and interaction. Jenny Lawton's mother, as Sara's caregiver during Jenny's school day, would do well to deliberately enable Jenny to enjoy a maximum amount of one-on-one time with Sara. This would mean handling chores such as baby laundry that would otherwise keep Jenny away from Sara. Jenny's day, already packed with classes and homework, left scant free hours. I'm not talking about "quality time," a hollow concept if ever there was one. I am encouraging sheer time in the saddle, the child in the company of the parent, doing things.

Another adult is not the same thing. Jenny's friend Bev could decide to develop baby-sitting skills and take Sara out. Stimulating, it might be. But a good source for Sara's language-skills improvement? No. A child learns to talk based upon the various inflections and experiences heard in the parents' voices, for it is those voices to which the child is most fondly attached.

Here are some specific things you can do to enhance speaking skills while playing and conversing with your infant, especially once he or she starts attempting actual words.

1. Converse with your child, not around him or her. By this I mean carry on a conversation to your baby's face. If you talk to other children or adults, occasionally include your child. You can send no unspoken message more powerful that the one that says your baby is a real *and communicating* human being who counts. Believe me, this is a message your child needs to understand from day one.

2. Respond enthusiastically to babblings and initial words.

3. Talk about things that interest you and your baby—that is, things the two of you have directly experienced. Know that a baby's attention span is short, and accessible memory even shorter. The baby may not remember seeing the big black crow come down and steal a potato chip in the park yesterday. But you never know, so talk about it anyway if you wish.

4. As much as possible, use specific, consistent words that name certain objects over and over. Each time you fix your baby cereal, say "cereal," not "food" sometimes and "cereal" sometimes. When you're going to the grocery store to buy cereal, say, "we are going to the store to get you some *cereal.*" And when the baby eats the cereal, ask him or her, "Isn't that *cereal* good?" Each time the baby will be hearing the word "cereal" and associating it with the gooey, tasty stuff that goes in his or her mouth. When the association seems consistent (kids are clever creatures; it doesn't take long), then you can branch out into *oatmeal, pabulum* and such.

5. Don't correct those first mangled words. Believe me,

your baby is trying his or her best to speak and hear. No one expects a child's first crayon attempts to look like Van Gogh (well, maybe some of Van Gogh); similarly, early speech attempts are stick persons with strange lines.

6. *Use animated gestures and voice inflections.* Overact! Babies love it. If you doubt that, play a game of peek-a-boo with wildly exaggerated hand movements and voice inflections. Then repeat the game using a monotone voice and a deadpan expression. Facial expressions and gestures add a great deal of meaning to the bare words; they reinforce the baby's understanding about what real communication is.

When Is Too Much Too Much?

Tom Jasper looked weary just talking about it. "My nieces visited us last weekend. A four- and six-year-old. They played house, using Brian for the baby. I don't know how Marsha lived through that. Talk-talk-talk, talk-talk-talk, talk-talk-talk. Marsha needed a can of tomato sauce for dinner and asked me to go next door and borrow one. Instead I got into the car and drove to the store."

I smiled. "I thought you were a strong environmentalist. Wasn't that trip wasteful?"

"My car," Tom replied, "doesn't talk."

Marsha's patience had worn thinner than Tom realized. "I'm not used to little girls talking so constantly at such a high pitch. I don't want Brian to be like that. Is there such a thing as slowing down a toddler's language development? Maybe channeling it?"

No.

Keep in mind throughout your child's early years, and it is just as true in this first year as at any other time, that your baby has an immensely intricate and demanding skill to master. He or she will play with sounds, experiment with what lips do, and see what happens when this attempt at communication or that one is followed. In one sense your child is learning from scratch what you do instinctively from long practice—communicate verbally. In another sense, your child already has a leg up on the task in the form of natural, innate linguistic gifts.

An incredible amount of investigation goes into this. The string of messy, slippery, spit-besmirched noises are serious attempts to understand what can be done and how to do it. In later years, the child's nonstop prattle will be that same investigative effort in new directions. Again, the goal of actual communication may be secondary to the goal of pleasure in the process of communicating.

May I suggest above all that, as you talk to your baby, pay attention to what you get back. I find endlessly fascinating the development of skills in eager little people. Literally listening to the progress will form a bond with your infant you can attain in no other way.

Is My Baby Normal?

Marsha and Tom carefully compared their Brian against the "average growth" charts in the child-development books. Sara read the magazines she bought at the grocery-store checkout counter.

Even Linda Mayron fell prey. "Look, Daniel. It says here that a twelve-year-old boy is supposed to be five-feet-four, and you're five-feet-six already."

"Mom, that's averages. Our family's supposed to have two-point-six kids too. We're point-six short."

Daniel has an excellent point. To quote the pundit, "No generalization is valid, including this one."

For the parents who absolutely must gauge their kiddie against some nonexistent norm, here is a list of words a baby will probably give evidence of understanding within the first year. Possibly the child might even say some of them. The absence of speech is nothing to worry about, and its presence is nothing to boast about. I hope that doesn't pop too many balloons.

Mommy	ball
Daddy	juice
shoes	hug
cracker	kiss
cookie	throw
dog or doggy	me
cat or kitty	no no
bye-bye	(sibling's name, usually
hi	mauled)

Adult Language 101

Equally as important as developing your child's language skills is developing your own.

"Oh, right," Jenny might whine. "Here we go. As

my toad-shaped English teacher, Ms. Bagby, says, 'English is the most important subject you will learn.' Of course, Mr. Damart says, 'History is the most important subject you will learn.' And Mr. Compton says, 'Math is the most important.' Get the idea?"

Clearly. But when I speak of language, I mean any language and any communication between any two people. Half of communication is making an idea understood. Transferring a concept from one mind to another necessarily involves both minds. The other half is listening.

Some of the people who listen best are the hearing impaired. They must depend on more than just ears. To discern meanings, they "hear" gestures, body language, positioning, facial expression, degree of agitation or gladness—a hundred things in addition to the voice and its inflections. The person of normal hearing ought to be listening to all those things as well.

Babies do. They also instinctively pick up on what Mommy and Daddy do. If you model good listening, they will learn better listening—particularly if you take the time and effort to listen to *them*.

Incidentally, just how good are your own listening skills? Every single day—and I am not exaggerating—I sit in my office as men and women discuss their children, and children describe life with their parents, and I am the only person in the room who's actually listening. Not only do they not hear each other, they don't even hear themselves. In so many cases, if they would only have listened to what one another were saying, they would not have needed me at all.

Linda Mayron, as we were discussing Daniel's problems, said, "Of course I listen!"

And her husband Alan added the postscript, "Daniel doesn't talk about anything worth hearing."

What did Alan really say in that sad statement? *Daniel doesn't say anything I'm interested in or agree with; therefore, I'll not bother to listen.*

I yearned to respond, *Whatever makes an adult male think a preteen has to enlighten or entertain him in order to be interesting?* I did not, of course. And yet, had Alan and Linda honed their listening skills early on, and heard Daniel from the beginning (a stultifying task at times, I admit), they would probably not be seeking help now.

I'll go a giant step further. If Linda and Alan would hone their listening skills now, it would improve their situation immensely.

"All right," Linda conceded. "How shall we go about it?"

As a start, play a game. Because listening is not based upon merely hearing the words, you'll want also to sharpen your sensitivity to all the sensory details the listener gets during an interaction.

The Listening Game
1. Select a partner to play this game with you. It can be another adult or an older child.
2. Sit facing each other without actually touching. Keep both feet flat on the floor.
3. Choose one of you to start out as the communicator; the other becomes the receiver.

4. The communicator thinks of a *simple* message to communicate to the receiver.
5. The communicator conveys the message to the receiver *without* using intelligible words (no foreign language either). It's fair to use as many gestures as it takes; just don't leave your chair or raise your feet off the floor.
6. The receiver then speaks, telling the communicator what the receiver perceives the message to be. The interpretation may be right on, pitiful, or hilarious.
7. Reverse the roles, communicating a new message.

The purpose of the game is to dramatize how little of what we communicate comes through words alone. An amazing amount of what we say to other people is expressed through our body language and unspoken thoughts.

Criminal investigators, job interviewers, and others who deal daily with strangers in verbal communication learn quickly that the words spoken may not reflect the true meaning. I've seen a study in which researchers measured the ability of various kinds of interviewers to detect falsehood. Sorry; listeners of my own profession tended to take words at face value and believe them. The best people (categorized by occupation) to pick up on unspoken thoughts counter to what was being said were police officers. But then, cops tend to expect and look for falsehoods.

This game also illustrates how to expand listening beyond words. It requires you to maintain focus on the communicator, looking into his or her eyes and watching facial expressions and gestures. That's what active listening is all about—completely focusing on the speaker. If you do that with a baby, really seeking communication of thoughts, what a blessing you will bestow on that tiny future speaker!

"Okay," Linda said. "I see the point. But how, specifically, do I go about improving communication, especially with Daniel? He doesn't want to communicate."

Permit me to offer some suggestions:

Body Position. Keep an "open" body position that demonstrates you're receptive to what's being communicated. An open position means legs or arms are not crossed. Hands are down at your sides or lying side by side in your lap. Your face is inclined slightly toward the speaker.

When you're talking to your baby, you can hold her in your lap and look in her eyes, encircling her with your arms. Or you can sit her up in an infant seat and face her with an open body position.

Eye Contact. How many times have you talked with someone and noticed his or her eyes everywhere but on your own face? When my son talked to me as he was growing up and I'd do that, he'd ask me, "Are you listening to me, Dad?" He was often right to suspect I wasn't. My mind would be a million miles away on some other subject. If you force yourself to really look the speaker in the eye, you have to focus on what he or she is saying. Maintain eye contact as much as possible.

Your baby is absolutely smitten with your face. Take

advantage of this adoration and look lovingly into his eyes while you talk to him, and listen to what he says in return, even if it is babble. In fact, especially if it is babble.

Repeating Back and Clarifying. This is an old psychology trick, although properly speaking it's not a trick at all. One of the best ways you can make a speaker feel listened to is to repeat back what you heard, making sure that's what he or she intended to say. Another term for this is *reflective listening.* This is an especially valuable tool for dealing with children. Even if you don't agree with what they say, just repeating it back to them makes them feel valued because they know you *heard* them.

For an infant, this is a little more difficult. Go ahead and repeat back the gibberish you've just heard. With an infant, meaning is not crucial. Communication is. So is the back-and-forth action of speech, the give-and-take.

Check Out the Meaning. Confirm what you've heard by asking questions. For example, "Is this what you meant to say? Because this is what I heard: . . ." Again, this isn't important to an infant, but in the Mayrons' case it would be essential.

Ask Lots of Questions. What's the best thing that can happen to a public speaker? Fielding lots of questions after a speech! That indicates that the audience was actually listening, always a heartening prospect for a speaker. It is just as true for the audience of one. In addition, questions following a presentation, however brief or informal, also get the creative juices flowing. They may open a whole new avenue of options and ideas that may come to you through this question-and-answer interchange. This is what conversation is all about.

Ask lots of questions of an infant? Why not? Here, communication of some complex idea is not at issue. Continuing the conversation is. Your baby loves your voice and loves to get your response, even to his or her gibberish. As you ask questions, you teach the child how conversation works.

There is, as you may have suspected by now, an important, overreaching bottom line here. As important as it is to hone language skills in both your infant and yourself, these exercises serve a wider purpose. They give your child, even at an age measured in months, a sense of value. *Ignored* or *disregarded* equals *low value. Attended to* and *genuinely regarded* bestows a *worthwhile personhood.* For the next eighteen years the child will be, in many important regards, a second-class citizen, earning wisdom day by day. But even in infancy, that child has value as a person worthy of attention. Please trust me on this: The lesson is not lost, even on an infant.

Another way a child feels valued is through the parents' practice of effective discipline. Discipline, by definition, is attention paid to him or her. Yet discipline can be ineffective when used wrongly or when it is not age-appropriate. In the next chapter, we'll examine how to discipline effectively.

7. STARTING OUT RIGHT

DISCIPLINE

We can't form our children
on our own concepts;
we must take them and love them
as God gives them to us.

GOETHE, *Hermann und Dorothea*

Daniel Mayron sprawled in the wingback chair in my office, pouting as only a preteenager can pout.

On the sofa, his dad, Alan, sat pouting.

Beside Alan, Daniel's mom, Linda, sat pouting.

I sat back in my own chair. "I take it this hasn't been a very good week. Daniel, can you explain why everyone's so glum?"

Alan opened his mouth, but I cut him off with a sharp look.

Daniel stared at me for a long moment. He licked his lips. "Uh . . . uh . . . just one of those weeks, you know? Some go smooth; some don't."

"Why didn't this one?"

Daniel's shoulders heaved in an exaggerated shrug, so I looked at Alan.

"He's bringing home Cs and Ds, and if he doesn't start applying himself, he could possibly flunk at least one subject."

"And it's his fault he doesn't apply himself?"

"Of course! Who else's fault would it be?"

I looked at Linda.

She melted into the sofa, utterly wearied by all this.

Alan rolled onward. "Now, Jessica applies herself and makes straight As. So it's not—you know—genetic or something. Daniel has the ability, but he goofs off."

I hear this over and over every day in my office. I am discussing it here in the discipline chapter, a case concerning a preteen in a baby book, because the roots go right to the newborn. In fact, we believe they begin about four months before birth. The problems growing from these roots usually make themselves known as discipline problems, and yet, no amount of discipline will solve them. What you do with a child like Daniel from the very beginning will profoundly affect your relationship with that child throughout his or her life. So the time to address the issue of variations in children is right now, at the beginning of things.

Discipline will improve some behaviors; the trick is knowing which ones.

The Mayrons considered Daniel's *differences* a discipline problem. They were not. Alan, in particular, thought he could browbeat Daniel into being "like other kids," especially the older sister, Jessica. But he could not—not in a million years. Had the Mayrons identified Daniel's special requirements early, they could have circumvented most of these problems. Of course, were they to refrain from comparing him with his sister, that would help immensely as well.

It was not too late to improve matters, but by seeing

the differences in their two children, the Mayrons could have tailored discipline to each child instead of trying a one-size-fits-all mentality. Then discipline would have been much more effective, with a much smoother transition from childhood to adolescence now. Daniel illustrates what you should be looking for right from the very beginning.

"Daniel, I understand you're very mechanically gifted—handy." I smiled at him.

Another of those oversized shrugs. He did not smile back.

I continued, "I'm always envious of people who can create with their hands. I was very good with academics in school. But had I been required to attend manual-arts classes, I probably would have flunked. For instance, right now I'm trying to assemble a rather elaborate needlework frame, a floor stand you clamp needlework in. I'm making it as a gift for my wife. It's giving me fits."

Daniel perked up slightly. "Yeah?"

"It's lying in pieces in my nurse's office right now. Say . . . do you think you could look at it?"

Still another shrug in size XL. "Sure."

"I'd really appreciate it. You know where her office is next door there." I nodded toward the door.

Daniel snapped to his feet and headed for the door.

"Daniel!" Alan barked. "You're supposed to say 'excuse me' when you leave the room."

"Sorry," Daniel mumbled. " 'Scuse me." Away he went.

Linda wagged her head. "He has the brains. I know he does. But he doesn't think."

"Are you familiar with attention deficit disorder—ADD?" I asked.

"Heard about it." Alan looked grim. "I don't believe in it. Look at Daniel. There's nothing wrong with him."

"I couldn't agree with you more that there's nothing wrong with him. But I disagree vehemently with the statement that he doesn't think. He certainly does. He just doesn't think the same things most other people think."

ADD is misnamed attention deficit *disorder.* It's not a disease, and certainly nothing wrong or evil. It's a *difference.* Children like Daniel view life in a different way. Whether or not Alan believed in it, it exists. And Daniel exemplified it.

Daniel forgot to say "excuse me" because his brain preceded him out my door by a good twenty seconds. As soon as I suggested he might help, his mind had shifted from the present in my office to the future and its prospects next door. His mind was not paying the least attention to things it had been told in the past. It was already diving into the promised puzzle waiting in the next room. In school, his teacher accused him of daydreaming. Not so, at least not deliberately. His brain shifted to another topic, and *he had no control over that.*

People with ADD do not want their minds to flit from subject to subject. It just happens. They can, as they mature, control that to some degree, but never does the situation disappear. They want their minds to remember information at the moment it's appropriate to remember, such as when Daniel rose to leave the room. Their minds, however, don't always do that. It's not a voluntary thing.

People like Daniel are genuinely gifted with hands-on sorts of skills. Fifteen minutes later he returned with the floor stand fully assembled and showed me how to adjust its height and tilt. I will confess here: I did, indeed, purchase the piece boxed, but my only effort at assembling it had been to open the plastic bag of hardware. My real intent was to kill several birds with one stone. I wanted Daniel to see that his gifts have value, and I wanted his parents to see that Daniel possessed rare gifts. Because Daniel's gifts were not the same as his sister's, the parents discounted his. We discussed that in his absence.

That is not an accusation of fault. Linda and Alan Mayron were simply not attuned to their children's differences. Never had been.

Attuning to Your Child's Unique Differences

You've heard before about right-brain and left-brain preferences. Left-brain people are supposedly highly intelligent and good at linear thinking (that is, logical or mathematical thinking—one and one are two). They are typically unemotional, able to memorize large quantities of facts, and good with words and speech. Their thoughts are organized and accessible.

Right-brain folks, on the other hand, are good at global thinking (nonlinear, where you pull a fact from here, a datum from there, and arrive at a realization or answer, often an unexpected one—one and one in this case are eleven). They excel at spatial relationships, intuition, and creative/manual endeavors. They are good at graphics and positioning, diagrams and maps. By reputation, they are given to emotional sensitivity, but they may not be particularly articulate in speech. They cannot always access what they've learned at the time they need the information. Right-brain people are every bit as intelligent as left-brain folks, but nearly all tests, such as the Scholastic Aptitude Test administered to high school students, are geared to measure left-brain thinking.

Fortunately, most people are a mix of the two, leaning a little to one side or the other. People who excel academically lean a lot to the left. People like Daniel lean a lot the other way. Neither is wrong or disordered. If, like Daniel, your child leans away from the left-brain gifts, no amount of discipline in the world will change anything. The wrong discipline, such as the kind Alan Mayron was attempting ("Apply yourself and be like so-and-so or else"), can only destroy.

Although it is not possible or even proper to try to diagnose incipient ADD in an infant, you can get an idea of a child's leanings almost from the beginning. There are several reasons to do so. One is to treasure the child's gifts. Only by doing so will you lead the child to treasure those gifts himself or herself, and unless the child does this, the gifts will go largely unfulfilled. Do one child's precious gifts differ from the gifts of his or her siblings? So much the better!

The other reason to consider the child's gifts during

infancy is to tailor your discipline appropriately to the child. This is an area in which I see so many potential problems—and, conversely, victories.

Here are some gifts to look for:

- Early dexterity; a gift for handling and manipulating. Able to put rings on a post.
- Early understanding of form, shape, and spatial relationships. Able to put graduated plastic rings on a conical plastic post correctly.
- Early verbal skills. Does the child sit still for a couple of minutes of board-book reading?
- Early level of activity. Is the child constantly on the move, physically active? When the child crawls, would the parents say "The kid is *always* into things"?
- Early impatience with life; does the child seem to find inability to do something or to get somewhere frustrating?

This age lays the groundwork for certain attributes, such as verbal skills, but those attributes are not yet particularly noticeable. A child younger than a year old is not really talking yet, for instance. Also, children's developmental schedules vary widely. A child who is actually very good at verbal skills might not show the least evidence of that for three years. The child beside him, a babbler from the beginning, may never articulate much more at age twenty than he does at age five.

In other words, you cannot assay a child's future by looking at the infant's present. You shouldn't try. On the other side, your baby at this age is extremely transparent. He or she has not yet learned to hide emotions or desires, has not yet learned deceit or restraint. Everything is raw and visible. What you see is what you get.

When you watch a baby you are not seeing faults to be corrected. You are looking at the attributes to be encouraged! In the future you will channel, you will cajole, you will encourage, but you will not appreciably change the child's basic nature.

Neither do you want to send the wrong self-fulfilling messages. ("What a dummy!" "You can't do such and so, and since this is the way you are, you'll never be able to do it.") But you can, and I emphasize this, you *can* find your child's uniqueness, celebrate it, and feed it.

Jenny Lawton would tell you that Sara shared many of Daniel's baby characteristics. "And how! She's all over the house, into something all the time, and can't sit still. Does that mean there's something wrong with her?"

Absolutely not! The point of this discussion of ADD, a situation that may become apparent in the future, is that children vary greatly in disposition and activity level, even in the beginning. The wise parent falls into the child's program rather than trying to shoehorn the child into the parent's preconceptions.

Babies love to please. The desire to succeed is built in. If you tell a baby to sit still (and the child is of an age to understand), perhaps adding to your request by physically holding and making still the busy little arms and legs, the baby will try. A naturally quiet baby will do better than a naturally squirmy one. Despite the different result, they will be trying equally.

"Yes, but . . . ," Jenny might argue, "there's this family at church, and their kids never squirm during the service. For a whole hour they just sit there. My Sara can't."

That may be more disposition than discipline. Consider Daniel. Both before and after his heady triumph assembling the stitching frame, he fidgeted and squirmed, constantly moving. This was not intentional on his part. Even while he wanted to sit still, his brain blithely sent his body off on its merry way.

How, then, should Jenny handle little Sara? For that matter, what can the Mayrons do for Daniel?

Fitting the Discipline to the Age and to the Child

Fitting Discipline to the Age

A baby less than a year old does not respond to discipline as we know it because that separation and individuation we mention so frequently has not really gotten rolling yet. The child is still essentially an extension of Mommy and Daddy rather than an individual.

Also, although the baby's conscience may begin to tweak toward the end of that first year, the child still has absolutely no internal sense of right and wrong. Right is what Mommy and Daddy forbid, and the baby has no clear notion of exactly what that is yet. An internalized concept of right and wrong won't appear for a while yet. All discipline and behavior control is external—outside the child's head and heart.

That means, bottom line, that when a baby disobeys, he or she is questioning and testing, not rebelling.

"Oh, yeah?" Jenny would be quick to disagree. "She's ten months old now and crawling sixty miles an hour. Take yesterday. I told her to leave the books on the bottom shelf of the bookcase alone. She looked at me, and I know she knew what I was saying. And then she deliberately pulled one down."

"So you yelled, 'No no!'"

"Right. And she pulled another one down. Hey, when *I* did that, it was rebellion!"

True. But not at one year of age.

Little Sara defied the clear instruction "no no!" not as a challenge but to see if that "no no" was firm. Did "no no" really include the books? Did Mommy really mean it? A test, if you will.

"It was firm," Jenny said, nodding. "I smacked her hand. Not hard, of course. And then she wrinkled up into the cutest, most heart-tugging little face and started crying. I felt so bad."

Redirect and divert the child.

Corporal punishment of an infant is unwise under any circumstance. Jenny learned that smacking a hand was painful for everyone concerned. Of course. Mother and baby are still essentially one.

A better response would have been a firm "No no!"

as Jenny picked Sara up and put her down elsewhere, facing a different direction.

Now babies and small children think symbolically of necessity; they have no verbalization for abstracts. That symbolic act of redirecting Sara meant more to her than it would to an older child. It would not have worked at all on a grade-schooler.

Let's say Jenny does that. Sara reverses direction and heads right back to the bookshelf. "No no." Another redirection. Back again Sara goes. More firmly, Jenny redirects her and then adds to that redirection a diversion—a toy or spoon or something. Sara will get the picture more clearly than she would were the corporal punishment a part of it.

Another friend thoroughly ingrained in her baby that one must never tear paper. The two of them would read books and magazines together, and whenever paper damage began, sharp words and redirection prevented further damage. "No! Like this, Honey. See? We *turn* the pages." Over and over, mother and child together, turned the pages, treating them gently. Eventually, the magazines and books were safe from little hands who mastered the lesson that reading was encouraged; crumpling or tearing was not. My friend was quite proud of the lesson she taught her little one. Her chickens came home to roost at Christmas, however, when her infant was afraid to open Christmas gifts.

Offer basic object lessons if absolutely necessary.

Another friend of mine lives in a remote, forested area where nearly everyone heats with wood. Their nine-month-old, Gina, was beginning to pull herself up on things, and there in the middle of the living room sat that woodstove, hot and dangerous. "We didn't want her to get hurt, of course," my friend said, "but it was November. We couldn't just let the stove sit there cold for the next year or so. We have to keep it going all day."

The first time Gina approached the stove, they barked "Hot!" sharply. To a baby, a sharp tone of voice indicates danger or anger (which to a helpless infant *is* danger).

Gina persisted, twisting around to sitting now and then, watching Mommy and Daddy.

"Hot, Gina! Very *hot!*"

Eventually, Gina touched it. Babies have great reflexes. So does my friend, who repeated, "Hot! Hot!" at the exact moment the object lesson was taught.

Gina cried, and her fingertips were red for a few hours.

Later, when she began vocalizing, she would grow wide-eyed and exclaim "Hah!" whenever she sensed that any object was warmer than a puppy. From then on, she carefully estimated the surface temperature of any object she reached for.

Now, I do not recommend this course of action. My friend followed it as his only option because circumstances prevented them from somehow fencing off the woodstove. The lesson worked. Gina never approached the woodstove again. But it was not discipline in the strict sense. It was conditioning.

Lessons of that sort (another example would be a dog that bites) stick with babies extremely well. They have a strong, strong sense of self-preservation. However, they live only for the moment. They do not understand the concept of tomorrow.

The future is now.

Jenny related, "There was this time I was trying to get Sara dressed and she kept squirming. So I said, 'Sara, if we get done here we can go down to the park. Won't that be nice? Feed the pigeons?' She was still for maybe ten seconds and then she started squirming even worse."

Ten seconds is a long time to a baby.

Promising goodies in the future means nothing to an infant. Babies anticipate in only the most rudimentary way. Jenny did very well to talk to her little one, but Jenny would have to keep in mind that promises of some treat in the offing would scatter and fall like autumn leaves, uncomprehended.

I do suggest promising something that will occur perhaps a minute in the future. This should never be in the form of a bribe but rather a verbalization to promote and teach anticipation. Jenny's "We'll go to the park and feed the pigeons" is a remote promise for a little one. "We're going to put our sweater on" is comprehensible. A minute later, here goes the sweater over the ears and face.

"We're going out to the car."

There we go.

"Let's get in our carseat." Jenny opens the car door, adjusts the seat, puts Sara in it.

As these lessons find home, Jenny will, with time, be able to use promises as rewards. They will be remarkably effective in encouraging obedience. But not while Sara is an infant.

Explaining why a rule is a rule does not work at this age either.

Detailed explanations fall on deaf ears.

With the speed of a galloping racehorse, eleven-month-old Sara thunders across the room, headed directly for that bookcase. Frustrated, Jenny scoops Sara up (good—redirection!) and carefully explains, "If you pull the books down it causes a mess and if you damage them we can't read them."

Sara does not care about messes—she makes hundreds daily herself—and if she comprehends at all about the reading and the damage, it's beyond her immediate circle of interest.

Explanations do not work on infants. It is not just that they do not care, cannot reason, have no interior discipline, and do not grasp abstracts. It's also that they are still part and parcel of Mommy and Daddy. If they do something, they are not doing it in their own strength and purpose. They have no individuality, no "me" yet. Explanations are superfluous.

All this is well and good for tiny Sara, but what about Daniel Mayron? Daniel, at twelve, is not going to respond to these devices; they are inappropriate for his age.

Fitting Discipline to the Child

As Jenny would eventually learn, attention deficit disorder, Daniel's problem, was also a factor for little Sara.

Both children would exhibit a number of behaviors that discipline does not shape.

Both will be active. Make that *overactive.*

Disciplining Daniel to keep him from fidgeting never worked; Linda and Alan would attest to that. Nor will it work for Sara. For both children, distraction, direction, or redirection will help. Is Daniel, as a five-year-old, constantly on the move? Give him physical action toys such as blocks, a good, well-anchored swing set well, a big sandbox. Jenny should do the same as Sara grows. At age twelve Daniel is probably ready to start working on a "beater car." It will take him four years of puttering to get the thing ready to drive when he gets his license.

I know of a man who loaned his twelve-year-old son fifteen hundred dollars to buy a riding mower, a trailer for it, and other lawn-care equipment. Over two summers, the boy built such an extensive clientele that he repaid the loan and put nearly a thousand dollars in the bank.

"Loan Daniel fifteen hundred dollars?" Alan roared. "You can't be serious!"

That is between Alan and Daniel. But whatever avenue Alan chooses, he should find something to direct Daniel's gifts. Channel the energy . . . because you cannot contain it.

Both will have trouble in left-brain situations, such as school.

Fortunately, as ADD and similar conditions are better understood, education methods are being developed to exploit them. For example, there are several excellent hands-on mathematics systems by which a child can handle and visualize math concepts. One system offers a set of variously colored cubes and bars that superficially look somewhat like building blocks. By manually manipulating those various cubes and bars, the child literally sees and handles the relationships between five and ten and one and a hundred and all. By adding, subtracting, multiplying, and dividing *hands-on,* a child like Daniel or Sara can see and touch math—the means by which such children learn everything.

Daniel, at twelve, was not too old to take advantage of such systems. Sara, at one, was not too young to start learning by physical manipulation.

Both will offer unique gifts to the world.

If I can drive home only one point in this whole book, it would be this: *Read your child. Emphasize his or her gifts. Celebrate them. Do not try to force your child into a preconceived mold.*

No amount of discipline will make a child something he or she is not. Period.

What Discipline Is *Not*

At 10 P.M. one night, four-month-old Sara precipitated a horrible fight. She did not participate. The fighters were Jenny and Jenny's mom.

After falling asleep at seven-thirty, her usual bedtime, Sara awoke and began to cry. Jenny was determined to pick her up and rock her.

Her mother insisted, "You'll spoil her! She has to learn

that we aren't going to cater to every whim. Let her cry it out. Besides, it's healthy for the lungs."

Jenny's mom had been taught that bit of pseudo-wisdom by her own mother when Jenny was an infant. It's not so. We've begun to see that infants who are "spoiled" by attention whenever they demand it thrive better and are happier as they enter the toddler stage. And, incidentally, they do not demand more attention than do babies who are left to cry it out. In fact, they require somewhat less.

Babies do not *demand*, in the sense that we use the word. They *need*—or perhaps think they need. When the need is met promptly, the babies, reassured, trust that their next need will also be met. Lesson upon lesson, they build a body of trust that will give them courage to step out boldly. Courage breeds confidence. In the end, the children feel safe to reach out and explore, knowing Mommy and Daddy are there.

When Mommy and Daddy ignore the perceived problem, failing to respond to those cries for help, the baby cannot depend upon the prospect that help will be forthcoming the next time it is needed (or perceived as being needed). In short: *Letting a baby cry it out is not, by any stretch of meaning, discipline.*

Letting the baby cry, unattended, teaches nothing positive. This is not to say that an infant must be picked up every time a squeak pops out. Jenny could serve the situation just fine by entering Sara's bedroom and speaking to her softly, rubbing her back or tummy, pronouncing her name. Sara then would know that Mommy was there for her. That's all that's needed.

One need not pick up a child in order to express love, tempting as it is to do so. A touch, yes. A word, please.

Jenny had cause in this case to hold her ground and respond to Sara's cries immediately. But she did not. She gave in to her mom because Jenny was a child herself under her parents' roof.

Tom and Marsha Jasper did not have that complication of life, and they had agreed in advance how to handle baby Brian's demands: equal requests, equal insistence. They agreed they'd take turns on a daily rotation. Sunday, Monday, Wednesday, and Friday, Marsha would get up during the night. Tuesdays, Thursdays, and Saturdays were Tom's nights on duty.

And they did, indeed, meet Brian's every cry. When Brian was distressed, you see, Brian was distressed. And because he was unable to anticipate well, especially during the first six months, lack of attention meant abandonment. During the last half of his first year he matured enough to understand that if his needs were not met instantly, they would certainly be met in the next few minutes. At no time was he "disciplined" by being allowed to cry it out.

That's not too easy when well-meaning relatives and friends anoint the new parents with the oil of wisdom. How might Tom and Marsha deal with such an outpouring of advice?

A smile and a gentle reminder telling the advisers, "We've worked this out and know what we want to do," should do it. If it doesn't, keep the smile, but keep the faith too.

As he entered toddlerhood, early childhood, and eventually, school, Brian knew without thinking about it that he could depend upon his folks to pick up the slack where he fell short. It is a wonderful, wonderful sense of security for a child to grow with.

But not all security is based on trust. Safety means surviving in the real world, and Mom and Dad must never trust to discipline for that. Discipline is never a substitute for safety.

Childproofing Your Home for Sane and Minimal Discipline

When little Brian took up crawling as a full-time vocation, nothing within his grasp was safe. That included the pets.

Identify Possible Problems with Pets

The cat learned quickly to stay at least three feet off the floor. In response, Marsha relaxed a house rule—that cats are not allowed on kitchen counters—so that Killer could escape Brian's onslaughts.

Dumkopf, their weimaraner, developed an amazing degree of patience, allowing Brian to pull his ears and sit on him without complaining or threatening. The Jaspers were lucky; their first item of childproofing more or less took care of itself.

Certain breeds of dogs are natural mothers (male and

female both), carefully protective of family members in general and babies in particular. Other breeds are in no way protective of babies, and mixed breeds should always have to prove themselves. As a general rule, weimaraners are natural-born baby-sitters as long as the baby is an immediate family member. So, as another example, are Labradors.

Tom and Marsha, then, in evaluating their pets, would take Dumkopf's breed into consideration. But neither they nor you should blindly assume that any particular dog automatically possesses all its breed's general characteristics. Dumkopf proved himself patient under careful supervision.

"Poor, Dum." Marsha smiled. "We had my cousins over one day; their two-year-old is a walking death star. They don't have pets—I can see why—and their Mark simply would not leave Dum alone. Killer hid until they were gone; I never did find out where. But one time I caught Mark dragging Dum across the floor by one hind leg, and another time, he grabbed Dum's tongue. There's Dum, with his eyes rolled up to me saying, 'Get this jerk away from me!' But he didn't make a move to harm Mark. He's a saint!"

Saint or not, the dog should have been protected from the child and vice versa.

If they had a dog whose breed characteristics did not include being "good with children," they would watch the dog especially carefully for any snappiness, impatience, growling, or such. Should any instance of hostility at all show up, they would keep the baby and the dog carefully separated.

Babies are incredibly clumsy, rough, little monsters. They hit, thump, sit upon, and fall upon pets. They tug fur and ears. A cat or small dog is in actual physical danger from a crawling baby. Big dogs fare better in that they're not easily injured. But *every* dog, including the smallest, can severely injure or kill a baby if the dog's nature or disposition permits.

Cats? The Jaspers' gray tiger-stripe, Killer, disliked the baby, stayed clear, and adopted an attitude of guarded truce. That's typical. Though some cats become quite motherly and protective, others never accept the new addition. The Jaspers were kind to pet and baby both by cutting Killer a little slack.

Don't worry about the old wives' tale that a jealous house cat will suck the life out of a newborn. Do, however, pay close attention to matters of hygiene. Cat litter boxes are magnets for babies, and infants can pick up some nasty infections by playing in them.

Never let a baby play with a bird or a small animal such as a hamster or guinea pig. The baby is simply too rough and does not yet possess the physical coordination to be gentle. Supervise encounters very carefully, with lots of talking and encouragement for both the baby and the animal.

Identify and Remove Obvious Hazards

"You can't protect a baby totally, so the baby just has to learn to stay out of danger. That's the only way to be

100 percent safe. So I'm not going to childproof my house the way some people say to. We're going to train our baby to stay clear of dangers. Then childproofing is unnecessary." This woman seemed such an otherwise intelligent and devoted parent, but her attitude about childproofing their home scared the daylights out of me.

A baby simply does not have the background knowledge or self-control to stay out of trouble. Even if the baby knows something is off-limits, if it is an attractive something, he or she will get into it. This is why the legal term for dangerous things such as swimming pools is "attractive nuisance."

I mentioned earlier the situation with the woodstove, in which the baby learned that hot surfaces hurt. That kind of conditioning works after a fashion in some situations, but it never works for sharp edges, poisons, and abrupt drop-offs such as stairs. In the case of the woodstove, the baby avoided the danger deliberately. But babies learning to walk lurch in a lot of directions they do not intend to go in. Also, infants do not think. The woodstove still presented a danger to the unthinking baby intent upon some other activity such as walking from the chair to the coffee table. The only good solution is to identify and either fence off or remove all obvious hazards. Check your home for:

Electrical Outlets and Cords. You can purchase protectors to insert into unused outlets so babies cannot stick pins into them. A couple I know who are university students live nine months of the year in married students' quarters and the other three months in a small mobile home in a state park, where they work summers. The first thing they do when they move in is slap duct tape over unused outlets.

If extension cords are necessary, make certain their unused outlets are plugged. Check all cords for breaks or fraying.

Stairs and Other Drop-offs. Babies have a natural fear of drop-offs. In a famous experiment, the researchers laid clear glass across an obvious drop-off. They then encouraged babies to crawl across the glass to them. The babies would not venture out beyond the drop-off they saw in front of them. Limited drop-offs such as sunken living rooms, therefore, present limited problems. Stairs are another matter. The baby sees people bound up and down stairs. The baby is carried up and down. Familiarity invites exploration. But if babies lose their balance on the top step, that sunken living-room floor is not there to catch them, and down they tumble. Fence off stairs with spring-loaded protective gates.

Make sure the vertical bars of stair and balcony railings are close enough together to prevent the baby's head from getting caught between them; this happens a lot. Drape attractive afghans or sheets over railings with widely spaced verticals, screening them from the baby.

Cabinets and Their Contents. Oh, so many cases of poisoning occur in infants, and they are all unnecessary! If your kitchen and bathroom cabinets have knob-type handles, slip a strong rubber band around the knobs to hold double cabinet doors together. If the doors have vertical loop handles, run a foot-long dowel through them and secure it with a rubber band. You can purchase latches that fit inside the cabinet doors and stop them about one-inch open. An adult can loosen the latch to swing the door clear open. Babies cannot.

Poisons include any caustic cleaning and polishing substances, the obvious stuff such as lye and bleach, medicines, and some vitamins. An adult dose of iron supplement can kill a baby or ruin liver function. Keep all such substances out of reach.

Protect babies from garbage; opened can lids can cut, and spoiled food may cause illness. Before Brian arrived, the Jaspers kept their trash can under an open shelf, easy to reach. When Brian started crawling they had to make room for the trash can in a closet, very inconvenient but necessary.

Things That Choke. Knickknacks within reach are sure to end up within mouths.

"How big is big enough?" Jenny asked one day during a pediatric visit. "I mean, what's safe, and what's small enough to be unsafe?"

Here's a general rule of thumb: If it fits in the baby's mouth at all, it's too small.

A fire chief for a small volunteer fire department told me, "Whenever I hear of a baby swallowing something, I find a similar object and drop it into this old cigar box." He pulled a battered old box out of his lower desk drawer and flopped the lid open. "It's a great teaching device to get young parents to pay attention to what their kids are getting into."

Inside it were a large, dead, very dry moth; safety pins and darning needles; buttons up to an inch and a half across; coins, of course; thumbtacks and roofing nails; and bits of toys and jacks. He stirred through the amazing array, picked out a razor blade, and held it up. "Now you'd think babies would know better, but they don't. That's the message. They just don't know."

The Bathroom. I recommend fencing off the bathroom. Children love to play in the toilet, and babies do not possess the coordination necessary to save themselves if they fall head-first into the commode. Drowning is a significant cause of infant death, and it simply does not have to be.

Things That Disgust. I've added this to the list, but not for safety reasons. It probably won't hurt your baby to get into the cat food or eat earthworms, but you'll want to prevent that sort of thing anyway, as much as you are able.

Identifying Potential Hazards

Since a baby can drown in two inches of water, child-proofing a home must include finding any water containers. Turn over all buckets, basins, and planter trays so they do not collect rainwater.

Check furniture, cabinets, and other areas for sharp metal edges that adults and older children handle safely and take for granted.

Try to think like a baby. Stand around, especially out in the yard, and mentally ask yourself, "Let's say the baby crawls over there. What can he find? Let's assume he found it. What's the worst he can do to himself?" Eliminate that potential hazard. Never assume, "Naw, he wouldn't find *that.*"

Oh yes he would!

The more you do to create an unencumbered home environment, the less stressed you and everyone else in your family (including the baby) will feel. Older brothers and sisters ought also to feel that their belongings are safe. They should keep their toys behind closed doors, and not just because small parts are choking hazards. A baby turned loose with a Monopoly game or a Tootsie truck can wreak havoc on the toy—not a pretty sight.

Babies are messy, squirmy, and loud. In that regard they are doing exactly what they're supposed to do. We cannot shoehorn them into an adult environment with any degree of safety. Rather we, as adults, must adjust our environment to their needs. Having said that, I remind you that no baby-proofed home, however thoroughly you try, is actually baby-proof. The child *will* find something. Believe it! Constant supervision is the only true safety precaution.

By the close of the first year, infants are becoming toddlers and persons in their own right. Their personality is clear and developing further every day. Coordination is improving. The stage is set for the next great stage, separation and individuation.

What Now?

"Brian! Brian, come back," Tom yelled from the comfort of his lawn chair. He loved this time of evening, the sun red on the horizon behind the trees and roofs and power poles, the evening cool descending, the breeze picking up. Tom and Marsha sat in the shade of the gum tree in their backyard and let life go on without them.

Without a backward glance, Brian took off across the front lawn with the speed and agility of a racehorse. He was walking now at eleven months, a pedestrian on the early end of the chart of development. Walking? Thundering! He giggled all the way until he tripped and fell face first in the grass.

Brian, the knees of his overalls thoroughly grass-stained, was beginning the long process of learning who he was and, more importantly, that he was separate from Tom and Marsha. Brian Jasper was a complete and total Brian Jasper, a heady realization that would set him at odds with his parents in the next year when the wills of three very different human beings began to clash.

Marsha had to jog to catch up to him. She put down her gardening trowel and scooped him up before he could gather his legs under him for another wild charge. "Look at you! How can somebody less than two feet high get so dirty?! Bath time as soon as we go in. Shall we go back to Daddy now?" She put Brian down and reached for his hand.

Instantly he was off and running in the opposite direction. Marsha yelled, "Brian! Come back here!" What had happened to Brian? He was certainly no pliant infant anymore.

The Next Opportunity

Already, at one year of age, Brian and Sara each exhibited strongly differing personalities. When Brian sat still, he sat still, often for relatively long periods of fifteen or twenty minutes. He was easily amused and amused himself well. He loved to explore, but he was not, by baby standards, particularly destructive.

Brian was learning well the lessons of trust and reality—that he need not fear abandonment—that would serve him so usefully throughout childhood. Bold and happy and easy to please, he was what many harried parents might call a nearly perfect baby.

Sara, Jenny would attest, was just the opposite.

How much of Sara's reticence and fidgeting and fussing were genetically based and how much of it was a product of her infancy? The experts debate and argue. On one thing, though, the experts agree: You play the hand you are dealt the very best you can.

For a child like Daniel Mayron, certain windows of opportunity are closed forever. As Daniel grows into adulthood, though, he can, through his own efforts, undo some of what was lost when his parents failed to recognize the opportunities that existed or the child's particular needs. No parent is perfect, and even if parents were, no child is perfect either. We have been blessed with the twin gifts of knowing God through Jesus Christ and of shaping ourselves closer to His likeness. That process never ends.

Other windows of opportunity are opening as your child enters the second year. You have built the foundation of trust and understanding that will make exploitation of those new windows easier and more effective. Your little person is well on the road!

An Incredible Little Person

As Tom and Marsha sat at ease in their backyard, Jenny Lawton sat on a steel folding chair in a stuffy gym. She was graduating tonight. The speaker, a businessman from the community, had just finished telling the graduates how commencement is not the end of school life but the beginning of real life.

Jenny knew that better than most people. Her school life virtually ended when Sara was born.

Her principal, Mr. Demond, stepped up to the mike and thanked the speaker more profusely than the businessman deserved. He explained how the graduates were to come forward to receive their diplomas. And then he added, "We have some special awards tonight. In the interest of efficiency we'll bestow them as the respective students come forward."

That was nice, but Jenny certainly would receive none. Her grades were okay—good, even—but nothing spectacular. Sports? She didn't even try out for varsity anything, not with Sara to get home to every afternoon. It was the same thing with extracurricular clubs.

They were taking it alphabetically. An *L,* she would receive her diploma about halfway through the ceremony. She glanced across the aisle to Darren over in the *T*s. Maybe he'd get "father of the year." Yeah, sure. His interest in Sara, fairly high at first, had dropped to zero. What did she ever see in him? Now, at the end of this last tumultuous year, she couldn't remember the vivid passion or even being in love. Another zero.

Somewhere back in the audience sat her mom and dad with Sara on Mom's lap. Jenny could just picture the constant squirming.

Her row stood up and moved to the far right. One by one they followed each other on stage as Mr. Demond announced the names. The system paused as Mr. Demond gave Jeffrey Hamer a special award for his work with the yearbook. Good. Jeff deserved it; he'd worked his tail off.

Jeff said a few words of thanks for his yearbook adviser and all the kids who had helped. Away he went.

Jenny stepped up on the stage following Marybelle Lantz. To her surprise the program paused again.

Mr. Demond cleared his throat as he fiddled momentarily with the knot in his tie. Jenny could see his neck muscles tighten up. "It's unfortunate that too many people like to think that students in a Christian academy such as ours make no mistakes and behave perfectly. I'm sorry; it's not true. Four of our girls became pregnant before graduation; three dropped out. As everyone here knows, Jennifer Lawton stuck it out in the face of a great deal of adversity. I've watched her juggle two lives, her school life and her home life. I've watched her grow in amazing ways. She acquitted herself well at school under very trying circumstances, and she is acquitting herself well at home as a mother."

Jenny felt her eyes turn hot.

Mr. Demond turned to her and smiled. "Jenny, your teachers and I wish to recognize your courage and determination in the face of difficult odds. On behalf of little Sara we thank you, and we ask God's blessing upon you both." He stuffed an envelope and her rolled diploma into her left hand as he shook her right one.

Was Jenny supposed to say something, like Jeff did?

She didn't want to, but her mouth opened in spite of herself. "I want to thank my parents for making this possible. I wouldn't be here if it wasn't for them." That was true, and she could feel tears threatening to overflow. "I hear all the rotten statistics about single-parent kids, and I can see what a rough time Sara's going to have. I'm sorry in a way that it happened like this. But since it did . . ." Her voice cracked. She jacked it a notch to strengthen it.

Out there in the first rows sat her teachers and their families, face after smiling face, so familiar. Jenny was losing her point. The past and the future were crashing together inside her, shattering her thoughts. The end and the beginning, and a long, long road. "Sara's going to be walking soon. And talking. Someday she'll walk across a stage and get her diploma too. She's such a . . . an incredible little person. I'm glad I can be the one to help her grow." Through blurry eyes she looked from face to face. "Thank you, all of you, for the support you gave me, and your confidence in me. God bless you too!"

May your child, an incredible little person as well, be blessed with the best life has to offer.

ABOUT THE AUTHOR

Paul Warren, M.D., is a behavioral pediatrician and adolescent medicine specialist. He serves as medical director of the Child and Adolescent Division and the Adolescent Day Program of the Minirth Meier New Life Clinic in Richardson, Texas and also has an active outpatient practice. He also is a professional associate with the Center for Marriage and Family Intimacy based in Austin, Texas.

Dr. Warren received his M.D. degree from the University of Oklahoma Medical School. He completed his internship and residency at Children's Medical Center in Dallas, Texas where he also served as chief resident. He did a fellowship in behavioral pediatrics and adolescent medicine at the University of Texas Southwestern Medical School and Children's Medical Center in Dallas.

An expert in child and adolescent issues, Dr. Warren is a popular seminar speaker who addresses audiences nationwide and is a regular guest on the Minirth Meier New Life Clinic radio program. His other books include *Kids Who Carry Our Pain, The Father Book,* and *Things That Go Bump in the Night.*

Dr. Warren and his wife Vicky have a son, Matthew.

Fighting the War
Against OCD:

A SEASON IN THE LIFE OF
GREGORY GENE CONRAD

An Autobiography

Also Available In eBook and Audiobook Formats
through Amazon Kindle and Amazon Audible.

**Published, Printed, and Bound in the
United States of America**

Reviews

"Gregory Conrad's 32-day accounting of life with Obsessive Compulsive Disorder is a journey into trials of despair and sweet respites of redemption. This is a true insider's chronicle of the treacherous inner workings of this oftentimes paralyzing disorder. While it entices the reader deep inside the mind of one with OCD, the author also boldly pulls back enough to invite a deep reflection with him. This is a touching and poignant slice of memoir told with humor, angst, and integrity. It evokes heart and compassion."

—MITCHELL LEVICK, Ph.D., *Clinical Psychologist*

"It's amazing. It's one of the most profoundly compelling pieces of writing I've ever seen."

—DAVE CONGER, *Accomplished Author*

"Gregory Conrad takes his readers inside his mind for just 31 days of his life, showing what his thoughts are and why they are reasonable to him while at the same time recognizing that they are the result of his OCD illness. His book shows his daily struggles to develop more self-awareness and implement the strategies he has learned through years of professional therapy. Some parts are painful and others humorous, but all are written with care and honesty in this captivating narrative."

—JANE ANDERSON, *Retired English Teacher*

To God, without Whom this labor of love never would (or could) have been written in the first place.

And for the benefit of the millions suffering from OCD throughout the world and the tens of millions who love them and struggle daily to support them and understand what they are going through.

◆◆◆◆◆◆◆◆◆◆◆◆◆◆◆◆◆◆◆◆◆◆◆◆◆◆◆◆◆◆◆◆◆◆◆

Table of Contents

Fighting the War Against OCD

Preface to 2nd Edition

This 2nd Edition was undertaken for a few reasons. The first was to update the front cover of the book to include the award seal, reflecting the fact that I am one of the fifty 2018 winners in The Authors Show Podcast's "50 Great Writers You Should Be Reading" competition.

The second was to adjust the text and layout of the book so that it correlates better with the now-available audiobook. The biggest change here is that the Explanatory Notes of the 1st Edition were moved from the end of the book to the end of each log and renamed Log Notes. This was necessary for a couple reasons. First, it would make the audio recording very "clunky" and somewhat confusing to vocally insert each note at its position in the text. Second, the odds of the listener remembering notes and their contextual significance would be much higher if they were placed at the end of that day's log, as opposed to the end of the whole audiobook.

The third reason was to fix some grammatical errors noticed after publication of

the 1st Edition and to better word certain passages in the book, especially in the reference notes.

I also needed to update the Acknowledgments and update the Title Page to reflect the fact that the audiobook is now "also available" instead of "soon to be available". Finally, I decided to break up Log Eleven into two separate logs, as they were actually written on different days, and the book's log structure is based on dates, not topics.

Acknowledgements

As one can see by a quick glance at the dates given herein, this book has been a work in progress for a very long time. And in those years, there have been a plethora of individuals who have, to one degree or another, helped in the development of this book...so many in fact that it fills me with trepidation to write this, for fear of not extending appropriate credit to one or many deserving individuals. However, I would be remiss to not specify my appreciation to any of the individuals. As such, this is my attempt at a complete list:

Thanks to my bishop Ken Armstrong for helping with the book's inception and preliminary editing. Thanks to my teachers Jane Anderson and Pat Barrette for helping with the many subsequent drafts. Thanks to my friend Dave Conger for helping to resurrect the idea of publication when it seemed impossible, helping with even more subsequent drafts, and providing the idea for reference notes. Further thanks to Jane Anderson and Dave Conger, along with my doctor Mitch Levick, for writing reviews for this

book so the public can know that this really is worth reading and not just an advanced monkey typing on a keyboard. Thanks to Central New Mexico Community College (CNM) and my teachers Nathan Saline and Joseph Sandoval for providing me with the advanced training in Microsoft Word so that I could make such a complicated and advanced document as this.

Thanks to my friend Walter Fazio for his fine photography of G.I. Joes on the front cover. Thanks to Katie Martin for being an able assistant in the photography process. Further thanks to Walter Fazio, Katie Martin, and Jake Martin for dreaming up the G.I. Joe idea to begin with. Thanks to my friend Jezzri Cochrane for using her advanced Photoshop skills to isolate every G.I. Joe and accompanying speck of dust and removing everything else so that the image would be easier to work with. Thanks to my friend Ryan Schofield for his help in assembling the front cover, back cover, and spine into one PDF agreeable to the specifications required by Amazon's CreateSpace publishing company.

Additional thanks to my friends Sean Crosby, Sophie Crosby, Jana Grass, Steve Grass, and Becky Grass for five truly awesome tanks carved completely out of soap. Further thanks to Walter Fazio for the fine photography of said tanks. Even though it didn't end up working for the front and back covers, I truly am grateful to them for all the time, talent, and effort they supplied.

Thanks to my friend Sean Crosby for handling the temporal practicalities essential to getting this book actually submitted, published, printed, bound, and available to buy. Thanks to the good folks at FedEx Office (formerly known as Kinko's) in the Albuquerque foothills for their skillful, professional, and remarkably inexpensive help in printing and binding all prior drafts of this work so I could have something tangible to give to my family and friends.

Additionally, thank you to all those who contributed to making the audio version of my book. Thank you to LDS Employment Resource Center for helping me secure the skills-based training and other temporal practicalities so

essential to the success of this kind of endeavor. Thank you to Jesse Korman from Elephonic Recording Studios for furnishing his recording studio and teaching me the ins and outs of audiobook recording, editing, mastering, and submission.

Also, thank you to The Authors Show Podcast, specifically Don McCauley, for helping me spread my book's message by interviewing me on his podcast, providing me with various marketing materials, and suggesting that I compete in the podcast's "50 Great Writers You Should Be Reading" contest. And a big thanks to all those who voted for me in that competition. Now I can accurately say that I am an award-winning author!

Finally, I extend tremendous thanks to all of my friends and family for reading the many iterations of this manuscript and giving their positive feedback. More importantly, thank you...especially to my friends of the female variety... for standing by me and remaining my (close) friends even after reading this proved to

you just how truly crazy my life and thought process actually are.

Finally, I express my sublime gratitude to my Savior and my God. Thank you for inspiring me and giving me the ability to help those in more dire straits. And thank you for providing me with the above-mentioned friends and family...along with doctors and church leaders...for comfort and cheer, and for keeping me going during life's darkest moments. In short, thank you for always being here for me.

Log One – Jul 11, 2005

These past two days have been a struggle. It's summer now in Provo.

Temperatures range from 82° to 92° Fahrenheit. And with the heat comes sweat. A trifle, insignificant fact, not even note-worthy. But not to me, not to one clasped with the iron bands of OCD. Sweating is a crisis. Sweat must be exterminated at all cost. Most of the time I don't even know why. I just know I have to kill it.

How? Simply whisking the sweat off my brow? No, no. It's far more difficult. Drenching my face, my hair in warm water. Scrubbing the perspiration off my face. Feeling each and every follicle on my head for the slightest bead of salt. Splashing water across the sink as I drown myself in the water that's getting hotter and hotter every minute.

Or maybe I will use the wind to blow it off. Sticking my head outside my car window desperate for a reduction of heat. Never satisfied until I feel the last bead of sweat blown away, cooled by the wind as it slaps across my face.

Still protruding out of the window as I drive faster and faster, giving the wind its necessary momentum. What's this? I feel the saturation of the hair just beyond the reach of the wind. It keeps moving around the cranial circumference. Now I'm struggling to keep the car moving forward even with the road while I strain to turn my head further and further around until I feel the swerve of my car and realize that I'm now looking directly at the car behind me.

Such a trite, insignificant event. Repeated over and over and over, forty, eighty, a hundred times each day. All to get rid of that building, escalating wave of anxiety. Anything to feel less anxious. Sweat must be terminated. It must be eradicated at all cost.

Or else what? I don't know. Salt dries up, giving me an exoskeleton of salt. It is like extraterrestrial ooze leaking out of my body, ready to kill me if I let enough of it out. Salty ooze. I might even to turn into a pillar of salt like Lot's wife[1]. Doesn't make sense. But that doesn't matter. Logic must never be applied. I must obey. I must follow the cry of my Tormentor lest he

whips me more than is necessary. He is always there, standing, itching to lash out, releasing several scarlet streams, bathing my back in blood. His whip is knotted, sprinkled with shards of glass and metal throughout the leather material. He waits in cheery anticipation to enjoy his work, laughing at me. Still he whispers lies to me, telling me he is there to protect me. But his whip, it cracks hard and swift. And the pain is unbearable even when I do what he commands. He whips me when I obey. But he whips me more when I disobey. Always filling me with pain and terror. Always using my flesh to carve his grotesque masterpiece.

No! I will not give in any longer. I'll let him whip me. Just long enough to turn and tear the whip from his grasp. Oh, the pain! The whip has never sliced into that area of my skin before. Blood is pouring. Oh, the pain, the pain! I must endure. For now I must endure until I can turn around completely and make the whip yield to my command. Oh, the pain, the pain!

This is what the past two days have been like for me. A victim of Obsessive Compulsive Disorder (OCD).

Log Notes

[1] In *The Book of Genesis* (in *The Holy Bible*), Lot and his family were told to flee from Sodom just before it was utterly destroyed. On their way out, 3 holy men issued the following command (found in Genesis 19:17): "Escape for thy life; look not behind thee, neither stay thou in all the plain; escape to the mountain, lest thou be consumed." However, when fleeing the city, Lot's wife disobeyed the commandment issued them. Genesis 19:26 reads, "But his wife looked back from behind him, and she became a pillar of salt."

Log Two – Jul 13, 2005

I'm getting closer to the whip. It's almost within reach. The new cuts are hurting less. Life is getting better.

The wonderful thing about resistance is there's a peak battle and then gradually, ever so slowly, a victory. I've won that war. I don't have to have the treaty. I just have to reach the peak intervention. Once the tide turns, it is only a matter of time. I win. Life gets better.

I have had a couple of these victories of late. Last Thursday I learned that my life-long love is engaged ... and not to me. I love her more than anybody I've ever known. She's an angel. Unfortunately, it was a long-distance relationship that grew further away because of the OCD. Two years ago I would have been holding a knife to myself. But I looked down at my hands and didn't see the knife this time.

Last Friday, I received a B+ on a test. Again most people would never understand the kind of anxiety this produces. However, a person with OCD understands. A perfectionist

understands how he could go throughout all of middle school, high school, and into college and never receive a grade lower than an A– on a test, much less on a report card. He would understand how the sight of an 87 immediately causes breathing to cease, his pulse to raise, his eyes to cloud with tears that he didn't order to come. That is I. Yet when I saw that B+ I took a breath and I realized I did my best and for the first time in my life it was good enough.

There is hope. Life can get better. It became better because I swore I would "not go quietly into the night ... Today [I] celebrate [my] Independence Day!"[1]

Log Notes

[1] This quote is from the movie *Independence Day*, released in 1996; starring Will Smith, Jeff Goldblum, Bill Pullman, Randy Quaid, and Judd Hirsch; and directed by Roland Emmerich. Specifically, this quote references the very end of President Whitmore's rallying speech to the fighter pilots right before they fly off for one last shot at destroying the alien invaders. In the movie, it's a cry for the right of existence. Here I use it in a similar vein, declaring my right to freedom and existence independent of the rule of OCD; it is my solemn declaration

that I too "will not go quietly into the night" (again quoting from said speech).

Log Three – Jul 15, 2005

My brain is being rattled, full of voices. Not schizophrenic voices—I do not hear any physical sound. Rather they are psychological imprints or shadows of voices that never enter the realm of physical sounds. At times they are all I can hear. Actually they are more than voices. They are entities, forms of life, beings I can see in my mind's eye. Sound a little bit freaky? I think it is. But it is all a part of this disorder, this disease.

What are these psycho-creatures? They are my songs. They are radio stations. They are my towels. They are my sweats. And much more. What's more, they are all shouting, angrily accusing me of one great sin—favoritism

"Remember me. What happened? I thought you cared about me. Where have you gone? Why aren't you using me? Do you love them more than you do me? I hate you! Why do you always ignore me?"

I hear them frequently, some days almost constantly. I see them waving at me for attention.

I feel guilty. I haven't used this towel for so long. I've been deserting it. What do I do to silence them, to show them I care? I rotate my towels, my sweats, and my shirts so I don't hurt any of their feelings, non-existent as they might be. Or do they exist? They seem so real!

Music is the cruelest. It inhabits far greater realms of OCD than do my apparel. I can never feel certain about which radio station to turn to. What do I really want—do I want to listen to country or rock and roll? What about station loyalties? I have that Big Oldies 98.5 T-shirt in my closet. What happens if I miss my favorite song because it was on the other station? What happens if I miss *the* song—the one song that could change my day and put me in a better mood? After all, that is the only song that could help me out of this OCD fit I am having right now.

Now it is even crueler. I'm listening to one of the 4,319 songs I have on my laptop. Yes, there is the usual accusations about favoritism and doubt about hearing the song, but this time it goes far deeper (and all of these have become

amplified a million fold). Everything is distorted ... so very distorted. What about all of the eternal, religious elements? Am I sinning by listening to this song? Does it include profanity? If so, which cuss words? (Oh, and I'm sinning for even asking that last question, as if one swear word is more innocent and acceptable than another.) What about drugs and sex? Is there any possible way something being sung could be construed as encouraging illicit drug use or celebrating fornication, adultery, or any other manner of lasciviousness? The voices are shouting at me. "You are sinning! You must stop the music! You are sinning!"

Then there are the legal doubts. Did I break the law? Did I infringe upon copyright? After all, 70% of my music isn't exactly mine. It's my brother's or my parent's or my roommates'. One cop friend of mine said I could burn, rip, and copy anything as long as I didn't sell it. (I definitely haven't been selling scalped music or movies.) Most other people (Latter-day Saint bishops, multimedia consultants, and Computer Science instructors) say that copying is

fine as long as it is within my immediate nuclear family or from someone that shares the same roof with me like a roommate. I haven't done anything outside of that. But what is truly right, truly ethical? Should I delete all of the songs that were not mine to begin with? I can't do that. That would include all of my Christmas songs and yuletide parodies; I can't celebrate Christmas without them.

OCD is screaming so loudly. I can hear its voices surrounding me. Yet it is not finished. It is not abated. There is more. It shrieks, commanding me to obey more of its twisted, miserable commandments. It wants to track, monitor, and record every bit of data that comes in its path. Who was this song's composer[s]? Windows Media Player has a table specifically for keeping track of the wonderful minds that compose music. This means I have to fill it in; I have to find and record all of the composers for all of my songs.

What about the singers, the players, and the lyricists? I need to know them, too. It is not enough to know that Handel wrote *The Messiah*;

I must also know that the London Philharmonic Orchestra performed his masterpiece when the CD was recorded. And audio books, sermons, or speeches—I can't just say "Track 01, Track 02, Track 03, … " I must assign a name to every single track despite the fact that I would have to listen to and come up with such a title for 267 individual tracks. I also must find the lyrics for every single song that I possess (and if it's instrumental, I must listen to the whole track to make sure that not the slightest vocalization was uttered before I can write the three uniform words "Instrumental—No lyrics") and write them in the lyrics window.

No longer can I listen to any of the songs on my computer (and I can't play any of my CDs for fear of showing my CD player favoritism over my laptop) in peace and enjoy it. I always hear the songs reminding me of any breach of conduct contemplated by my OCD. I always hear the voices yelling. They will never be satisfied.

Log Four – Jul 18, 2005

The past few days I have engaged the enemy, my Tormentor. I decided to wipe out one of his key data facilities. I wiped out most of the compound, taking out thousands of its occupants. Of course there were some bloody moments for me, as well. I was captured for a little while and transported to another underground facility. There I was beaten, and I received two gunshots (one in my right knee, the other in my left shoulder) and a bloody nose. However, it wasn't long before I regained control. I took advantage of the enemy's arrogance in taking me inside to their headquarters. I have propelled grenades into several rooms and am proceeding virtually unchecked into thousands of others. The enemy is crumbling before my feet.

What have I been doing? Well, I logged into Windows Media Player and have erased 75% of the composers. The other 25% erased were inconsequential artists, which were then replaced by the more prominent composers such as Beethoven and Handel. Once finished, OCD coerced me into making sure that the artist

folders inside "My Music" were still accurate, as some of the artists had changed and then drove me to expand the music file database by adding new artist folders. However, I soon realized the downward spiral that OCD was leading me down into and figured out how to escape its hold and then do the most damage to it. I am now deleting all of the artist folders and am sending all 3,439 songs directly into "My Music," exterminating all of the hundreds of sub-folders.

It took three days to delete all of the composers and some lyricists. I expect it to take another three to erase all of the subfolders. Anxiety has actually been relatively low while fighting this battle, but I'm not getting cocky; I don't expect the really bad anxiety to start until I am done. The real trick for me will be to resist rebuilding everything. To not start over will be the real fight. (Submission to this urge is what gave me my few wounds of late.) And I am feeling sorely tempted to resurrect an old Access movie database. Yet I will fight on; I will continue to resist despite momentary lapses. But I will *not* underestimate OCD.

Log Five – Jul 20, 2005

Last night was abysmal. Loneliness and depressing darkness were everywhere. The ironic thing was that I wasn't alone. I was with my roommate, and we were watching a movie (normally my favorite past time). I should have been happy, but I wasn't. Everything was shrouded by a cloud of darkness.

For the past month or two, I've generally been in a state of depression, a darker depression than what usually accompanies me through life. I feel friendless and rejected. I feel like I don't have a home or a family. My social life is for the most part non-existent. Why? Because of all the delightful complications that OCD presents in my life. There's so much that I can't do.

I'm afraid of grass, dirt, vegetation, and every other element associated with the "great outdoors"—at least that's what most people call it; to me it's more like a mine field in the scorching wastelands of Perdition. I don't even like to walk on lawns. Grass is great to look at, but not to interact with and certainly not to feel.

It pricks at my skin, affording a bridge of passage onto my epidermis for the bugs that grass is laced with. Each prick or tickle brings on the familiar pangs of formication. This is the scientific term for the phenomenon of literally feeling insects, which do not exist, crawl along the flesh and between the follicles of your body. Mostly this phenomenon is experienced by drug addicts who are going through rehab after taking massive amounts of marijuana, cocaine, LSD and other hard hallucinogenic drugs. However, it is also fairly common for people suffering from OCD to experience this created super-sensitivity to bugs. As such, every time I set foot on grass, I would begin to feel a dozen bugs spreading up my legs, each winding its way up a labyrinth of hair.

Dirt isn't much better. Underneath its layers lies something much more menacing than bugs—snakes. With each step that I make comes the possibility of stepping onto a snake's hole, giving its wicked venom the excuse to come out and exact vengeance and leave me wallowing out in the desert sand all alone, screaming, laying there as its painful venom courses its way

through my blood stream, poisoning my heart, and leaving a pus-filled, swollen wound.

Snakes, however, aren't the only threat that lies await on the dust-bitten mesa. There are Gila monsters, coyotes, rabid dogs, rabbits, and vermin who leave a destructive pile of excrement laced with the presence of hanta virus[1]. There are also scorpions, centipedes, and other desert insects.

Then again, there's just dirt itself. Get it under your fingernails and your fate is sealed. After all, this dirt is the same that has been there for hundreds of years. Who knows what happened to that dirt in a hundred years? Who knows how many pounds of solid waste have been deposited in that time? Who knows how many dogs have peed and pooped there? Who knows how many murdered bodies could be just below there? If it's one thing we know about desert sand, it's that hot sand is the best preservative in the world. There are enough mummies buried under the Egyptian wilderness to prove that point.

And all this is preserved on each and every particle of sand. Get that stuck in your nail beds and whatever disease preserved upon that granule will enter into your bloodstream and infect you, killing you. Why, it can even do its dirty work if it just simply stays on your arm. You can't brush it off. That spreads it to your hands. Even water won't do any good on its own. Without soap, water is more likely to aid it along in its journey through your epidermis.

This restricts my fun to the indoors, taking out a big chunk of social interaction. However, the social problems and limitations don't end there. I hesitate to even play indoor card or board games because I'm afraid of losing and all of the horrible things that people are going to think of me because I didn't end up owning the most on a Monopoly board. I'm hesitant about joining any activity because I'm afraid of showing social ineptness. Even more than that, though, I hesitate to join any new game because I'm afraid that it will turn out involving anxiety-provoking behavior and then my freaking out in front of everyone because of it.

If it's a board game, I'll start asking too many questions and start breathing heavily. I'll probably start shaking. Inside I'll feel short of breath and my thoughts will be rushing to no conclusion whatsoever. I'll become paranoid when people start talking, immediately reaching the conclusion that they're talking bad about me. If it's a card game, I'll be too slow as I seek to sort out my cards and mull over which option will guarantee me victory (and thus keep up my social dignity); do I take the red 2 or the green 7, the king of hearts or the 4 of spades? I won't be able to cope with the desired speed, and my mouth will begin to mutter unceasing apologies.

But the worst is the other games—the ones where you have to interact with other people *physically*. Am I running around? If so, my legs will work awkwardly and I will feel my blubber start flapping around. Once again, I will nauseate girls to the point of swallowing their own vomit. Do I have to hold someone's hand? If so, is the girl an ugly hag who will fatefully interpret my touch as my commitment to our relationship? If it's a cute girl, then she'll feel the cold dampness

of my hand and will shudder away. What if it's a guy? Will I suddenly turn him gay by the touch of my hand? Will he suddenly feel an uncontrollable desire to make out with me? Does the person look funny? Do they have Down Syndrome? If they do, they will inevitably end up transferring the disease to me, or I'll become even uglier and more socially inept than I already am. What if they ask me to do something that I feel morally or obsessively against? Will I have to play some kind of kissing game? How can I explain that I don't want to play without either giving my OCD away or being falsely perceived and accused of being gay and not liking girls? What if I have to contaminate myself, and then I start raving like a lunatic? What if? What if? What if?

At the climax of a game, I once discovered to my horror that the girl mischievously ended up pouring water down a guy's leg; supposedly it was done in a modest way. In another game, the players were tucked under a blanket and told that they were in a desert and to take one thing off that would enable their survival in the desert. My

goodness, what would I take off? I learned that one girl got down to nothingness; her pants, shirt, bra, and underwear came off. How was I supposed to know that the player was supposed to take the blanket itself off?

The only thing that generally works well is to go out and see a movie; however, this quickly becomes a burden on my wallet, especially because I'm unemployed because of, you guessed it, OCD. Even this can end up being quite cantankerous, when it is the voice of a crowd, and not mine, which chooses which movie we should see. This presents two complications. First, I cannot ever, ever, ever see a movie more than once in the theatre. And second, my religious views prohibit me from seeing 75% of box office shows, as they're rated R or have too much nudity, sensuality, profanity, horror, violence, and/ or drugs in the content.

At any rate, last night should have presented no problems. I was watching a rental video with my roommate that both of us picked out. However, OCD soon made up new problems that could only be worried about. One—I had

seen a lot of movies of late (as it was the only social enterprise that I could venture into), and it was somehow a sin for a person to watch movies all the time. Two—I had chores, homework, and other rituals to attend to. Three—It was late, and this movie was intruding upon my perpetual fear that whatever action I ended up taking would violate my body's laws with regard to sleep and would produce insomnia. Four—There was a problem with the audio portion of the TV, VCR, and/ or VHS; a continuous high-pitched static rendered it impossible to hear and clearly make out any of the dialogue to my satisfaction. Five— My roommate was asleep on the couch next to me. A normal person might have just interpreted this as meaning that my roommate had a long day and was tired. OCD, however, didn't permit such a simple and trivial explanation. No, no. This meant that he was upset with me for choosing a poor film. Six—I had looked away for an instant and missed the most pivotal two seconds in the entire movie.

Tonight I am alone again with no friend anywhere in sight except you. As such, a toast to my ever-present reader, with me till the end.

Log Notes

[1] Dictionary.com defines 'haunta virus' as "any of several viruses of the family Bunyaviridae, spread chiefly by wild rodents, that cause acute respiratory illness, kidney failure, and other syndromes, following exposure to the virus in airborne particles of rodent urine, feces, or saliva or directly by the bite of the rodent." It occurs most in the dry, dusty climate of the Southwest. It is mentioned here because rodent waste litters the ground when out walking in the desert brush.

Log Six – Jul 22, 2005

I was tricked. They lured me into their trap and then snared me. It was me, not them, who was arrogant. They took me to their headquarters, it is true. I blew up several of their rooms and killed several men, it is true. But they were waiting further down into their complex, drawing me farther and farther down, until they had surrounded me. Now I am once again their prisoner of war. They have resumed torturing me from where they left off, and they have bludgeoned my head with the back of their guns, shot me deep in my side, and are now preparing to electrocute me as I sit chained to a metal chair.

Deleting all music subfolders seemed wise at the start, but I was soon rudely awakened to the fact that OCD had managed to twist my battle to its advantage. I was killing a fear by moving all of my files directly into the "My Music" folder, but I wasn't killing the greatest fear—that my music files could stay as they were in folders sanctioned for the wrong artist. Additionally, it wasn't too long before I discovered that Windows had a neat little feature that could

group all of my folderless songs alphabetically according to title, genre, and artist. Thanks to this little feature, I was accomplishing next to nothing by deleting all of my artist subfolders. Plus, the process of deleting over 150 subfolders was enormously long and burdensome. My continuing to labor for such a tedious and worthless cause was another testament that this process had turned to OCD's advantage. After all, I couldn't leave my subfolders only partially deleted. I had started this process and that meant that I had to finish it no matter what. Also I now had to finish the process so that I could once again group all of my songs according to artist, genre, and title.

Now that I've completed that process, I discovered to OCD's absolute horror that I couldn't group the songs by title after all. Why? The computer had put a track number in front of two thousand of the song titles. Now instead of reading Johnny B. Goode, it read "02 Johnny B. Goode." As a result, the songs were grouped numerically instead of alphabetically. I am ashamed to say that I am still working my way

down the list, deleting all of the track numbers. I'm just not fully satisfied that I don't need to do this ritual yet. More accurately, I am cowering before the terrifying presence of my OCD. I trust in your understanding and faith that I can overcome this in time.

But maybe I can unstrap just one of my harnesses. I can gain one little victory. I will stop for tonight. I will make my OCD wait. Victories build from small beginnings.

Log Seven – Jul 23, 2005

This evening was absolutely miserable. I spent the last 4½ hours trying to write a single page. For my assignment[1], I was supposed to pick one verse or section from the scriptures to write about. That's thousands of verses. It's like finding a needle in a haystack. Anyways, once I found the section I was going to write on, I was supposed to write a one-page analysis of the verse, analyzing the importance, context, assumptions, and doctrines found therein. I couldn't do it. It took me almost two hours to finally decide upon and write down my first sentence. From there, it continued to be absolutely miserable. Before I wrote any word down, my mind had to cut it, stretch it, skewer it, fry it, and send it through the washing machine. I had to think, worry, and obsess about every possible way it could be wrong. I hate OCD! Augh!

Now, lest I leave you hopeless, some good things did happen today. To start off, I went and worked in the temple baptistry[2] today. Six months ago I would never have been able to do

that. I get anxious just walking through the doors of the temple because my mind starts filling me with all kinds of "I'm not worthy, I'm a sinner" religious obsessions. Yet today I worked at the temple for four hours.

Also, I have not touched my "My Music" folder once today. See. There's good stuff, too. It's just harder to see.

Log Notes

[1] This assignment was part of my REL C 325: Doctrine and Covenants II class at BYU. It covered the second half of *The Doctrine and Covenants*.

[2] Temples are holy edifices, believed to literally be the House of God, where members of The Church of Jesus Christ of Latter-day Saints in good standing make sacred covenants to obey the word of the Lord and receive sacred ordinances necessary to one's eternal salvation. Here these blessings are also extended to those who have died without the opportunity to receive the fullness of Christ's Gospel. This happens when members perform and receive these saving ordinances while acting as proxy for these individuals, who then may decide whether or not they want to accept the work that has been done on their behalf. One of these ordinances is baptisms for the dead, where the deceased may be baptized through this proxy work. The area of the temple where this takes place is called

the baptistry, comprising of the baptismal font, baptistry chapel, and confirmation rooms, where the dead, if they so choose, are confirmed as members of The Church of Jesus Christ of Latter-day Saints and constitutes the baptism of fire (also referred to as the gift of the Holy Ghost).

Log Eight – Jul 25, 2005

Today was a fruitful day. I went through several different experiences that were another testament to the fact that I am getting better. First, I took my car into Midas to get the brakes fixed. When it was done, I took care of the payment all by myself and utilized my first ever debit card for the first time. Then, I drove the car away without ever having asked them to make sure to wipe down every part of my car that they (and oil, grime, and grease attached to them) came into contact with.

Then after dinner I used a public restroom to defecate. Not only that, I chose not to put my clothes on as if I were distributing uranium all over the material. I chose not to wait until everyone else had deserted the bathroom before exiting my stall. I chose not to wash my hands too obsessively (no elbows, arms, fingernails, and lasting only one minute). I chose not to use paper towels as a barrier in order to turn off the faucets and open the door. And I had a conversation with the guy who was in the bathroom with me.

Later I went to a church activity, where we played waffle ball on a goathead-infested dirt mound. This presented yet another opportunity for me to demonstrate progress. I actually touched the bottom of my shoe (and unobsessively at that) to pull out the thorns that had fixed themselves into my shoe. Then I made an even bolder move. I reenacted one of my previous exposures from the hospital[1]. I grabbed onto the bottom of both shoes with the whole of both hands. Then I wiped the whole of both hands from my cheeks to my lips.

My final feat was sitting in the grass, watching firecrackers go off while a gazillion bugs hovered around me. And I endured a good portion of it without wiping and shooing the bugs away. Then when I got home, I didn't inspect every single square centimeter of my body to make sure that no bug, egg, corpse, or bite was there.

A little explanation is needed here. I wouldn't go outside much (the only times I did was because of insensitive coercion on the part of others) for years for fear of bugs. When I looked

outside all I could see were massive clouds of bugs, and these I could see individually counting into the thousands. A good portion of these bugs were real, but an equally great, if not greater, portion of them were not actually there. Again I experienced severe formication. I experienced it just about every time I stepped outside, and every time I actually had a real encounter with a bug.

Now to explain the feeling: It wasn't just a vague feeling of traces of movement. I literally felt the bugs. I felt the scope of their matter—their surface area. I felt the space created by their body as it moved along between my socks and my feet. I felt the hairs covering the spider's body. I felt the prick of all six of their legs individually. I felt the hardness and roughness of their exoskeleton. I felt them weave slowly or run quickly up my leg, brushing past my own follicles and up into the place where all bugs are attracted to—my groin. Then again, assuming that it was a tick, I felt it bite into my flesh and slowly insert its cranium into the hole that they were gnawing. I felt my skin close up around its head, enveloping it. I felt its suction as it begin to

suck the blood out of my veins. I felt all of this from something that never really existed. All of this was a creation of my own sick mind.

So is there cause for exuberance of soul? Is there cause to bask in the light of a new world forming? Is there cause to be glad? Yes, I believe there is.

Log Notes

[1] The hospital mentioned here refers to Rogers Memorial Hospital. It is located in Oconomowoc, WI and has an OCD Treatment Center, one of only 3 hospitals in the nation which specialize in the treatment of advanced forms of OCD. (The other 2 hospitals are located in Texas and Massachusetts.) Rogers Memorial Hospital, also abbreviated "RMH", is the hospital where I went and lived for 3 months while undergoing intensive treatment for my OCD at the end of 2003. Its OCD Center was completely separated from the main hospital and consisted of two 2-story houses at the edge of a lake. "Lake House 1" housed male residents, while "Lake House 2" housed female residents. Each house had from 4 to 6 rooms, allowing for the possible occupancy of 8 to 12 patients per lake house. It should be noted that, while the main RMH facility is still located in Oconomowoc, the OCD Center was moved some years later to two new buildings of roughly the same size located in nearby Delafield, WI.

Log Nine – Jul 26, 2005

Today the toilet clogged. This gave me some exposure opportunities. I reached for the plunger, and I didn't use a barrier to hold it, and I didn't hold it as far away from me as humanly possible. Then I went at it. I really hate toilets with low water pressure. I wish I could upgrade, but I don't know how, and it probably would be impossible for me to do since I'm in a rented apartment. Anyhow, I pumped and I pumped, and I pumped and I pumped. Pretty soon water from the bowl splashed onto me. Nevertheless I pumped on. Pretty soon I realized the toilet water had already touched my skin, my pants, and the seat, so what would a little more be? So I put my shoulder into the pumps, making them harder and faster. It took ten minutes until it finally started working again, until it was finally unplugged and the toilet water resumed its spiraling downward course.

By that time most of the floor was covered with toilet water along with the porcelain seats, back, and bowl. So I hunkered down and started wiping the water off of the floor, toilet, clothes,

skin, and shoes. Immediately the water seeped through the toilet paper and the toilet paper was filled with the grime that always exists on a bathroom floor from wear and tear. I really don't know how on earth it gets there, but there it was staring at me, with only a soaked, degrading surface of shallow toilet paper to block it from touching my hand, my fingers. But I wiped on. I even wiped up the urine that elusively manages to get along the back base of a toilet. But I wiped on.

It took about five minutes to finish the wiping. Then I sat back down and finished my business and wiped up. Then I washed my hands for the first time during the entire ordeal, and resisted washing up to my elbows; I only went to my wrists. Then I dried off with a towel that may or may not have had toilet water flung upon it, and I stepped out.

Then I went to a movie. I figured I kind of deserved it after a big battle like that. And yes, I was still wearing the same clothes that had very clearly been soaked with water (in certain parts).

I probably even rested my hands on that spot while I was in the theatre.

Now two years ago I would have washed my hands thirty different times up to my armpits in near-boiling water. I would have thrown my toxic clothes and the hand towel into the hamper, making sure that no part of them actually touched the hamper. I would have taken out all of the cleaners and sanitized every inch of the bathroom. I would have spent four minutes knocking the water off the plunger and anxiously looking inside every inch of that plunger to make sure there was no fecal material in it. And I would have screamed, cried, wailed, and howled ritualistic prayers up to the heavens, asking God for forgiveness from several horrifying sins that I had never committed but believed concretely that somehow I did and He was punishing me for these blood stains on my metaphorical garments.

Oh, and when it was all wiped up today, I was pouring out streams of perspiration from the enormous physical and mental exertion. It collected in pools on my glass lenses and plummeted down onto my skin and clothing. I

knocked the beads off my glasses, but I never washed them, I never cleaned them, I never rinsed them, and I never wiped them dry. And I resisted wiping away 95% of the sweat off my clothes, as well as washing my face and brushing it with a towel. I just let it stay there, glistening and streaming. Finished, I walked past two beautiful girls that were visiting my roommate, having hardly wiped any of it away. Then I went to the aforementioned movie and let the salt dry on my face.

Log Ten – Jul 29, 2005

It's been a few days since I've written—a few anxious days. I've hit a 7^1 several times, and have stayed at or above a 5 for as much as three or four hours.

For starters, I'm taking another dance test and yesterday, the day before I took it, I was a mess. The last test I earned an 87% which freaked me out of my mind. It wasn't so much that I received a $B+^2$ as it was that OCD was convinced that since my grade dropped to a B+ it would keep dropping until I failed and flunked all of my classes and I would be kicked out of BYU. Plus, for this test, I would be dancing with my teacher and, as I have never been able to figure out the timing for the music and previously had dance partners to help tell me when to start dancing, I was worried that I'd start off-beat and stay off-beat for the entire test, as my teacher wouldn't help me on account of it being considered cheating.

Then, I went to a mandatory dance lab, which was really like a social dance except you

were expected to do ballroom dancing instead of the usual freelance jump-and-jive. Anyhow, this required me to gather up my courage and ask a girl to dance with me, and I had to ask her to dance knowing full well that I had two left feet. Another snag was the fact that the room was packed and my dancing got considerably worse because I had no idea how to dance *and* navigate through a crowd at the same time. Hence I was at a 7. I was so nervous that I felt like vomiting.

It was right before the test when another problem presented itself. I had had to pay $10.00 to take the test (don't ask me why) and I had forgotten the receipt. I was sure this meant that I couldn't test. It turned out I could but I would not be able to get my scores. As a result, I had to rush home, get my receipt, and rush back to claim what rightfully belonged to me. However, I couldn't remember where I had left the receipt. No sooner had I realized this than OCD blew it out of proportion and I became as worried about finding this receipt as I would have been about finding a wedding ring two minutes before a wedding. Immediately I started ticking off the

OC-prayers. I was convinced losing the receipt was a punishment from God for all of my vile, fictitious sins. By the time I got home I was repeating "O God, have mercy on me who am in the flames of Hell and torture" over and over and over and over.

Despite all of this, I found the receipt within one minute of entering my room. Was OCD satisfied? No! I still had to present the receipt to the Ballroom Dance Office and then meet with two people about an academic map (a plot of all the classes I had left to take until graduation) that I had spent six hours on the day before and make it to my dentist appointment all within just under one hour.

Then, the bus was late. It was twenty minutes late! This again increased my anxiety to exponential proportions. This was made even worse by the fact that I'm always at a 4 or 5 every time I have to wait for the bus because I'm standing the whole time (a major problem due to severe spinal injuries) and am convinced beyond any fraction of a doubt that I already missed the bus and will be late to class; I always feel on the

verge of kneeling down and shouting out pleas to God from the bus stop. It wasn't any better this time. Finally, when the bus arrived, I had only 36 minutes until my dentist appointment, which meant I was not going to be able to meet with my academic counselors.

Then another dilemma presented itself. I had forgotten to take my heart medication that I have to take exactly one hour before my dentist appointment or else risk having heart infection. Great! Clearly God was orchestrating life to my disadvantage, to put it mildly. Clearly I had committed some kind of evil atrocity though I had no idea what it was. By this time the self-abasing phrase "Spawn of Satan" was rattling off my tongue every twenty seconds. By the time I got home I only had five minutes left. I called up the dentist to see whether I should take my medicine now and still have my teeth treated or reschedule. The answer was to reschedule. I was very definitely at a 7. I felt like hurting myself, so I called the bishop. Thirty minutes later I was fine.

Thank heavens, the next day (today) has been far less exhausting, though depressing. I found out I will not be able to go see my Wisconsin family. They were the ones who basically adopted me into their family when I was at my worst (in the hospital) and they showed so much love to me, a stranger. Anyhow, I am deeply saddened by this unfortunate turn of events. I know they have good reason—they are busy with their own family's life, but OCD can't let me go without wondering if they don't love me anymore. I miss them so much! I was so looking forward to this trip.

I need somewhere to go that's away from here during the coming school break, somewhere where I can feel relaxed, safe, and wanted. I can't go home to feel like this, not with all the awful physical and emotional abuse I was forced to suffer "under the safety of my own roof" for so many years. I know he's better now; I'm pretty sure that he won't hit me now. He's made progress, but I will never be able to feel safe and loved around him for the rest of my life. Abuse[3] has a deep and very personal lasting sting to it. I

can't enter into any new or old relationship or friendship now without wondering if "every one's going to hate you if they really knew you, if they had to live with you," as was said to me multiple times throughout my adolescent and early adult years.

How I wish I had a home! How I wish I could feel safe! How I wish I had a family! How I wish I had a refuge that I could dock in to wade out the hurricanes of my life! How I wish I could feel loved! How I wish! But if I had a dollar for every wish I wished, every dream I dreamed, I would not be a poor man.

Log Notes

[1] "Hitting a 7" or "staying at or above a 5" refers to a numeric system of rating the intensity of anxiety that one is currently facing or expects to face in a certain situation. 0 means no anxiety at all of any kind (a very rare score for someone battling severe OCD). Hence, the scale more often starts at 1, the first occurrence or manifestation of anxiety. A score of 7 refers to the most anxiety one could imagine facing/enduring. Theoretically, this would be the top of the scale, but there is still one score higher than this: a 7+, which would indicate more anxiety than the patient could even imagine facing. This

0 to 7(+) scale is the scale used at Rogers Memorial Hospital's OCD Treatment Center, differentiating Rogers from most psychological/psychiatric offices, which use a 0-to-10 rating scale.

[2] This is the same 87% (or B+) that I mentioned previously in Log Two. I received it in DANCE 180: Beginning Social Dance at Brigham Young University (BYU).

[3] References to abuse are not used lightly…or, maybe more accurately…they are not used maliciously here and in other places throughout this book. I admit that such references were voiced out of deep anger at the time these passages were originally penned, but, in preparing this book for publication, I have done my best to redact explicit or superfluous details (particularly the identity of the person and descriptions of the more abusive encounters, in as much as possible) from the manuscript. However, I did not remove such references completely for the following reasons: First, the reader cannot sufficiently grasp the reasons why certain events and decisions present me with the deep amounts of conflict, trauma, and uncertainty that they do. Second, such references provide the reader with a firmer understanding of the reasoning behind subsequent responses, reactions, and decisions. Third, it is impossible to accurately ascertain the genesis of certain obsessions, along with their respective compulsions, without them. Fourth, it helps relate a critical warning to those who will feel the temptation to either dismiss actions as non-abusive simply because they aren't physical or because they don't leave any visible scars on the person's body. Fifth, it warns against the well-meaning, but highly fallacious, tactic of

providing or generating something "real" for the affected individual to fear, in the hopes that such a comparison of rational fear against irrational fear will result in that individual's loss of fear and OCD, either totally or with regard to that one particular phobia. Sixth, it illustrates the enormously dangerous fallacy behind the similar, initially well-meaning approach of simply "beating the OCD out" of an affected individual.

Log Eleven – Aug 4, 2005

I'm in the process of moving, quite to my dismay. When I moved here, I thought that I was going to be living in the same place (the same room, the same apartment, the same complex) the whole time. I even recontracted for another year. However, my apartment (Old Mill Condos # 306) got bought up by another owner. She bought it for her sons to stay in along with their two friends. Well, this would have been fine and dandy (for the most part) except for the fact that the apartment only had four rooms. The new owner had only one term—"You're kicked out at the close of August!" (They had found a 30-day loophole that allowed them to reject my new contract and leave me out in the dust.) Great! This was not good in the slightest. Status quo is good. Change is a nightmare.

Well, I reluctantly found a new habitat. I was going to move across the stairwell to Old Mill Condos # 305. It just goes to show how against the grain OCD is to change. I was changing apartments, but I was staying attached to the same stairwell on the same floor. Of course

it had to be on the top floor because bugs don't climb tall walls. Yeah right! Yet it was the rule. This law, like all the others, was carved into stone by OCD and could not be rubbed away. This was truth unalterable against the face of sanity.

Then there was the matter of which room to move into. The first possibility was a translation in mathematical terms; I would pick up the entire floor plan for 306 and drop it right on top of 305. This would put me in the front right bedroom. This also kept my bedroom the same topographically; I would still be facing northwest. However, a problem quickly presented itself—my bedroom had actually landed on top of 305's kitchen. Well, the next option was to translate the floor plan for 306 and then rotate it 180 degrees. This would put the kitchen in the same place, but this would also move my room to the back left bedroom.

This posed two other problems. This new bedroom had one window while my old bedroom possessed two. Also this new window's panorama was limited to the street 1720 North;

neither of my own apartment's windows faced this way. My windows faced Carterville Rd. and a Quiki Mart gas station or a back view into more of the apartment complex. In order to have two windows I would have to take the back right room; this would also allow a cooling cross breeze during the sweltering summertime. Now I maintained my view of the Quiki Mart, but I still lacked the view out back. Then again what about during wintertime? This would be the coldest room in the apartment. To solve this I would have to move into the front left room; its only exterior wall faced into the solarium. Then again, once summer returned, this would be the hottest room in the apartment. Well, after much deliberation I reached a decision. I would go with the rotation. I would take the back right. This seemed the most similar and proffered the benefit of thinned-out noise as foot traffic would be denser in the front two rooms of Apartment 305.

Then another complication came. Someone new had moved into the apartment, striking claim to the back right bedroom. Now I had to come to terms with another choice and

another room. I quickly struck the front left room off my list, vetoing the sweltering inconvenience of the present summer months. So now the question was back left or front right. The front right retained a practical advantage. It was the only room in the house with a deep windowsill, enabling me to perch my printer, alarm clock, tape player, trash boxes, and literary and cybernetic volumes. However this would be noisier than the back left as it took in more traffic than the back. Also the back left bathroom was further back in the room away from the hallway wall. This allowed me to cover or mask any unpleasant noises that could arise from using the bathroom. With the front right, the bathroom wall was alarmingly adjacent to the hallway.

Well, after much more thought, I decided on the back left bedroom. Yet this didn't mean my problems were over. I still had plenty of concerns regarding my roommates. Would they like me? No! Once they got to know me and, more to the point, my OCD, they would hate me. They would never tolerate any of my OC Questions like my last roommate did. They

would think I'm a freak. They would avoid me or they would hurt me. To make matters worse, the apartment got bought up after I had signed a contract with 305, and the owner's son was living there. Translation: The son would hate me and get back at me by having his father kick me out as soon as possible. There was no other way to see it. I would be out cold on the street in a year. He already hated me because I had been asking questions about the mutability properties of the front right room. Yep, he hated me and thought me a freak, and I hadn't even moved in yet.

Then there came the matter of timing. The electricity at 306 went out. My roommate had called to ask that his name be taken off the bill since he was leaving to get married. He had assumed that the new 306 owner's name was also on the bill, but it wasn't. Plus, the electric company wouldn't let him put his name temporarily back on the bill without paying a $60.00 deposit, and we weren't sensing any move on the owner's part. So the answer was to move early. I would move the next day while the

electricity was still off in my old apartment. This way I would have access to the electricity that powered my life and made living possible in the age of laptops, printers, Palm Pilots [1], alarm clocks, CD players, and so much more. Despite this, no one was home at 305 and I didn't have a key. So I waited in suspense and anxiety all day until someone showed up at around 7:00 pm. When the power suddenly turned on at 4:06 pm I was in such a single-minded frenzy that I absolutely had to move that night.

The actual move was exhausting, as I kept being confronted by little and big challenges. The first one was that a good portion of my room was taken up by a former tenant's piles of stuff. It would have been in the front right except for two things. The new owner had been misinformed as to which room I would be moving into, and I would have to wait till the next day for the occupant of the front right to move out. Then there was the unexpected discovery that the hanger shelf in the closet was of wire mesh and not wood like my 306 bedroom, and the shelf was on two levels instead of one. This meant two

things. I couldn't keep all of my videos and DVDs on one uniform, easy-to-reach shelf with the necessary width to it, and I couldn't stand them side by side without having the one-disc DVDs falling through the mesh to the ground. Then there was the question of where I should put my printer as this new room had no deep window alcove to put it on. And where was I supposed to put all of my other electrical appliances, books, and miscellaneous belongings?

And there was the order of things. The books had to all be placed from tallest to shortest, and everything was measured with the utmost scrutiny to fractions of a centimeter. Everything else had to follow one great rule: THE POSITION OF EVERYTHING MUST BE THE SAME. I had to take ten or more trips back and forth so I could line up my pencils and pens in the same order in the relative drawer. My shoes had to be meticulously organized. My appliances had to remain in the same relative position insomuch as possible. My pants had to be stacked in the same order as in their old drawer.

My stack of books and CDs had to be poised the same—on my computer desk as neatly lined up to the front left corner in the same order from top to bottom. Everything I did had to be positioned at the same relative place geographically from the vista of someone standing in my doorway looking into my bedroom. Every time such order was violated my anxiety would increase and bewildered confusion and doubt would enter into my life.

Log Notes

[1] Palm Pilot is the brand name most typically associated with PDA (Personal Digital Assistant) devices, most commonly used around the turn of the last century. Essentially, the Palm was the rudimentary predecessor to almost any handheld computing device used today. It was approximately the same size as today's smart phones, and consisted mainly of a screen with a few buttons at the bottom and a pen stylus used for writing on the screen. Typically, its functions included basic programming like Calendar, Address Book, To-Do List, Photos, Word, Excel, Solitaire, Minesweeper, and Adobe Reader.

Log Twelve – Aug 7, 2005

I'm still not fully moved in. I have to have my old roommate help me move all my bedding without it touching the ground, and then I need help holding the sheets and blankets apart so I can make my bed. I also still have to get my doorknob replaced so that I can lock it the same as before, keeping my new roommates out from stealing any of my belongings. If the new 306 manager had known how catastrophic this was for me, I wonder if she would have kicked me out. Unfortunately, I don't think it would have made any different.

Oh, and yesterday I had another big worry added to my already massive list. I saw the note on the fridge. It said "Monthly Cleaning Inspections." It listed the whole slew of everything to be cleaned. It's a white glove inspection once every month. Some of the things like sweeping were tolerable. Depending on the levels of my roommates' hatred toward me and lack of understanding, I might be able to finagle my way out of the more anxiety-provoking items. But there's no escaping the hardest—the

bathroom. Not only do I have to clean the toilet and sink (which cause a good amount of anxiety by themselves), but I have to clean the floor. This will mean collecting large amounts of hair, grime, and who knows what else, picking it off my sponge mop with quickly degradable toilet paper, and somehow washing the spray and collectibles off of the sponge itself (probably in the toilet bowl) which will require extra hard sponging to make sure that no part of me contacts any area that could have been contaminated by the filthy sponge. Plus I have to clean the shower, something I have never done, I don't know how to do, and I wish I never would.

Isn't life so cheery?

Log Thirteen – Aug 10, 2005

It hurts to sit. It hurts to stand. It hurts to walk. It's all of my own doing ... or rather it's all OCD's doing. Hemorrhoids. Yeah. Ick, gag, gross! It's an awful thing to consider, to think about. So for all of you with a faint heart and a superficial need or desire for understanding, you've read too far already; please skip to Log Fourteen. I know people are never going to look at me the same once I write this. Actually it shouldn't be that much different from the way you look at me up to this log, but I know this'll be worse. It's embarrassing.

So why do I write it? For the same reason that I write everything else. I want to help. I want disaffected people to understand the complete hellish hues of OCD, to understand why people do irrational, even downright putrid things. They don't want to. No one with OCD wants to do what they do. As a matter of fact, they all hate to do what they're doing. But despite this they do it because they have to. They don't see any alternative. They feel frightened and powerless to fight back and retaliate against a relentless,

soulless Gestapo. They want to survive. So they keep following the devil's orders for the minute chance that the flames won't burn as hot in Perdition that day.

I think I've given you enough warning and preparation, so I'll draw your attention back to my original thought—hemorrhoids. I didn't used to have them. As a child, they weren't there. They crept up on me somewhere in my adolescence at about the same time that everything else went haywire. They were a result of the horror that I had of any bodily secretion or excretion. Anything that came out of my body somehow possessed a toxic nature. A whole score of plagues were living inside of me, waiting for the first chance to come out and infect and murder me.

At the top of this list were feces. Nothing was more hazardous to my survival than poop. And nothing had any greater social stigma that I was aware of than did feces. So you can imagine somewhat the terror that seized me every time that I had to defecate. Then when I sat down I pushed and I pushed and I pushed. I would push

so hard trying to force every single spec of feces out of me once and for all. Of course, this never happened, but that didn't matter. I had to push, shove, huff, and puff until my face would turn purple, internal blood vessels would pop, and I would all but pass out and wake up with perspiration coating my body, and then I would start all over again.

Yet nothing gave me a greater surge of anxiety than to clean up. I had to wipe, but I also had to avoid the slightest feeling that I had touched my poop or my butt. Yet OCD still had another whopper. I had to not only wipe my butt, but I had to go inside my anus and wipe around in the rectum. Why? OCD had totally convinced me that if I didn't wipe as far as I could inside my butt that poop would just fall or leak out during the proceedings of the day and, of course, it would happen when I was at school or at seminary[1] talking to a girl that I had a crush on and in front of every Chairman for the Board of Gossip and Social Humiliation. This had to be prevented, so I dug … no, drilled in … for the

sake of security because I had been so horribly brainwashed by my disease.

Actually brainwashed isn't quite the right term as much as internal cerebral sabotage. My own mind was doing this to me, but it wasn't "washing". No, no, it was unplugging stems and nerve endings and creating a chaotic system of intricately misplaced neurons in something somewhat resembling the web that a spider with a blood alcohol rating of 4.0 would have created.

I digress. So I drilled on in. I soon discovered that I was getting more and more talented at shoving my finger further and further in, twirling and rotating my finger as I wiped down the entire inside. Of course this did two things. It brought me into far greater contact with poop than a normal person would ever have. I would account for this by scrubbing flakes of skin off in boiling hot water for about thirty minutes. Secondly, all the pushing and the in-wiping had given birth to hemorrhoids. I had actually managed to make my fear come true while in the process of attempting to prevent it. I

had pulled skin from inside my rectum to the outside.

And that's how I got hemorrhoids. Wonderful story, isn't it? I told you you'd experience some nausea. Now, I don't do as much in-wiping as I used to thanks to my experience at Rogers[2], but I still have a good ways to go. I have an even higher cliff to climb with regard to the pushing. Things would be so much easier if I were not completely constipated all the time. Things are made even worse by the fact that I have a low-flushing toilet. Because when poop comes out, it comes out. Then I either have to plunge for 45 minutes or I have to pull out my stockpile of wooden pencils to slice, carve, and break apart my gigantic, rock-hard waste deposit.

Why? You're afraid to ask. Really it's quite simple. I was terrorized (and I use that word knowing full well what it means, as related to places like Iraq, Iran, and Palestine) by the process of using the bathroom. When I stepped inside that bathroom to defecate I experienced the kind of terror that was experienced on 9/11 as

individuals felt 36 floors crumble beneath their feet, felt the first weight of the upper 44 floors tumble down on top of them, felt their skin blister and erupt as it caught fire and they were enveloped in temperatures above 200 degrees Fahrenheit, felt their lungs gasp for want of air, heard the screams of women and children all around them, witnessed those in the adjacent room jump out of the windows from nearly two miles off the ground, saw the second plane hit the adjoining tower, and realized that their country was under attack and had been hit on the mainland for the first time since the War of 1812, and pictured their family and friends being blown up by enemy fire or a mine while lost in the Arab deserts. Yes, yes, yes. I know what I'm doing when I use the word 'terrorize'. And because of this terror, I avoided the bathroom at all costs until my insides would fill with pain and I would be forced to enter that tower again. At times I would even go a whole week without defecating.

Log Notes

[1] In The Church of Jesus Christ of Latter-day Saints, the young men and young women have the opportunity of enrolling in a class (called seminary) that centers on Christ and His Restored Gospel. Seminary is held either before or during school and is only offered while the student is in high school.

[2] 'Rogers' is short for Rogers Memorial Hospital.

Log Fourteen – Aug 14, 2005

Well, I'm back at home[1]. I'm trying to relax during the school break. I'm not sure if it's working, though. Today I saw two close high school friends that just got back from their missions[2] not long ago. It's the first time I've seen them in two years. I should be happy, but I'm not. I'm wallowing in the familiarity of depression. Two thoughts just keep running through my mind. First, they hate me. Of course, this shouldn't be any shocker. I think everyone hates me. Still it's worse with my friends because they served missions and I didn't. I couldn't because of OCD. My "mission" was to go off to the hospital for intense psychiatric treatment.

Losing my real mission was the biggest loss I've faced in my whole life, and I've experienced lots and lots of losses. It was something that I'd planned for, looked forward to my whole life. It was my purpose, my dream. It was the thing that I lived and breathed for. It was the greatest desire I had in life, but OCD crushed it. I don't blame the church for not letting me go. I wouldn't have lasted a day in the MTC[3], much

less in the field. I don't think I even blame God for it. It was inevitable in my rational and irrational opinion. Rationally, I recognized that it would not work for the mere sake of time. It would have been impossible to be an effective missionary and wash my hands for six to eight hours each day. Irrationally, I was being justly punished for horrendous sins, crimes, and abominations. I believed I was "the spawn of Satan," worse than Judas Iscariot, Charles Manson, and Adolph Hitler. I had killed, stolen, raped, molested, committed genocide, adulterated, fornicated, consumed alcohol and illicit drugs, taken up devil worshipping and witchcraft, took on all manner of "unnatural affections," and transacted in the rank business of pornography. So it was justice, it was bound by heaven and earth to happen.

Still I never apostatized[4], I never went inactive. I kept going to church. I kept abiding by the precepts and doctrine I had been taught there. Mostly, I kept living and resisting the continual desire to kill myself. I did all this, even though I was 200% certain that I was damned to Hell no

matter what I did. But I kept doing these things because I loved God and I loved the gospel, all despite my belief that God and the church had turned their backs on me. Naturally when my close friends took off on their own missions, I thought that they would never be my friends again. They would go off and serve, become saturated with the Spirit of the Lord, and have it confirmed to them that I was the demon I believed I was...and still believe I am. They would recognize evil for evil and stay away.

Now I no longer believe that I've committed all of those horrible and rank sins, but OCD won't let me get away from the notion that anyone who serves a mission will come back and pronounce me evil. Today I was welcomed warmly by two wonderful friends, but I still can't shake the feeling that they're going to accept the truth that I'm a monster and leave me. Somehow it just hasn't taken effect yet.

Secondly, in reference to the first paragraph of this log, I am overwhelmed by the feeling that I don't have a life. All I have is OCD. I mean I'm so much better, but I have a long,

steep climb ahead of me nevertheless. Certainly I don't have a past. They spent their past two years living lives, making progress, growing, and having the experiences that people should have. I have no past...nothing except OCD. True, I've had an eventful two years where I have revolted against OCD. But they have lives, real lives. My friends have spent the past two years in heaven. I have spent the last several years in Outer Darkness, in Perdition.

I often speculate that I feel like Frodo (you know, from *The Lord of the Rings*) in the last book *The Return of the King*. I've spent what seems like a lifetime carrying an oppressive burden (a ring) on my way to Mordor. I feel like I have a deep, painful scar that will be with me for eternity. It will never go away. Oh, I might return to The Shire[5] once again, but I will return a far different creature than the one I was when I left. I will never fit in again.

I'm sure there is great hope, but I feel as though I have no light to guide me. My eyes are open, but I cannot see.

Log Notes

[1] 'Home' here refers to my parents' house in Rio Rancho, NM, where I was raised. This is not a reference to my apartment in Provo, UT, where I was living at the time in order to take classes at BYU.

[2] Because we recognize the need for people to have saving ordinances both for themselves and their deceased ancestors, The Church of Jesus Christ of Latter-day Saints calls thousands of its members each year to serve full-time missions in most locations spanning the globe. Their purpose is to proclaim, teach, and preach the gospel to all of God's children around the world. Typically, missionaries serve when they turn 19 or some time in their 20s. Males are expected to serve and do so for two years. Females, however, serve on a more voluntary basis and do so for a year and a half. Additionally, senior couples are afforded the opportunity to serve missions, though usually in a different manner, running various auxiliary programs of the church in various locations, by teaching foreigners to speak English or in their native tongue in their native lands, or serving as tour guides at locations significant to the early history of the church (such as Palmyra, NY; Kirtland, OH; and Nauvoo and Carthage, IL). Individuals who cannot serve full-time missions for whatever reason may also elect to serve in part-time missions, where they can live at home and help in local auxiliary programs. For purposes of this book, however, 'missions' is a reference to the standard two-year, full-time proselytizing missions served by young men.

[3] MTC is an acronym for Missionary Training Center. This is where missionaries go to get taught how to be an effective missionary, as well as learning how to speak in the language native to the part of the world they will be serving in. Generally, a missionary's stay is only a couple of weeks, though that is generally longer for missionaries that have to learn a second language. The main MTC is located in Provo, UT, but there are a few other MTCs around the world, including ones in England and Brazil.

[4] Simply put, to 'apostatize' means to turn away from and/or rebel against God, His church, and the leaders called to preside over His church. Apostasy is most often and most clearly signified by the individual's choice to stop attending church, though these individuals are generally referred to as 'inactive' (or the less-stigmatizing term of 'less active'). Apostasy in its truest and most complete sense happens when the individual also either asks for their name to be removed completely from all church records or is excommunicated from the church. In either case, their names are blotted out from the records of the church so that they are no longer as accountable for failing to live by covenants that they cannot or will not keep. People who leave the Church are always welcome to return and re-enter the Church through baptism. I should probably add that the above is only one context of the word apostasy—that of an individual person. Apostasy, however, also applies to a whole group of people turning away from God, whether that is a small community, a nation, or the whole world. When apostasy is applied to the latter-most situation, it is known as a Great Apostasy. As members of The Church of Jesus Christ of

Latter-day Saints, we believe that the martyrdoms of Christ and His Apostles led to a Great Apostasy, when no more prophets were called and the priesthood keys enabling the governing of God's kingdom here on Earth were removed and taken up into heaven. We believe that this Apostasy didn't end until the prophet Joseph Smith ushered in the Restoration and was given the Aaronic and Melchizedek Priesthoods by John the Baptist, as well as by Peter, James, and John (respectively) and The Church of Jesus Christ of Latter-day Saints was established on April 6, 1830.

[5] The Shire is the green, fertile land found in the world of Middle Earth, as created by J.R.R. Tolkien, where hobbits dwell. It is from here that Frodo starts off on his burdensome journey to destroy Sauron's One Ring of Power in the fires of Mount Doom in the wicked land of Mordor.

Log Fifteen – Aug 15, 2005

I fear my last several entries have been a bit depressing. For this I apologize. I do not wish to promulgate the false notion that there is no hope. There is. There's a bright, beautiful horizon shadowing my life and yours, dark as moments may seem. I suppose a better analogy would be to use the sun. It's always there shining, beaming down, giving life, directing our paths. We just don't always see it; but it is always there. At the risk of sounding cliché and cheesy, "The sun *will* come up tomorrow."

Anyhow, I've had two victories of late. The first involves a license plate. About a month ago I was notified that my automobile registration would shortly be expiring and I needed to renew it. More than this, it quickly became apparent that I needed a title change as well, seeing as I would be living in Utah from now on rather than my former home in New Mexico. Accordingly I went to the Department of Motor Vehicles and waited for fifty minutes (a remarkably quick amount of time seeing as there had to have been around 150 persons in the

DMV when I got there) to be told that I had to come back another day. I couldn't get a title change until I had passed a safety and emissions test.

A couple of days later I arrived at a car shop where the tests could be performed. Again I was told that I had to come back again; the tint on my front two windows was illegal in the state of Utah. I took off to a glass shop which in turn redirected me to a tint shop. By the time I had arrived the shop was closed, so I came back the next day to get it removed for twenty bucks and returned to the auto shop where he passed me.

Now one minor backtrack is necessary. I hate car oil. I hate grease. I hate grime. I hate everything to do with the inner workings of my car, or any car for that matter. I'm afraid of it, and two, three years ago it scared me to death. Oh, I would commit great feats worthy of a contortionist act. Upon returning home from the gas station or auto shop, I had to open the front door, which of course was shut to the bolt (but not locked). I had to twist and push on the doorknob with my elbow pit fearfully making

sure that my hands, my wrists, my forearms, and my sleeves did not spread the pollutant to the door, in which case I would have to take a soapy rag to the door. You see, all of that car stuff was a toxin that would eat through my skin, poison me, make me go blind, and kill me (ironically a fate I wished for with every breath every time I heard the commanding voice of OCD).

As a result of all this, I learned to fear car shops. I could barely set a foot into them. Even after I got my car back I would worry endlessly about any possible mark that the workers could have left in my car. On the way home I had to sit forward and erect to avoid bathing my hair in gasoline and simultaneously suck in my gut as I drove the car home with one napkinned hand to avoid contacting the steering wheel that I absolutely knew they had touched. Upon my arrival home, I would have to scrub the entire car down with a wash cloth covered in suds. Next I would drown my keys in soap and water.

Then I would madly buff my shoes with the grass on the front lawn. Finally I would have to deposit all of my clothing into the laundry

hamper and then shower for 45 minutes. After I went to Rogers, much of these rituals went into hiding, but one remained. Every time I took the car to Jiffy Lube or any other car shop I would ask them to make an extra effort to wipe down my keys, my seat, the steering wheel and anything else that they had touched. At these times, I could hear OCD's voice in the background saying, "Ritual? What ritual? They're just wiping it up, that's all. You're not doing it. It's small. It's not like you're going to go home and wash the car. They're doing it for you." Oh, the cunning, lying voice of OCD!

Anyhow, finally, I will get to my point. When I picked my car up from the auto shop, the tint shop, and a week previously the brake shop I didn't ask them to wipe anything down. I opened the door normally, sat normally, drove normally, and went on with my life. I had shut out the continually withering voice of OCD.

I sent this message again a week later when I returned to the DMV. For three weeks I was contemplating getting a special license plate for my car, as I was tragically informed that I

couldn't keep mine. Why? Did I want to look cool? No, not really. I had given up on the idea of cool a long time ago. I wanted to get a plate with the word "FEZIC" on it. Why? My old license plate had been "FZC 952". I had named the car Fezic to help me remember what my license plate number was. It meant nothing more. So why was I gritting my teeth? I didn't want to hurt my car's feelings by putting a license plate on it that didn't contain the letters F, Z, and C. I mean, that's what the "evil white man" did to the Indians, the Cherokee especially—They assimilated them into the American way of life and the first thing that they did was to take away their identity and change their names. I was being racist against my car. Well, when the time came I resisted. I received a new license plate "251 VUJ". I had saved myself the fifty bucks that I would have thrown away in order to nourish my disease.

Log Sixteen – Aug 16, 2005

My anxiety spiked some time ago. I'm playing Risk with my friends. I have been looking forward to this all day. What better than a classic game of world domination with your two close friends? Yet as always OCD has intruded into my life, and I don't know how to shut it up. What kind of exposure can I do? I suppose the only one would be to keep playing and not say anything. I so much want to quit, but feel I cannot for the risk of appearing a poor sport.

They're whispering. They're forming alliances. I hate alliances. I hate secrets. I hate whispering. I know they're saying bad stuff to each other. They're laughing at me, they're laughing. They're laughing at all of my flaws, at my OCD. They're saying how they hate me. There's no other explanation but this irrational conclusion. Help! I need help. I feel like screaming for help. I wish I could make them understand. I'm not good with games, even the ones I like. I'm not good with anything social. Hence I don't have any friends. I feel like I'm

never going to get any new friends. I can't even maintain the ones I have. One thing is certain. All of my friends will leave me, every single last one of them.

The only other thing I can do is a ritual. It's so strong. I feel the beckoning call to rip[1] everything, every CD that my family has. So when I came over here I brought seventeen CDs. It takes so long to rip them all. The thing is I don't like a lot of the songs. I just feel compelled to hoard every single song that crosses my path.

I got into an argument with my brother earlier. I lost a computer program he had allowed me to copy a year earlier. I lost it when my computer crashed. Now he won't let me copy it. He's quoting the copyright laws. I am already battling (and most definitely losing) that ethical battle. I know I won't be happy if someone else pirates this book I am writing. Yet I am being driven to copy other artist's work. How hypocritical a being I am! I wish I had never asked that cop about the copyright laws. I keep going back to the one voice that repeatedly told me that it was legal to copy anything as long as I

didn't turn around and sell it. I know he had the best of intentions, but it's hurting me. I was looking for rationalization and I got it.

Still I believe it would have been perfectly legal and ethical for me to rip. To rip my five favorite CDs would have been alright, but instead I copied everything, the entire library. I just wanted a definite line that told me without any hesitation where right became wrong. That's the problem with OCD. It wants everything to be black and white despite the fact that we live in a world of gray ambiguity.

Log Notes

[1] In this context, 'rip' has nothing to do with tearing something up. Rather, it is used in the jargon of modern technologies. Here it means the act of taking a CD, sticking it into your computer, opening up your media player, and then making a duplicate copy of the CD's contents, storing it inside your computer's memory. In short, 'ripping' means taking what's on a CD and putting it into a computer, eliminating the need to insert the disc every time you want to listen to it.

Log Seventeen – Aug 17, 2005

Today was a good day. My progress was put to the test when I visited my fourth grade teacher. My opportunity came in the form of two dogs. I was able to sit comfortably and have a normal conversation while actually petting the dogs. I could not have done so a few years ago. I couldn't touch dogs, much less any animal, and they in turn could not touch me. They were too full of bugs and diseases. This was very problematic considering my family had a dog. True, I didn't hold some of the fears about him as I did with other dogs. I knew more or less where he had been. I knew he was not carrying rabies, but other dogs were always "rabid until proven innocent". I couldn't even venture to pet a good friend's dog until I had received satisfactory answers in the affirmative to these questions: "Does he have all of his shots? Is he carrying rabies? Are you sure? So can I touch him? You're sure he's safe? No diseases? Are you 100% positive?"

While I did not have to worry about whether my own dog had rabies, I certainly

carried a whole host of other worries. First of all, had he contacted any poop? This was a common question as he shared the common repulsive tendency with other dogs to eat his own poop or that of another dog's. I was sure to be flying high at a 7 or 7+ when I saw this. Where had his mouth been? Where was his mouth? Where could his mouth possibly end up? The same questions could be asked for his nose. Of course the answer to the first was always evident. I had seen where his mouth and nose had been. I had beheld it with my own two eyes. It was the other two that provided endless checking. I had to anxiously maintain proximity to the infested dog in order to make sure that his face didn't come into contact with anything. Were it to touch the tile or the carpet I would have to file a memo in my brain telling me never to touch that place ever again. I couldn't even walk on that spot for a whole week or two.

Were it to contact a cupboard I needed to open in the near future, I would have to send myself the same memo. This way I would know not to touch (or ever brush up against that spot

while washing dishes) the left edge of the cupboard in between the one- and two-foot area from the bottom edge. If this didn't work I would have to bring out the soapy washrag again.

This still left the dog's mouth and nose contaminated, so I would have to trick the dog into sniffing the ground once outside and then apprehensively force his mouth and nose to the grass or the dirt and use the grass or dirt to wipe off any last trace of it. Then I would have to feed him a dog biscuit to clean out his teeth and inside his mouth despite the fact this might encourage the dog to commit the same sin again. Of course this practice also extended to any time he used the bathroom; I had to force him to sit in the grass or dirt while I anxiously moved his posterior around from side to side, acting as toilet paper in my mind's way of thinking.

Now all of this made it hazardous for me to ever pet or touch the dog. Why? Dogs also have the habit of licking their fur. If that mouth had just ate poop it would now be spreading the poop all over his fur, creating a glossy coat of feces. It was also anxiety-producing if the dog

were to, with all poop aside, lick his private part. Now he was adding urine to that fecal coating along with elements related to canine reproductivity.

In addition to all of the fecal stuff which brought around the usual plague of hepatitis, there were bug problems. Dogs were naturally full of parasitic insects from being outside and brushing up against all of the desert shrubbery. Specifically this meant ticks, fleas, mites, and lice. I was already convinced I had lice from leaning my head up against the back of the seat in the theater two nights before. I mean where hair is, lice is sure to exist. At least that's what OCD told me. I could not believe in the rational converse—that is, where lice are, hair is. As far as fleas they were always trespassing on a canine or feline body. Where fur was, fleas were. After all, that was the case on the cartoon I had seen two years previously.

Then there were ticks. They had haunted my every-day existence since the time I had gone to a family reunion in Nebraska when I was ten years old. One had stowed away in my parent's

luggage. When it was discovered, they searched through every piece of luggage we'd brought with us, as well as a thorough search of every part of our bodies. That was when I gained awareness of that awful monster. Once I learned that ticks burrow into our flesh while infecting us with a lethal sickness by the name of Lyme disease, my mind went to town. This awful fact was made even worse when I recalled watching *Star Trek II: The Wrath of Khan*, wherein a hideous-looking bug chewed its way into Chekhov's ear and proceeded to latch on to his brain with the prognosis that it would take control of his mind and drive him mad, even until death, as it grew up inside his head.

This fear was further reinforced in my late teens when I saw scarab beetles eat their victims from the inside-out in *The Mummy,* starring Brendan Fraser. Anyhow, I couldn't go outside without feeling bugs crawling on me, as mentioned in a previous log. And where did all of these bugs go? They went straight to my crotch or up my butt crack. They say that ticks do this because that's where your underwear clings

tightly to your body, preventing the tick from going anywhere else. This was the worst possible place for a couple of reasons. One—I couldn't see my entire butt, much less into the crack. Two—This would be the perfect place for a tick to go due to the fact that ticks could camouflage themselves amongst all of my pubic hairs, preventing their detection. Three—These were the only two areas of my body that I could not ask my mom to look at to provide the final confirmation that I was bug-free.

Anyhow, my dog was certainly ushering the return of ticks into my life by his presence. Now I was at risk even though I had stepped on nothing outside but concrete and asphalt for the past three weeks.

So, to return to my original thought, I was able to pet both of my teacher's dogs today. I also was able to do so without asking whether they were up to date on all of their shots and without washing my hands. The dog even licked my hands and pressed its nose against my hands and I didn't wash my hands. Nor did I change my clothes when I got back home, since the dog had

also licked my pants for some unknown reason for quite some time.

I took this victory to another level by deciding that I would not only resist washing when I got home, but I would also resist washing before eating something. I even licked some pickle juice off and picked my teeth with my unwashed hands. Then I took the exposure to a new peak when I decided that I would take this as an opportunity to maintain my overall gains against hand-washing and general contamination by re-implementing my four-month hand-washing ban. I decided I would not consciously wash my hands for an entire week (or until I legitimately forgot). This decision was put to the test a few hours later when I defecated without washing my hands. And I didn't. So "Hello, hepatitis; I'm open for business!"

Log Eighteen – Aug 20, 2005

I'm really anxious. My eighth grade teacher just came by to visit, and she brought her two-month old with her. Man, I hate babies. I know; it sounds terrible. I know babies are important and they cause great amounts of joy for most people. However, for me, all they do is cause anxiety. I've said it before and I'll say it again. "Babies are just big sacks of germs." Really, it's all I see. I have never looked at a baby and started cooing over it like so many people do. I have never looked at a baby and had the desire to hold it or play with it. All they do is poop, pee, barf, spit, and mouth things that shouldn't be mouthed. They're just a plague waiting to happen. I'm honestly surprised that two-thirds of all people are not dead because of the Baby Plague. The way I see it Eve should have been killed when she became the first mother exposed to a baby. I'm surprised Adam didn't keel over and die. By my estimation of things (and it's always right) mankind should have been wiped out by the first newborn. I mean Lucifer's plan[1] would have worked—get them to

take a bite of the poisoned apple, get them kicked out of the Garden of Eden, let parenthood happen, and bring about offspring. This would have put a stop to all humanity.

So my big, burning question is "How come we're all still alive?" At least the fecal component should have killed us. Hepatitis should be rampant. Not an hour ago the baby filled its diaper with the toxic material. Then they started telling my mom (who was holding the baby at the time) how to hold the baby and where to place its blanket so that the poop did not come spurting out of its diaper. They just went on with life, pretending it didn't happen for the next ten minutes. Finally the mother decided it was time to change its diaper, and where did she decide to do it at? She did it inside my house on the entryway tiles. The feces now took the opportunity to sink into the tiles and create a radioactive zone where I have to walk every day. True, this was better than choosing to change it in my room or in the front room, but couldn't she go out front and change it on the concrete driveway?

Anyhow, once she had finished changing its diaper they put the soiled diaper in the kitchen trash, in my own garbage receptacle. Next my mom and she took the kitchen trash sack out front (thank goodness they weren't leaving it inside the house) to deposit the substance in the big trashcan. This meant that one of them had to have touched the doorknob, which now meant that the doorknob had diarrhea streaming down to the ground. Finally, to top it all off, neither one of them went back to sanitize all the contaminated areas. I really don't even know if they washed their hands afterwards. I'm going to go with believing they did because I'm not sure if I can handle another, stronger stomach ulcer. My goodness! They went about it like it was no different than putting away the groceries. The final result was I had to take a soaked, soapy washrag and wipe off the inside and outside of the front and back doorknobs, as well as wiping it all around the area where I think the diaper-changing took place.

One should notice that I never referred to her baby as "he." I only referred to the baby as

"it." This surely is not meant as a reproach or a rude comment as to their son's grotesqueness. It is merely meant to revert your attention back to the fact that people with OCD cannot see the wondrous life for the presence of a flashing neon sign that reads: "Dangerous. Stay away." I wish I was at the point where I could see a baby instead of just a big amoeba of death.

Someday I would like to have a family of my own. However, I really don't ever see this happening. I doubt I will ever be ready for parenthood. I know really none of us are, but at least your brains allow you to register the sight of a baby as a baby. To me, he or she remains an "it" that must be avoided at all cost. How am I ever going to be ready?

Often I think the only solution is to adopt a toddler once it has been potty-trained. Yet I severely doubt my wife would agree with me. Women are born to be mothers. That's the way God made them. How can I ever have a family of my own? My one hope is recognizing that there is a living God of Miracles to whom nothing is

impossible. I suppose that should be worth a good deal of something.

Log Notes

[1] The Church of Jesus Christ of Latter-day Saints teaches that while in the Garden of Eden, God commanded Adam and Eve not to partake of the fruit of the Tree of Knowledge of Good and Evil, "for in the day that thou eatest thereof thou shalt surely die" (*Genesis 2:17*). Sometime after this, Lucifer (more commonly known as Satan or the devil) tempted them to eat of the fruit of the tree. By doing so, Satan hoped to foil God's great plan for the development of us, His spirit children. For if Adam and Eve were killed, the rest of us could not have been born and received a body of flesh and blood, a gift essential to our progression in becoming more like our Father in Heaven. However, in reality, when Adam and Eve transgressed God's given law and were thus cast out of the Garden, their bodies became mortal and fallen, and gained the ability to procreate, allowing the rest of us (in due time, over subsequent generations) to come to Earth and gain a body, ensuring the fulfillment of God's great plan for our development and salvation. My point in the referenced text, however, is that if OCD was true, Adam and Eve would have had to die once she had her baby. And, if this were the case, God's plan would have failed. Without anyone to nurture the baby, it would have died. And without anyone left to carry on the work of "multiplying and replenishing the earth", no more babies could come into existence. Thus, the rest of us would not be able to come to Earth and receive a body. Thus, God's plan (again)

would have failed. Of course, this would then also mean that Satan's purposes would be accomplished and he would win.

Log Nineteen – Aug 23, 2005

I'm about to go out of my mind. I have nothing to do. I still have two days to go until I return to Utah. Thank goodness I came here for the break. If I had stayed there, I would have gone out of my mind about ten days ago. Oh! I've visited most of my close friends. As for others, I can't call them now. They'll ask, "Why didn't you call me a week ago? Now we don't have any time to get together." I can't hang out with the friends I already spent time with. Two of them are leaving tomorrow, which means that they are probably busy packing for all of today. The plus side, though, is they're going up to BYU as well.

So the only thing left to do right now is ritualize. When there's nothing else to do, that means that I need to make lists and databases. I've been busy trying to find a chiropractor back home in Utah. As a result I've been pouring through the Provo phone book and making phone calls. Now, however, I have found one I think will work out, so the only thing I can do is wait till my first appointment.

My one savior today has been Maria. I've been reading *Maria: The True Story of the Beloved Heroine of The Sound of Music* aloud to my mother. It's really quite enjoyable. What a woman! She's had quite a life and been a touching influence for good in the lives of so many. To add to the value of the book, it was even autographed by Maria von Trapp herself. This occupied numerous hours today.

Notwithstanding all of the boredom, I have had a couple victories of late. Ever since I got home I've been feeling an overwhelming anxiety to rip all of the music that I haven't already ripped. I submitted to the OCD last week in a big way, copying between ten and fifteen CDs. Some of them I didn't even really care for or want, but I was compelled by the ruthless dictator and taskmaster called OCD. Well, yesterday I discovered a big stash of CDs that I hadn't noticed before. Again I felt the whip of OCD digging into my back, commanding me to copy these as well. But today I faced the torturer and grabbed his whip. I resisted the compulsion.

Another familiar anxiety appeared last night as I walked around the block. Formication set in. I could feel the bugs crawling all over my body. This proves the resourcefulness of OCD. Since I have not been outdoors of late, OCD has had to move its place of attack. Now it has developed a new strain. I feel bugs even when walking on concrete and asphalt. The demand, however, remained the same—scour my body, checking or give into trichotillomania. Trichotillomania is a disorder wherein the victim pulls out huge amounts of his or her hair in order to diminish anxiety. For me, this means constantly pulling out eyelashes, eyebrows, head hair, pubic hair, and arm and leg hair. The fear behind it is that I have lice, scabies, spiders, or eggs nesting in my hair, even in my very own eyelashes. I pull and pull and pull and check and check and check and the anxiety only gets worse and worse and worse.

Despite my submission to this last night and today, I've made considerable progress. I can now rest my head on the back of a chair in a movie theatre. I recall a time only a few years

ago when I went to the local dollar theatre to see the movie *Two Tigers*. Things were going relatively fine until a couple moved to the seats right behind me. Suddenly my OCD was a-rage. All I could see was the woman's long red hair filled with lice. Yes, the lice weren't there, but still I literally saw them, and that vision would not leave my mind. I slumped and twisted in my chair until no part of me could be seen, and, more importantly, no part of me could be touched, by the woman's perceived collection of lice. My behavior must have seemed very rude, but I had no intention of offending the couple.

When the movie ended I continued behaving like a mad man. I rushed out of the theatre grabbing my hair as hard as I could and pulling. I was jerking my neck about violently with the force of each pull. I couldn't even get in my car to drive home for fear of transmitting the lice into my car. I distinctly remember running away like a mad man pulling the hair out of my head as I cried and prayed and screamed, filled just as much with recognition that my behavior was irrational as I was filled with the fierce

power of OCD. I knew my behavior was wrong, and I desperately wanted to stop, but I could not; I literally could not. I remember my dear mother following me as I ran up the road trying to catch me, trying to help, but proving as helpless to alter my thinking as I was. Today the trichotillomania was very present, but it was nowhere near where it had been just a short while ago.

Log Twenty – Aug 28, 2005

My mind is groaning under the oppressive weight forced upon it. There's too much anxiety. Yes, OCD even has the power to make you feel pain. It quite literally wears on your body. Thus you're not only gifted with that pain which stems from ritualization, i.e. the pain one feels when washing in boiling water, but you're also gifted with obsession-based pain over which you have no power to inflict or remit. As such I am experiencing a terrible headache caused solely by worry.

So why does my head ache? Primarily it's anticipatory anxiety. I'm worried about tomorrow. I'm wrenching under the consciousness of a new semester with two new, very hard classes. I will be taking Fundamentals of Literary Interpretation and Criticism, as well as Physical Science. Thus far I've only had easy courses at BYU, although they seemed anything but easy at the time. I've only had Acting, Religion, or P.E classes so far, whereas these new classes will be more grueling.

Mostly I'm worried about the English class. My eleventh grade teacher told me it will be easy and that I already do that stuff with my writing, but I still have OCD's doubts. For one thing, this will be my first course under the English major; if I don't do well, I'm toast for the next four years. Plus, poor performance in an English class would mean only one thing—that I'm not good at writing and nobody will ever want to read this book. Another dilemma I'm anticipating is getting through all of the assigned readings. I still do a good amount of re-reading. If I had to keep re-reading *Maria*, there's no way I'm going to resist re-reading *Pride & Prejudice* or *Backpack Literature*. Of course, there's also the writing. I can see it now; I'll have to turn in an essay every single week.

How am I going to do that? Sure, I did well with all eight essays for REL C 325, but I struggled big time with a couple of those essays. Plus, those were only one-page essays and were on the scriptures, not five- to ten-page papers on the meaning of Kafka, Tennyson, and Sophocles.

Then there's the problem of a social life mandated by my doctor. How in the world can I afford to make friends and do stuff if I have to read a book, write a paper, and memorize scientific terms and theories every week? It's either homework or friends. That's how I see it. Yet my doctor remains firm. I need friends, especially if it means sacrificing an A grade for a B. It's good exposure, right? Wrong. I don't have time for football games that I don't even care for.

Additionally my mind's weighed down over sleep. I thought I finally found the perfect amount of medicine, but I was wrong. Either I sleep at night and feel drowsy all day long or I have insomnia and feel tired all day long. I just can't wake up until about 10:00 or later. How can I afford having insomnia at night *and* my being comatose during the day when I have classes and oodles and oodles of homework to do? I'm so tired of experimenting with new drugs and new doses. I have OCD. Why does God deem it necessary for me to have so many other medical problems? OCD consumes away enough of my life. Can't we just draw the line there?

Log Twenty–One – Sep 3, 2005

Well, the first week of school has now passed. It went much better than expected. I was sure I would be at a 7–7+ on Monday (the first day), but I never even hit a five. That just goes to show that what the doctors say is true. Anticipatory anxiety is always greater than the anxiety experienced when actually confronting your fear. The less you stew over something and the quicker you actually confront it, the better off you will be.

Despite this fortune, the battle rages on. At this very second I am fighting my seemingly infinite battle with sweat. It still amazes me how much terror wells up inside of me as I feel my body perspiring. The only workable comparison that I can use to make you understand is that it feels as though someone were lightly gliding a machete across my own flesh. OCD is convincing my mind that I am in that much danger, that much peril, and that is all because of a single bead of sweat. For every other bead of sweat, the harrowing torture is magnified that much more.

This time OCD is having even more fun. I just finished lying on my traction unit; it's a kind of foamy wedge that I lie on to stretch my neck out and more closely align my upper vertebrae along the line of curvature that should exist in my neck. The problem is that while I am using it, the top of my head is touching the carpet in my bedroom. What's wrong with my carpet? It's full of little specs of debris—hair, carpet threads, sand, paper, and other stuff that I can't even begin to classify. To make matters worse my head also brushes up against the traction unit itself, and that unit is made up of foam that just loves to attract and collect all of the debris, primarily hair, from whichever spot of carpet that it rested against during its usage over a period of about a year.

Why do I have problems with hair? It's for the same reason that I fear fiberglass, insulation, and carpet threads. I am convinced that somehow these small units of fiber are going to fall into the pores of my skin and wreak havoc, clogging the pores and cutting open my blood vessels. If the obsession wasn't so real, I would be laughing,

but instead I cringe and endlessly brush them away from the surface of my skin. And in the meantime I worry about the nasty little bug that has taken up residence and laid a hundred eggs in my hair because it crawled onto one of those itty-bitty pieces of debris while my head was against the floor.

I've become a lot more agreeable to carpet in general because of my experiences at Rogers. One of the very first exposures that I was assigned when I got to the hospital was to just touch the carpet with both hands, palms flat against it, knowing that I couldn't wash my hands afterwards and I couldn't search my body for bugs. Most trials would last between fifteen and thirty minutes and would offer no removal of anxiety.

After all, the floor had been walked on by who knows how many hundreds of people. Someone's shoe had touched this very spot with the same shoe that had walked amongst the leaves in the grass, left its print on some patch of sand or mud, and stepped into a pile of dog poop. That shoe had popped off of the ground in a

movie theatre where someone had spilt sticky soda and slick butter from off the popcorn. That shoe had knocked against the base of a toilet where diarrhea had overflowed the night before. That shoe had touched the dark circle in a store parking lot where someone had spilt car oil and possibly antifreeze an hour earlier. That shoe had smashed a cigarette butt. That shoe had stepped into a white substance on the floor of a high school restroom where a marijuana addict had puked just twenty-three minutes before. That shoe had jarred a tick from off a branch of sagebrush. That shoe had been to every infested, infected spot on this green earth. So heck yeah, I was scared to touch the carpet. But I did the exposure and I kept doing it until the fear had dissipated to a slightly more manageable level.

Today I wasn't worrying about this. The only reason I worry now is because there happened to be fibers on the carpet and my head hair had touched them. That's a lot of worry made, but looked at with hindsight, that's also great progress.

Log Twenty–Two – Sep 7, 2005

Tonight I went out to the theatre. I saw *Herbie: Fully Loaded*. It was good. I like movies. In fact, I like movies a great deal. I like getting swallowed up into the story and feeling as though I'm right there beside the characters as they go forward to conquer whatever conflict that they come across, be that taking a ring of power to the pits of Mordor to save all of Middle Earth or trying to get back a baseball signed by Babe Ruth from a monstrous gorilla dog. Mostly, though, I love to be sucked away from my life. Let me live their lives. Let me fight their battles and their demons because I know that in the end, I will have proven victorious, gained true friendship, and fallen in love.

Oh, how I ache to reach a happy ending in my own life! Oh, how I wish I could progress like others. I desperately wish that I could turn back time, erase OCD from my life early on, and reclaim my long lost and long obliterated life. I wish that I had had a childhood and adolescence like other people do (mind without dipping into the pool of filth that Mammon[1] has to offer). I

115

wish every day of my life that I could have gone on a mission for my Church. I had prepared and waited eagerly more so than anybody else that I know for that day when I could wear a name tag that said "Elder Conrad"[2] on it. I wish I had a family that I felt safe with, and loved. I wish I could go to college without the heavy burdens that I carry.

I wish I could fall in love. I wish I could know that there was a beautiful girl out there who for one minute felt in love with me. I wish I could take her in my arms and say "I love you. I love you more than anything in this world," and to be able to look her straight in the eyes and say, "I can take care of you. Whatever it is, we can make it through it." I wish I could marry that girl and raise a family, knowing that I had a good job that could provide for them. I wish desperately that I could have a family, that I could have kids, that I could hold a baby in my arms and take care of it. I wish so many things!

Still I know that I'm immensely blessed. I have more friends than I can remember the names of. I have wonderful friends that surround

me and lift me up. I am at BYU, my dream university. I was blessed to be born in a day when doctors know what OCD is and how to treat it, and when people are accepting of my quirks and eccentricities. Just a couple centuries ago I would have been branded a witch or someone possessed by the devil. There are medicines today that can help me deal with my disease. Just thirty years ago such medicine didn't exist. OCD hadn't even been recognized and properly diagnosed.

I have a mother who is the greatest person that I will ever know. She's the most kind, loving, supportive mother ever, possessing the true love of God, and I am proud to say that she is *my* mother! I have been blessed to have a father who is able to financially take care of all my medical needs. I was blessed to be guided to Rogers Memorial Hospital, where I lived for three months, obtaining the tools to help me conquer OCD and gain the freedom that I needed to exercise them. I am an American, and I will always be grateful to be a member of this great nation.

Most importantly, though, I was born into a church that is organized and sanctified by God Himself. Christ is the head of it. I know Jesus Christ. I know that He is my Redeemer. I know that He took upon Himself the sins of all the world. More importantly, I know that He took upon Himself all of our sicknesses, our infirmities, our trials, and our weaknesses "that he may know according to the flesh how to succor his people according to their infirmities"[3].

I have a personal testimony that He suffered all of the agonies brought upon us by OCD. Christ took upon Himself OCD, so that you and I would never be forced to bear the burden alone and it is through this atonement that we can one day be healed. He knows what it's like. He's been there. He's done that.

Above all, He knows the way out from the captivity of this disease. He knows how to help you regain control of your life. He will heal you. And of this I know and testify, with the surety of God's true and unchanging word.

Log Notes

[1] Mammon is another name or title of Lucifer or the devil. It is a scriptural term that also refers to the natural world in all of its wickedness and greed. The word originates from the Aramaic and is translated to mean 'riches'. Probably its most famous usage is found in *Matthew 6:24* and reads "No man can serve two masters: for either he will hate the one, and love the other; or else he will hold to the one, and despise the other. Ye cannot serve God and mammon."

[2] Elder is an office in the Melchizedek Priesthood. Because missionaries are official, full-time representatives of The Church of Jesus Christ of Latter-day Saints, they are referred to by the priesthood office they hold, followed by their last or surname. This is done out of respect, reverencing their sacred calling to serve as representatives or ambassadors of the Lord Jesus Christ in proclaiming his gospel throughout the world. The only other members of the church who are referred to in this sacred manner are the members of The Quorum of the Twelve Apostles and the members of the various Quorums of the Seventies. As such, a missionary always wears a nametag, reading "Elder ['So-and-So']" on the first line and "The Church of Jesus Christ of Latter-day Saints" on the second line. This, however, will be altered if the missionary is serving abroad, translating everything but his last name into the tongue native to the country or area he is serving in. It might be useful noting that this change in wording also occurs if the missionary is called to serve in a foreign-speaking mission inside the U.S.

[3] "And he shall go forth, suffering pains and afflictions and temptations of every kind; and this that the word might be fulfilled which saith he will take upon him the pains and the sicknesses of his people. And he will take upon him death, that he may loose the bands of death which bind his people; and he will take upon him their infirmities, that his bowels may be filled with mercy, according to the flesh, that he may know according to the flesh how to succor his people according to their infirmities." (The citation for this quote is Alma 7:11-12.) Alma is one the books contained in *The Book of Mormon: Another Testament of Jesus Christ*, which was translated from gold plates given to the latter-day prophet Joseph Smith by the angel Moroni. It gives a record of the ancient inhabitants of the Americas, a people brought to this content by the hand of God, preserving them from the destruction of Jerusalem by Babylon's King Nebuchadnezzar. Most of all, though, it is additional holy scripture, which joins *The Holy Bible* in bearing testament of Jesus the Christ and contains many more insights into the Lord's gospel. *The Book of Alma*, specifically, gives an account of the prophetic ministry of Alma the Prophet and an account of the many wars and dissensions that happened among those same ancient inhabitants.

Log Twenty–Three – Sep 9, 2005

I'm lost. I've been wandering blindly through a dark mist of lies, blanketed by irrational dictations. Even now it is hard for me to breath, to see, to reason. I can't break free. I'm too disoriented. I see faint glimmers of sunlight in the distance, but they elude me, appearing here and there, never in the same place, as it whittles its way through the shroud of mist. Why can't I get out? Why can't I get out? Forces pull on me, guiding me close to the chasms of the precipice. My mind is going mad.

I am experiencing classic brain lock [1]. Obsessions loop infinitely through my mind. I pause as I read the line just one more time. I read it over and over, desperate to catch the meaning. No, I don't want to catch the meaning. I want to memorize it, every syllable, every rhyme, and every connotation. I want to have it dissected to the smallest quark. I want it branded into my mind. Yet I fumble, I fall. I do not understand, not everything. How can I let go? If I don't do well in this class, I will fail my major and I will never graduate from BYU.

Now I grip my stylus, continuously carving letters into the bits and bytes of my Palm [2]. I'm creating a To-Do List. It sounds innocent enough, but I've been inputting data for at least an hour now. What homework will I have and when is it due. The syllabi have these things stated already. Yet I must write them down again and again. I must have it in my computer. That way it will alert me when time is near. Due dates are too scattered on the syllabi. I might not notice. I might forget. Yet my beautiful piece of machinery will never let me down. It was made to remind me, to eliminate all possibilities of casualty on the road to academic success. Still my mind whispers I may have entered the wrong date. I must go back and check. And then check and check and check. Still this will make my life easier, speaks fallacy. Meanwhile all of my reading, my warm-ups, my printings, my experiments, my studying remains loomingly undone.

I write in this book. What words should I use? Which ones? Which ones are perfect? They must be perfect. Else you will think me a hack.

"You can't write. You're terrible. The words you are using are all wrong. They don't communicate what this disease is like. You will help no one. No one will understand. No one can understand if you are the one who is writing. Rather you do OCD injustice. You do health a crime." Which word must I use? I must get it right.

I use the bathroom, a particularly gooey time. I feel feces splattered everywhere in the toilet and on my butt. I try to wipe it away. I try to eradicate the feeling but it won't go away. So I wipe and I wipe and I wipe. No particle must escape me, in my crevice or out. The toilet paper slowly shreds away. Now there is the matter of the toilet. I felt poop on it, but now I can't see it. There must be something wrong with my vision. Perhaps my eyeglasses are broken. Only one command is given. Wipe. Wipe the top of the lid, wipe the bottom, wipe the top edge of the bowl, wipe the inner edge of the bowl. Wipe. You are missing something. Wipe.

I wash my hands. Water will knock the poop away. Soap will exterminate it, every single trace. I must wash my palms. I must wash the

back. I must wash the fingers all about. I must wash the fingernail front and back. I must wash where the back of my fingernail sticks to my flesh. I must wash the whole tremendous mound that is my fingertip. I must wash every part of my finger and fingernail. They are clogged with feces. The feces are seeping through my finger into my veins. Soon some plague will arise. I don't know what. It can't be hepatitis. I got over that. Yet a voice whispers that it can. I am slipping. I am regressing. It is comparatively minor when gazed through the lens of yesteryear. Surely it's nothing. Surely, but my mind keeps slipping, slipping away.

Log Notes

[1] The term "brain lock" was first introduced to me when I read Dr. Jeffrey M. Schwartz's seminal book of the same name. It was the first book that I was introduced to in the wake of my original diagnosis as having OCD. Its complete title is Brain Lock—Free Yourself from Obsessive-Compulsive Behavior: A Four-Step Self Treatment Method to Change Your Brain Chemistry. It was co-authored by Beverly Beyette and was published in 1996 by HarperCollins.

---

[2] Used here, 'Palm' is simply the abbreviated version of 'Palm Pilot'.

Log Twenty–Four – Sep 14, 2005

The past couple weeks have been trying and crazy all at the same time. A deep depression had settled over me, plucking all hope from my vision, distorting all perspective. The name of the cloud was school. All I could see were hopeless times in the near future. I could never stop and enjoy where I was because I was in a nice situation. Things were going nearly perfect; it was as good as it gets. Nonetheless, I only felt a harrowing sense of the calm before the storm.

I saw science chapters, warm-up quizzes, mini-experiments, homework questions, articles, pretests, and exams. More than this I saw tough times in the English department. Right now all I'm doing for English is reading one eight-page chapter at a time filled with several poems each. Between that and the science homework several hours are consumed. I can't read fast. Even when I resist re-reading, which wasn't happening, I crawl through my reading, focusing and sounding out every single word in the book.

That really is as good as it gets. I have never been able to read any other way. Still it takes forever. Then, to compare with this, I looked at the second half of my semester and all hope exploded into oblivion. I will be required to read a whole book or whole play, like *Oedipus the King*, in two or three class days. That gives me a week at the most to get through sixty, seventy, eighty pages, and the next class we'll be moving on to the next book or play. This way if I fall behind (which I fully expect to), I'll drown as assignments start to compound. Eeeeegh! Then there's the issue of the two who-knows-how-many-pages-large essays critiquing the critique of some other critic about who knows what.

Anyhow, this just hammered me into the dust, and all I could do was obsess! It really was just a nasty situation. All I sensed was this doom in my future. The taste of pizza, the smell of donuts, the touch of a soft fur blanket, the sound of rock and roll, the sight of a really gorgeous woman, all were overridden by a very real, very tangible feeling of oncoming catastrophe. My head ached, and I quite literally felt my brain

ache under enormous physical pressure. My brain was overheating, sweating under spiking energy currents. It's ironic that the very organ that is the most responsible for this monster is also the most battered victim of its own assault.

Still you should notice the use of the past tense. I was under siege, but not right now. I'm not completely sure how it happened, but all of that left me. The one thing I do know is that it had to do with a conversation I had with my mother. She empathized and then told me that I didn't have to worry about the future; I should just think about today. Face one day at a time. Not too long after that I remember being released and my brain quit hurting. I stopped looking at the future, and I saw today. I don't know how it happened. I suppose God answered my prayers; the burden passed from me to Him. It sounds crazy, but He did say, "Come unto me, all ye that labour and are heavy laden, and I will give you rest. (Matt. 11:28)" Maybe God knew what he was talking about.

Log Twenty–Five – Sep 18, 2005

Ah, the taste of Skittles is so good. The feel of the sugar-filled balls of joy melting in my mouth, lazily meandering against my tongue in a stream of fruity sweetness is one of the great pleasures of mortality. There's nothing in the world like it.

Just about anyone who knows me knows I love Skittles (just as much as I hate chocolate, I might add)! Why, one of my dreams for growing up was that I would own all the plants that manufactured Skittles. Every chance I got growing up in high school I was relishing them as I ecstatically digested them. Every chance I got I was praising the candy masterpiece from my own personal soap box, pointing out the somehow-lost link that eating them would heal a cold, cheer you up after getting dumped, improve your grades, enrich your church stewardships[1], and make you just that much better of a human being. I even created my own design for the bag, introducing a Halloween/Batman special edition wrapping as a prop for a skit that functioned as an ode to Skittles. I even e-mailed the makers of

Skittles with my new design, but alas they thought I was asking for free candy. Yes, I was in love.

What most people don't know is that it's been eight months since my last Skittle. What's more, I have for the most part given them up. I haven't bought a package of Skittles for about two years now. I know it's shocking to those of you who know me.

What, pray-tell, is my reason for betraying the colorful rainbow? Do I now loathe their taste? The answer to that is: No, I still love them. What's changed is my health. You guessed it. OCD has taken them away as well. Now I fear them. I stand back in dread.

This new obsession was given birth in the well-meaning censures of one family member. He did not like me eating them, and he swore up and down for months that I would get diabetes. He was trying to introduce a "healthier, better" obsession into my already plagued mind. Well, at first, it didn't bug me. This individual was clearly out of his mind and seemed to be against

anything that I liked. However, his vocal drill was gradually opening the passageway for OCD to snap and take over. Plus, I was meeting more and more people that had diabetes (mind none of them were my age), I was learning more and more about diabetes, and then one of my grandparents got it. Aha, now there was family history to the viral bugger!

So I stopped eating Skittles. I'd still eat them with applause around my friends to cover up my deteriorating mind, but even then I wouldn't dip down deep into the bag. OCD had stolen them from me. Ironically, however, OCD only applied the scare of catching diabetes to Skittles. It didn't apply it to other candy. Now if I was going to go to the theatre to see the latest blockbuster, it was sure as money that I'd have a half-pound box of Sugar Babies (ooh, I loved that caramel) and it would be consumed before the day was over. However, this too was doomed from the moment it took over. OCD was bound to eventually generalize the fear.

One of the first problems I ran into was the mind-made rule that everything had to be eaten

within twenty-four hours. This obviously led to a mouthful of sticky, caramelized sugar, and here the fear took off. That night I had to brush my teeth like I hadn't been able to touch a toothbrush for two years. I brushed and brushed and scrubbed and scrubbed, applying the greatest amount of force that I was capable of, and I went at it. I still have to do this, but now I have to do it if I eat any candy or drink any soda. I have to brush my gums like there's no tomorrow. I furiously scrape my teeth and gums with the force of sandpaper. If I had some and I wasn't afraid of touching it, I think I might actually use sandpaper. After all, that would be much more efficient than a common toothbrush. Worse yet, when I don't have a toothbrush handy, I use my own fingernails to slice along my gum line, scraping away any hint of sugar. I scrape along my teeth and gums, slicing them with my fingernail. Naturally my gum line has receded significantly since I started this ritualization. As a result, I now obsessively avoid all candy and try to never consume soda pop.

Yesterday, though, I just wanted something sugary to eat. So I bought my first bag of Skittles in years, and man, does it taste good. As for the ritualizing, I'll just have to see how I feel tonight. I should resist, and maybe I will, but chances are pretty likely that I'm going to power-brush. I'll try not to use my fingernails, though.

Log Notes

[1] Here, stewardship refers to one's calling (or position of responsibility) in The Church of Jesus Christ of Latter-day Saints. Most callings are for positions within a member's own ward (a congregation of members determined by the given LDS population within a certain geographical boundary). These callings can be anything from bishop, ward librarian, or Relief Society president to Sunday School teacher, scoutmaster, or nursery worker. Some callings, however, are for positions within the stake (a geographical grouping of around a dozen wards). These generally consist of the Stake Presidency, his counselors and clerks, and the stake's high council, although they are not limited to these. Those with callings concerning geographical areas larger than those of a ward or stake are usually referred to as the general authorities or general officers of The Church. It should be noted that every member of the church is extended a calling, so that all might be edified of all, as they learn together as both teacher and pupil. Another

important element of callings is the source. While it is true that the callings are extended by members of the bishopric or stake presidency (or even by general authorities), as members of The Church of Jesus Christ of Latter-day Saints, we believe that callings are really extended by God. His servants here on Earth pray, seeking revelation to know which person God wants to fill which calling. Once the revelation is received, the call is then extended to that person by that church leader to the appropriate member. Thus, every calling is extended to each member by God himself, with that particular leader serving *really* as the instrument in God's omniscient hand.

Log Twenty–Six – Sep 20, 2005

I've made a few advancements of late that I haven't gotten around to reporting yet, so I will now. Probably the biggest advancement has to do with flies. For years I was deathly afraid of flies. They're just so nasty. More importantly to my OCD, however, is the fact that they land every place they desire, including dog poop. To them, I suppose feces are a delicacy, one of the finest substances that they consume. Yet from behavioral observations I am led to believe that it is a *common* delicacy. It isn't eaten in restaurants filled with insect patrons. No, their rambunctious behavior suggests that they eat while on something like a picnic, for they fly around, darting this way and that, skipping from poop to poop in an endless game of tag.

To me, however, it is a thoroughly disgusting lifestyle. To OCD, the flies were attacking me, fervently seeking to eliminate one more human as they laid maggots in my hair and transmitted plagues of hepatitis, Ebola, and hanta virus onto me. It was war—a war that they were winning. All that I could do was attempt to

quarantine myself from them. I couldn't use a fly swatter to kill them; it was already a breeding ground for all of their diseases. I couldn't transmit that to the kitchen table or the wall that I might lean on. No, all I could do was isolate myself and when that didn't work, explode in an ecstasy of prayer, checking, and mad jerking movements that were supposed to drive the flies away.

Of course I would experience the greatest anxiety when they would approach my food, which they were always doing in between their picnics. There was no way in heaven or hell that I was going to eat something that a fly had succeeded in landing on. No, sir. It didn't matter how much I had eaten of it. I would call out the food's time of death even if I had just reached to take my first bite. That fly had planted its plague deep down in that bit of food. If I ate it, I would be inviting the disease right on into my bloodstream. From there, death was only a couple minutes away.

That's how things were. That's not how things are now. It took over a year and a half for

me to break through that obsession, but a month or two ago, it all came tumbling down. Its ruin came as a big shock. One day out of the blue I was at a restaurant and I realized that a fly had just landed on my arm. Slowly my mind began to assess the situation. "There's a fly on my arm. I should be afraid. It probably landed on my food. I should be freaking out. But I'm not. Huh?!" Then I decided that the food was too good to let a fly ruin my dinner. "I will let it crawl on me and I won't even move to shake it off."

A few weeks later, I reacted in a similar manner. A fly had landed on a roll that I was reaching for. "There's a fly on that roll. I should be anxious. But I'm not." Then in a daring move that I would have been physically incapable of two years earlier, I reached for that roll and I ate it. I even *enjoyed* eating that roll. Minutes later, I was still alive. Nothing bad ever resulted from that impromptu exposure.

My second advancement came a couple weeks later. I had just used the restroom and was heading over to wash my hands when I heard my shoe strike against something metallic. I looked

down to see that I had stepped on a drain pipe. I quickly realized that its purpose was to stand ready to drain if any of the toilets started overflowing. Suddenly my anxiety gave a little jump. What if the toilet had overflowed just an hour before and it spewed out urine and feces? I walked to the sink and tried to wash as un-ritualistically as I could. Then I took a deep breath and did an impromptu exposure. I stepped back onto the circular drain, making sure both shoes had firmly contacted as much of the drain as possible, also making sure that my shoes had touched the most contaminated area—the center. Then I reached down and successively clasped as much of the bottom of both shoes as possible. Then, to put the cherry on top, I took both my hands (now contaminated) and smeared them across my face, giving special care to wipe them across my lips. Then I walked out. Minutes later, I was still alive.

My third advancement similarly deals with the bathroom. I have recently made the decision to not in-wipe with regular toilet paper, postponing the in-wiping until I use a Wet Wipe.

I had gotten tired of pulling out strand upon strand of dry toilet paper from my rectum with the Wet Wipes, after failing to complete the whole (in-)wiping process using *only* toilet paper, each time I had to defecate. Most importantly, I have succeeded in *following through* with that decision. What's more, the in-wiping I have allowed myself to do has mostly gone down altogether since I stopped in-wiping with the toilet paper. I know. It's gross... But it's also progress. Hours later, I was still alive.

Log Twenty–Seven – Sep 25, 2005

The past couple days have been severely trying. Most of it started on Friday. I was on my way to the school library to do some reading for English when all of a sudden it hit. I was pummeled backward as a tsunami of light-headed exhaustion broke across my entire body. I immediately recognized it as a medication-induced coma. It's happened enough times. A second later my anxiety spiked. I hadn't changed any of my medication recently. I was taking the same pills with the same dosages. If my medication hadn't changed, why was I feeling this way? I tried to read, but soon gave up and tried to nap in my little study cubicle (a hopelessly uncomfortable environment) until class started. Luckily I only had one class today due to a previously-taken test in another class. Still I had to fight to maintain consciousness for the fifty minutes I had to endure of English.

When I got home, I called my psychiatrist so he could diagnose what was wrong me. He didn't know, but he thought it was likely an infection. "What do you mean an infection? An

infection of what? A cold? The flu? No, no, that can't be happening to me. I can't handle being sick! I especially can't handle the flu, you know, barfing and all? I can't barf! I can't. I need my mother for that kind of thing. I can't do that alone, on my own! I can't get that intimate with my toilet bowl." He persisted. It was probably an infection. I could see Urgent Care the next morning, but I would have to make it through the night.

Then unwittingly I found the source of my problem. I had taken my evening meds that morning instead of my morning meds. Whoo! I felt relieved. I wasn't sick after all. My relief was short-lived however. I couldn't sleep that night, but worse than that I felt nauseous. I guess I had an infection after all. All my arguments to the doctor came back, filling my head, with no place to go except around and around in my own little brain. I wanted to scream. I couldn't do this. Finally, around five the next morning, I asked for a priesthood blessing [1]. After that, I had to defecate—the worst possible position to be in when you have the flu. I mean, what would

happen if I was in the very act of pooping when the flu hit. I couldn't kneel before the toilet as was the usual custom when I was barfing. I would have to puke all over myself. Thankfully, however, that didn't happen. Feeling a bit better, I laid down on the couch. Half an hour later, I was asleep.

When I awoke I felt better, but I was still a little nauseous. Nevertheless I plowed on with my morning routine—showering, getting dressed, eating breakfast, and brushing my teeth. At 10:40 I arrived at the chiropractor for my normal adjustment and then headed to Urgent Care. Unfortunately, they were about to close (in half an hour, though) and they wouldn't help me. They would have to run extensive blood tests to determine whether I really was sick (and if so, with what?) or whether it was just a matter of mixing up my medications and then not taking any at night for fear of tampering with my health the next day. All they offered was the suggestion that I call a pharmacist. I did so, and was told that it most likely was the meds. However, he still wasn't able to tell me for sure whether I had

the flu or not. With this, I opted forward with my life, feeling cautiously healthy.

The next ordeal arose a couple of hours later when my landlord came by. He was replacing our broken microwave and needed help doing so. I eagerly offered my limited services and we lifted the microwave out of its box and onto the stove (which was turned off). Shortly after that my roommate appeared and opted to help as well. He immediately took over for me, bearing most of the burden as the landlord and he worked to get it up and settled into place. I gratefully accepted, already feeling the burn from the limited work I had been able to do, and rested a hand against the microwave to help keep it in place as they lifted it into position.

That's when it hit. I was again pummeled, but this time by a vertebra that I had somehow managed to knock out of place, pinching against a nerve. Undaunted, I pressed forward with my services until it was clear that they didn't need me anymore, and then I retreated into my room to stretch and twist my back, swallow Ibuprofen, and lay on my traction unit for twenty painful

minutes. At the conclusion of that time, I was out of my wits. I had tried everything I knew how to do and I was still writhing in excruciating agony. Finally I found my chiropractor's home phone number and called him in desperation. He said would be at his office in an hour.

At that news, I got in my car and drove to the Cannon Center for dinner, but found it closed. Hungry I turned to the pizzeria next door and forked over money for the heftier price. By the time they called my name, I had just enough time to make it to the chiropractor's office in time. However, instead of being greeted with my pizza, the cooks greeted me with the news that they had messed up my order and had just barely stuck in another pizza for me. When that pizza was finished baking (suspiciously fast, I might add), I only had two or three minutes to make it to the chiropractor. That's when I began to crumble.

I was going to be late. He was making a special trip to the office outside of his work hours just to help me, and I was going to be late! As I drove, ritual compounded upon ritual and I became an ever-worsening, unsafe driver. I was

going to be late! I couldn't be late! Yet the traffic lights kept turning red. It was time for OCD to take action.

I have a ritual I do when I'm running late to an appointment (which frequently occurs due to the nature of OCD). I will start speaking to the stop lights animatedly in Italian, saying, "Verde! Verde! Verde! (Green! Green! Green!)," and commanding the cars in front of me, "Va! Va! Va! (Go! Go! Go!)." Why? All I will say is it has something to do with a scene in the film *La Vita E' Bella* (*Life Is Beautiful*). Then as time drags on, I will start to raise my volume until I am shouting as loud as I can. I will also speak faster and faster. Then I will repeat my commands more and more times until I am continuously shouting out rapid-firing orders in Italian, regardless of whether my car is moving or not. I do all this as if the stoplight is deaf and suffering from ADHD, as if increasing my volume and speaking continuously, as fast as I can, will somehow manage to make the stoplights actually hear me and recognize that a change in their behavior is necessary. When this fails to work,

which it will, I start madly praying, begging forgiveness for screaming at God through the stop lights He controls.

By this point, I was gone. I completely lost it. And that's when the self-mastication started. I started bludgeoning my head, punching it as hard as I could. And once I started hitting myself, I couldn't stop, not by my own powers. This was particularly problematic because I was also driving at the same time. Things quickly became worse when I realized I had completely missed the intersection where I was supposed to turn. Now I was a rotten, poor mess of a creature, pounding against my cranium over and over and over and over and over and over, sweating a flood of perspiration, pouring out tears, and madly pushing against the gas.

Now there's an important lesson to learn here. Self-mastication, or self-harm, is just as much outside an OCD victim's control as hand-washing or checking is. The person who is hurting himself is obviously not enjoying himself or herself. They're inflicting harm on their body! Yet they are driven to do so. OCD has become so

powerful that the only way to gain any sense outside (and yet inside) their misfiring brain is to overwhelm it with some other signal. They are trying to escape their tormenting tyrant's grasp, and self-harm is the only way that they know how to do it. The cruel irony is that it's just another ritual, and since it's a ritual, it will worsen just as much (no, more) than if they were performing any other ritual.

This ritual, however, is so consuming that the person undergoing this hell can only be saved by someone else. The most important thing then is to realize that if you're angry or you're mad, and you don't really care about the victim, you are of no good use to that person. You can only make it worse by driving the message into them that they are being bad…and thus need further punishment. You have to be calm, cool, collected, loving, and willing to do anything you can to get them out of this nightmare. It is also critical that you do not forcefully grab that person to make them stop. Contact may be necessary, but it should not be a strong and reproaching hand. Rather it must be a tender hand, reaching in

softly to save them. Remember that they want to stop even more than you want them to stop. Be calm and talk them through it, away from self-mastication. Often the realization that they can talk to someone who isn't going to be mad or chiding toward them will be enough. They need reason and love communicated to them, as it has physically become impossible for them to send that message to their own selves.

I was lucky enough to have a wonderful bishop to help me through it until I was able to reach my chiropractor, at which point my chiropractor wonderfully took over. These two men saved my life (and perhaps the lives of others).

There is one last message here for the victims themselves to hear. Remember (and it will be hard, extremely so) that God will not suffer that you shall fall to your death in this abyss. He will lead you out of it.

And the most important thing for those not suffering to realize is that they themselves are

usually the means that God uses to save the sufferer. Please be there when you are needed.

Log Notes

[1] A priesthood blessing is an ordinance performed by a worthy holder of the Melchizedek Priesthood, where the person requesting the blessing has hands laid on his or her head and a blessing is pronounced through the power and authority of God as delegated to the individual giving the blessing. These blessings generally fall into one of three different categories or types. The first is a blessing of healing for the sick. This is administered by two different priesthood holders. One of them anoints the sick person's head with pure olive oil (which has been previously consecrated for the specific purpose of healing the sick and the afflicted). After this, the second person seals the anointing and then typically pronounces a blessing, as directed by the Spirit. The second type is a blessing of comfort. This is given to an individual who is not sick but *is* seeking inspiration and comfort from the Lord as they struggle to deal with a certain challenge or obstacle in their life. Two priesthood holders may administer this type of blessing, but only one is required. Furthermore, no olive oil is used and, as such, there is neither a sealing nor an anointing in the blessing. The third category of priesthood blessing is a father's blessing. As the name suggests, this type of blessing is administered by one's own father. While a father's blessing can include blessings for the sick and/or blessings of comfort, they are not limited to these. Father's blessings typically occur at various important junctures in his child's life. Some examples of when

this might take place are at the beginning of a new school year, at the start of a new job, before a mission, or before one's marriage. In all three categories, it is believed that the person giving the blessing is literally speaking for God. Thus, as is the case with our church callings, personal revelation is the greatest key. Without the Holy Spirit's inspiration, priesthood blessings would lose their power and validity. Worthiness on the part of the ministering priesthood holder is thus the most crucial component and prerequisite of these blessings. Without it, one cannot be adequately in tune with the Spirit, and, therefore, cannot speak the mind of God.

Log Twenty–Eight – Sep 29, 2005

I have a great weight lifted from my shoulders. It's been eating at me, overshadowing, and suffocating me for so long. Of course, this should not come as a surprise to you. I've been worrying about my major for a long time. Really it's been on my mind since May when things weren't working out with my Theatre degree. That's right; I was going to be an Acting major. It had always been my dream to be on the big screen. Unfortunately, I had to adjust my plans when I wasn't passing any auditions and my teacher said my abilities were primitive. She was the first person to ever speak badly of my acting abilities, but she was also the first person who actually worked in the business. Fortunately I had some guidance from up above. That's when I started this book. I now know that this is what I'm going to do for a living—help.

But I still didn't know what to do for my major. It was obvious that I should scrap Acting. I decided I would major in something that had to do with literature, so I picked English. It fit my new career best. However it wasn't long till that

choice started giving me grief. There was way too much reading required for all of the classes in too short a time span and affixed to that were several essays critiquing the author of the book or some other critic who wrote about that book. None of it had any merit in contributing to my new career in writing and public speaking. More than that, I would have to wade through fire and brimstone every semester until August 2009 (my projected graduation date). Plus, to foreshadow it all I was taking ENG 251: Fundamentals of Literary Interpretation and Criticism, and that required the same back-breaking performance in the here and now. As time went on, the anxiety just continued to mount as I trudged through the class, always laden with nearly impossible due dates. This led to all the aforementioned pressure on my brain and had I'm sure a very present role in underlying all my recent self-mastication.

It was time for a change. It was time for a new course of action. I met with my counselor and discussed the possibility of taking another major, but none of them were practical if I wanted any degree of mental health in the next

four years. There was Linguistics, but that was an in-depth look into grammar—boring and not helpful. There was Psychology, but that included a lot of science and experiments, which I am not gifted in. Looking at public speaking, there was Communications, but those majors all had an emphasis on print journalism and news broadcasting. I couldn't really choose something that I enjoyed. I had received a rejection letter eliminating the choice of an Acting major because of too many "unfruitful" credit hours. Next to that was Theatre Studies, but it consisted of a lot of directing, crew work, make-up (can you say toxic?), and critiquing playwrights.

The more I looked at the other options, the more I understood why I had chosen English, but the more I looked at English, the worse my mental health became. The only answer left was to transfer to another college—one where I could graduate without a major (with an Associate's Degree). Yet where could I go? I couldn't go back to TVI[1]. It's a great school and I didn't need a major there, but I wouldn't feel safe and welcome at home. Lately it seemed so saturated

with anger and shouting. It felt like living in a room full of volatile explosives, like everything could blow up at any moment in time. Another option was to attend Eastern Arizona University, near where my best friend lives. They wouldn't require a major there, but that would also mean moving.

That's when my bishop [2] presented the answer. I could go to Utah Valley State College, just down the road in Orem. There no degree would be required. I couldn't believe that I hadn't thought of it sooner. Finally I had an answer that worked. Now I wouldn't have to wait until 2009 to graduate; most likely I would accrue all the remaining credits needed by the time I fulfilled their requirement for 20 residential hours.

Some might see this as a retreat, but I see it as progress. True, I will be leaving BYU, but I don't see it as giving up my dream. I fulfilled my dream. God knew it was important to me to attend BYU, and He blessed me with the ability to complete a full year here and gain what I needed to move on. However, my mental health

isn't worth sacrificing just so that I can have a Bachelor's Degree for the sake of having it. I'm so glad to have this weight off my shoulders and, more importantly, off my mind. I'm ready for the next chapter in my life.

Log Notes

[1] TVI refers to the Albuquerque Technical-Vocational Institute, now renamed Central New Mexico Community College (CNM). It consists of around five different campuses sprinkled throughout the Greater Albuquerque Area.

[2] A bishop is the leader or head of a particular ward. While a bishop is similar in office to a minister or a pastor in other Christian religions, the office is very distinct in that the bishop is not paid for his ecclesiastical service and does not necessarily preach from the pulpit every Sunday. Rather he presides over the ward, making sure that correct doctrine is taught by the members of that ward and "governs" the various sub-auxiliary organizations of the ward in their various policies and functions. In addition to presiding, the bishop has also been called as a judge in Israel, and, thus, judges, with the help of his counselors and other ward leaders, in matters concerning individual worthiness, offering counsel and assistance to the members of his ward as they face the various challenges and tribulations common to mortality. Another primary responsibility of the bishop is to oversee the ward's welfare program and help meet the temporal needs of people (both member *and* non-member) in the geographical

boundaries of his ward. Bishop is also the highest office in the Aaronic Priesthood. He thus has a special duty to watch over the spiritual development of the young men in his ward. It should be noted, however, that while this is true, bishops *also* hold the office of High Priest in the Melchizedek Priesthood.

Log Twenty–Nine – Oct 1, 2005

What a burden OCD is! Even when you are unaware of any specific fear, it is at work and it is at work to destroy. Oftentimes a wind of worry and anxiety will come out of nowhere and I won't know why. I just know that I'm worried—no, disturbed. My body is put on yellow alert, and I begin to fidget. My knee starts bouncing at an astounding speed. I cannot even guess how many times per second my leg shoots up and falls down. I hear strange noises in my head, which sound somewhat like: "Aiiiieee! Aiiiieee! Uheee! Ohhh!" It is the reverberations of words that I never hear constantly filling my head.

Tonight such a manifestation appeared. I was at general conference[1], listening to the words of a beloved prophet, along with the Twelve Apostles, and other general authorities from the Church. Yet my enjoyment in hearing the word of the Lord was disturbed once again by my OCD. I felt like screaming, both to declare my need for help and to drown out the rattlings and hiccuppings of my brain.

At these times it is particularly distressing because I don't know how to intervene in the name of sanity. There is no exposure possible when you are forced to fight an invisible enemy. All I know is that my brain is on fire, overheating. It is caught in a loop and cannot get out. It is expending amounts of energy that I sometimes muse could light an entire city for a week, if not a month.

As I was so vexed, I conjured up my own feeble cure. I would fill that noisy void with the toneless repetitions of the words the speaker was speaking. It was amazing how quickly my dismal attempt at first aid ended. In fact it backfired. Now I couldn't stop—not even for a minute. I had to repeat each and every syllable out loud in my mind. My efforts were adding to the fury of the subconscious gale. I wanted to bite into my tongue. No, I *yearned* desperately for the taste of blood to fill my mouth as I bit my own tongue off. However to my dismay, this wouldn't even affect a solution to my problem as I was not actually using my tongue to speak these words. It all was in my mind.

With added frustration, I wished I could harm myself, but I did not possess this luxury as I was in a public, ecclesiastical setting. I wanted to dig my fingernails into the palms of my hands. I would not stop until my hands were pouring out blood. I would keep digging until I forced open a hole through my hand. I wanted to grab my leg and hold it still. I would carve a firm handle into my leg so that I could hold my leg still. Then I would push down until the bones in my leg buckled under the pressure and caved in. Then I would be happy. Then it will have stopped. Of course it would come as no coincidence that I would have died at that same moment.

Log Notes

[1] General Conference refers to a special group of meetings held for 2 subsequent days every 6 months (in the beginning of April and in the beginning of October). They consist of sermons delivered by the general authorities and general officers of the Church of Jesus Christ of Latter-day Saints. The most notable speakers are the prophet (or president of the Church), his 2 counselors, and all the members of the Quorum of Twelve Apostles. While these meetings are actually held in the Conference Center on Temple Square in Salt Lake City,

UT, they are also broadcast to the many LDS chapels around the world, as well as via television, radio, and the internet. Herein testimony of the Lord Jesus Christ is born and instruction is given to the millions of LDS members around the world on matters of doctrine, teaching, policy, stewardship, and priesthood office. Conference is divided into six two-hour parts (or sessions)—Saturday morning, Saturday afternoon, Priesthood, Sunday morning, Sunday afternoon, and Relief Society/Young Women's. All are welcome to attend, both member and non-member alike.

Log Thirty – Oct 2, 2005

I have a few new exposures [1] I've been forgetting to mention. The first is to not eat everything that is on my plate or that is available at the cafeteria. Why would this be an exposure? There are many rules designed around eating. The first is you have to eat everything that is on your plate; lick that sucker dry. It's bad form to leave food on your plate. Society demands that you never waste food. Just think of all the work that the cook put into making that food that you're not eating. More importantly, think of all the children starving in Ethiopia. Why, just think of all the homeless people in your own town.

The second rule is that you have to get enough food to quantify a meal. You must be full when you are finished eating your meal. If you're not, then you'll go hungry, starve, and become just like those children in Africa. This holds true even if you are just one bite short. Of course, this rule beckons the question: How do I know when I've had enough? The answer is you can't, and as such, you must eat far past the time you are full.

You must eat until you start to hurt. That is the only way to really know.

The third rule is you have to get everything that you want or like. After all, should you fail to do so, you will not be able to consume another piece of pizza or bowl of tapioca ever again.

The fourth is to eat your money's worth. You paid for that Fresh Value Meal or that buffet or that plate at Red Lobster, as well as that cup of Sprite. Now you have to consume it all; otherwise you're just throwing your money (or someone else's) away.

The fifth (temporary and more optional) rule is that you must eat the foods that your body needs to operate well. You have to eat those vegetables on top of everything else or you have to eat those six bowls of fruit, so that you'll have healthy bones, good eyesight, and you won't be constipated.

This has given me plenty of work to do, but the exposures have been going really well. For the past month I have tried to make it a point to always leave something on my plate when I'm

done eating. Most of the time this means a couple of bites of something and that's all, but a couple of times I've left something totally untouched. Tonight, for instance, I got a bowl full of Cinnamon Toast Crunch (which I love) to end my meal, but then I recognized that I didn't really want to eat any of it. I just got it because I felt I *should* have it. So I decided to take advantage of the opportunity and take my tray with the whole bowl untouched back to the conveyor belt where the dishwashers were waiting.

Now someone was going to see that I got a bowl full of cereal and didn't lift my spoon up once. A couple of weeks ago I did a similar exposure. I bought a pizza for lunch with money from my own pocket, and when it came time that I was feeling in the direction of full, I threw away the quarter that I didn't even touch. A few days ago I threw out a three-pound bag of pretzels with one whole pound still remaining because I decided I really didn't want to eat it anymore. As a result, I've been feeling a good

deal better come the end of my meals than I have in a long time.

I've also had considerable success with the gum-tracing. I've had a couple slip-ups, but on the whole I haven't run my finger inside of my mouth to knock all the particles away for almost three weeks now. As a result, I've been feeling less socially conscious than before.

Success has been the byword of another exposure—my fear of bad breath. This fear owes a great part of its existence to a member of my family. Time and time again growing up, he would exclaim with exasperation, telling me that my breath smelled just like "dog *!@#". Often this appraisal was even given when I had just brushed my teeth two minutes earlier.

OCD has taken advantage of his 'tact', and ritualizing began to take the form of constantly chewing horribly tasting gum (because I couldn't betray Big Red to another gum whose likeability was completely unknown), as well as gum-tracing, breath-huffing, tight-jawing [2], hard-toothbrushing, liquid-swishing, spitting,

praying, checking, worrying, and maintaining an obsessively felt distance from those around me. So what's my exposure? I can't chew gum of any kind (and I have to throw all of my packages of Big Red in the trash to counter a money-wasting obsession). I can't swish water. I can't do gum-tracing. I can't brush my teeth extra-hard or extra-long. And I can't avoid social situations.

Finally I have also been making progress with re-reading. For six chapters now, I have been listening to Microsoft SAM read me MP3s of my science textbook. In so doing, I have, for the most part, been able to listen to each track all the way through, thus resisting the desire to stop or pause the track in order to facilitate my re-reading some part of the actual text, as well as the desire to rewind the track and re-listen to part of the tape. Now this would have been good progress even if I went back and re-read or re-listened to the textbook after I made my way through the entire chapter. Yes, it would have been progress in and of itself to get through a single chapter without any such ritualization. Still I wanted more progress than just this. I

wanted for me to have only read the chapter once, period.

I needed to see if this quick run-through was good enough. So I did the exposure, and then I went to class. What I didn't understand, I got through class notes and asking the teacher questions. After that, I didn't go back and read...ever. Even when the test came, I didn't go back and re-read the book. I read all of my notes once, memorized a couple of equations, and traipsed off to take the test. I don't know my grade yet, but I know I felt good about how I did. I did well in spite of only reading the chapters once. Hallelujah!

Log Notes

[1] Exposures are psychological exercises intended to help someone with OCD get better by assigning them to face (or expose themselves to) their fears and then assigning them to resist performing the ritual[s] that OCD will then compel them to complete in an effort to negate the effects of their previous therapeutic actions. Technically, the complete name designated to these exercises is Exposure and Response Prevention (or ERP). One component that is paramount if ERP is to produce any real, positive, lasting results—repetition. The patient

cannot get better without exerting enormous persistence in caring out each and every individual exposure over and over again. While the approach is rather simplistic, the positive power of its use is not to be underestimated. Similarly, if ERP is misused either out of a sense of domineering impatience or complete ignorance, the result can be extremely destructive in its misdirected, negative power. The best safe-guard against this consists of two, equally important steps. First is to have a competent psych specialist construct a pyramidal hierarchy of exposures that is based on the degree of distress that each deliberate, gradual step causes the individual. Second is to assign the individual to work from the bottom-up, slowly progressing from the lowest-level-anxiety exposures to the highest-level-anxiety exposures. Starting with the higher-level exposures is not advised, as these attempts at "flooding" will overwhelm the patient's ability to work through their fears and activate their brain's flight-or-fight responses. This will then elevate their feelings of peril and distrust toward the person administering the exposure and present yet another, greater obstacle to the patient's well-being and progress.

[2] 'Tight-jawing' is my personal description for my compulsion to clamp my jaw down so tightly that no breath can escape my mouth, so as to prevent those in my immediate physical presence (or sometimes just myself) from smelling my bad breath. This practice puts significant pressure on my teeth and jaw and is meant to produce the same degree of tightness that someone suffering from the 'lockjaw' associated with a severe tetanus infection would experience.

Log Thirty–One – Oct 4, 2005

It's winter now. Yes, I suppose to most people it's autumn. It's only October, and Halloween is still to come. The leaves remain green and do not yet possess their autumnal cornucopia of colors. It's raining, not snowing. However, I'm cold, and therefore it must be winter. Jack Frost is gently grasping my arm, chilling the very marrow of my bones.

My hands draw back in offense when they touch my 60° steering wheel. The goose-pimpled hair on my arm is standing with rigid erectness. There's the sound of a sniffle, and the cold migrates by, floating threateningly close as did the destroying angel over Ramses' Egypt.

Fortunately I am far more equipped to deal with this bother than ever before. I still cringe, but I persist onward with my life. Two years ago, I would say the usual repetitious prayer asking for forgiveness so that I wouldn't sink into my grave with the infection of a cold. To be accurate, though, I wasn't afraid of a cold; I was afraid of pneumonia and tuberculosis. Their peril was

equivalent to a cold...yes, just a mere common cold.

Every time I heard a cough or a sniffle, my body recoiled with fear. I would dance around the person so I wouldn't be required to shake their hand. Then I'd rush nonetheless to the bathroom to wash my hands and quite often the sleeves of my shirt, coat, or jacket. If I was sitting in a theatre and someone behind me coughed, I would sink down in my chair. I would scooch my arm down through my sleeve and I would madly start wiping away the germs from off my head and my neck, and in the process I would offend the person behind me.

When the children I tutored[1] would cough, I would pick up the bottle of evaporative soap and rub it on my hands and, when they were gone, wax the table and whatever other object had been contaminated with it. One day one of my students finally perplexedly asked why I was always washing my hands. I couldn't think of a suitable answer and changed the subject. All of my kids thought I was weird anyway.

Worse than any of this, though, was the sneeze. It would send a conglomeration of snot, saliva, and germs whisking through the air in all directions and splatter onto everything and everyone. I knew this was true because I had seen it on some hygiene filmette in sixth grade Biology. Commercials nowadays do a good job of propagating this truth ... no, more than truth, it was an image that got locked inside my memory and was played over and over again.

Then one night it happened. I was at a friend's house staying the night when all of a sudden his sister felt one coming on and turned directly to me. The putrid waterworks shot across the short distance of air between us and spewed itself all over my face. I rushed to their bathroom, but found little comfort there. The bathroom was a disgusting mess. Now I had to deal with tuberculosis *and* hepatitis. If my recollection is correct, that was the last time I ever stayed the night at his house.

Now the whole business is back... all but being sneezed at in the face. However, this time I won't wash, I won't wipe, and I won't pray.

When I was out to conference[2] on Saturday night, already dealing with all of the generalized anxiety, the person next to me coughed and sniffled. The sound was horrifying; I could see great long tendrils of snot hanging from his nostrils and falling onto my shoes. I could also feel the bitter sting of tuberculosis.

At first I didn't know what to do. On one hand, it was obvious—never touch that shoe again, at least not until I had thrown it inside the washing machine and then the dryer. Only then would it truly be safe and clean. On the other hand, though, I knew from past experience that doing so usually also ruined my shoes, what with all the chemicals, the water, the constant tumbling, the heat, and the grinding friction from all the other clothes pressing against them. Still, the shoe would be safe, clean, and sanitized. Yet I knew that I should resist. So I switched into ERP-mode[3]. I reached down and grasped my shoe, rubbing my hand over the "contaminated" area. Then, for extra measure, when no one was watching, I rubbed that hand over my jaw and

cheekbones. Finally, to really drive the message home, I finished it off by licking my lips.

Then yesterday, my teacher declared she was getting over some sickness. Of course, she said this *after* she had been handling my textbook, flipping through the Index to find an answer to my question. So I immediately made a mental note of where it had been touched and decided that I would never suffer myself to use the Index again. Yet I knew that I should resist. So I switched back into ERP-mode. I slid my hand along the closed pages and opened up the Index and rubbed my hands against the front and back of each infected page. Lastly, I wiped my hands over my face. Two hours later I had forgotten about the whole ordeal.

Log Notes

[1] From September 2002 to August 2003, I was employed by Rio Rancho Public Schools through AmeriCorps. During that school year, I worked with 1st, 3rd, and 4th graders at Ernest S. Stapleton Elementary School, tutoring them in reading and math. During the summer months, I subsequently tutored math

to the 8th graders attending summer school at Rio Rancho Mid-High School.

[2] Used here, 'conference' is simply the abbreviated version of 'general conference'.

[3] ERP-mode is a shortened term of my own creation to help indicate when I have entered into the process of an exposure.

Log Thirty–Two – Oct 7, 2005

Yesterday was a trying day. I was driving to the bank when I thought I felt my car wobbling. When I got to the bank, I looked at my tire, but I couldn't make up my mind whether it was flat or not. I accordingly went into the bank and asked one of the employees to come out and appraise my tire. He said it was flat, so I jumped back in my car and took it to the Tire & Lube Express at Wal-Mart. They looked it over, said they couldn't find any holes or punctures in the tire, and they filled it up to the right pressure.

Still they couldn't tell me why it had suddenly deflated overnight. I asked them again whether they had found any holes, and they said they didn't and my tire was fine. Not wanting to worry, I decided to take their word for it. I left feeling good that I was able to take care of the whole business pretty much on my own (besides the bank guy looking at my tire).

However, later when I related the story to my parents they both said that it wasn't fine and the tire's inexplicable deflation proved that there

was a leak in the tire and Wal-Mart was unskilled and incompetent when it came to finding a tire leak. They further said that this would mean my looking my tire over regularly to see if it was flat, and that I would probably have to fill it up a few times using the pressure pump at a gas station. This news completely wiped away all my earlier progress in handling the affair on my own. All that effort, it seemed, was now in vain. This also greatly distressed me because OCD would significantly limit my own ability to independently discern the pressure of my tire. Remember I had to have the bank worker come out and look at my tire for me to *positively know* that my flat tire actually was flat and that it wasn't all in my magnificent mind.

As I considered this news from my parents, I looked down at the offending tire with uncertainty. It already looked flat, but it also looked full. A more significant problem loomed. I would be forced to use a gas station's pressure gauge/pump. First problem—it was at a gas station. Second problem—I would have to touch the pressure pump. Third problem—I didn't

know how to use a pressure pump. Fourth problem—I would probably have to kneel on the asphalt of a gas station. Fifth (biggest) problem—I would have to touch my car tire. There was no way I was going to touch that tire. I didn't know all of the stuff that that tire had run over. Worse still, I *did know* some of the stuff that the tire had run over…like road-kill of more kinds than I care to name.

The second ordeal was reading my science textbook. I tried listening to the MP3s as usual, but I wasn't picking up a darned thing. It was describing the details of all these experiments that this scientist or that scientist did to prove the structure of the atom as we know it today. I decided the only thing to do was to read the book on my own. This turned out to be a huge mistake! I immediately got trapped re-reading. I read some sentences more than ten times. It took me between 2 and 2.5 hours to read 9.1 pages! Awww!

The third ordeal came on the heels of talking with my parents about the car. (I read my textbook in between taking my car to Wal-Mart

and talking with my parents.) As a result, I was significantly agitated, making what happened next so much worse than it would have been. I came into the house to eat dinner and get ready to go to the church for my calling [1] when I discovered my roommate chopping up raw meat...on what I can't remember. I just saw that raw meat and I rushed back out the door to sit on the steps of our stairwell. There was no way I was going to deal with that now. Just the sight of it had already compounded my anxiety.

No, I would sit on the steps until I could reach my bishop (who's become very much my father figure). I would tell him all about the tire and the meat, and he would reassure me that everything was going to be alright, and then I would go on about my business. However, I couldn't reach the bishop, so I sat outside in the mild cold waiting for about twenty minutes! By this time, that want had turned into a need. My anxiety had gone up every minute that I sat out there, performing the ritual of avoidance [2]. When I finally talked to him, though, he didn't give me that reassurance. Instead he was going to send

someone to get me and take care of me (how I didn't know).

This response further sent the message that my fears were valid and I needed someone else to intervene physically for my protection. Now I was caught between a rock and a hard place. I didn't want to bug someone else. I knew that I could handle the situation on my own. I just needed to summon up the resolve and the desire to go through something that I knew was going to be extra painful and unpleasant.

On the other hand, the fervor of my OCD was growing proportional to every minute of avoidance and reassurance-seeking[3]. Plus, the bishop wouldn't be able to reach someone else for help until he reached his destination twenty minutes from now. It was all so stupid! I didn't want to stand out in the cold, putting my life on hold for another twenty minutes, and I didn't want to involve someone else who would realize the kind of cowardly freak that I was. Now I couldn't just suddenly go into my house and face everything. I had brought the bishop and someone else into the whole thing, sending the

message that I couldn't do it without their help. I didn't want to be a liar.

So I waited for their response, each minute hating myself more and more. Finally the response came. I would go over to a friend's house and eat dinner there, so that I wouldn't have to worry about microwaving and eating my dinner in the contaminated confines of my own kitchen. I coiffed at the thought, not wanting to be such a burden to my friend, but I went, obliged to eat my whole dinner at their house, so that I would not appear to be the liar that I feared I was. Now my ritualizing had made me significantly late for my calling, had cost me the first twenty minutes of *Smallville*, and took away the tiny bits of respect that I allowed myself to possess. I felt terrible!

All of this had made it abundantly clear what I needed to do. I had known it for some time, but again was unwilling to face something so anxiety-provoking and painful.

I needed to uphold my already-been-assigned total ban (from Rogers) on

reassurance-seeking. I had let the ritual come into my life and take over, and I was tired of paying that price. I went in the house and wiped my hands over the entire counter space where my roommate had been cutting meat. Then I wiped them all over my face, a move that was trite in comparison to another exposure I had done a year earlier (actually touching the raw meat). Still I had exposed myself to my fear and prevented myself from both washing my hands and asking my roommate whether or not he had sanitized the area in question.

Unlike yesterday, though, today has gone well so far. I know what to do, and I'm doing it. I didn't call my mom to see whether I would sleep tonight even though I didn't wake up until 9:00 A.M. Plus, I didn't ask my one roommate whether or not the other one hated me. I've decided the number of my phone calls home and to the bishop are going to significantly decline, as most have been for reassurance purposes. I've also succeeded in leaving my fingernails alone when I wash my hands (as I've also fallen into deep, extreme fingernail-washing lately.) Finally,

I've also figured out a solution to my re-reading. I'll do what I had previously been doing; I'll listen once all the way through and then be done with it.

All in all, I have a pretty good feeling about today.

Log Notes

[1] Calling is another word for stewardship, which term is explained in greater detail in Log 25, Note 1. It's probably useful noting that at the time this entry was recorded, my specific calling was that of Ward Assistant Executive Secretary. Therein, it was my duty (or commission) to wait outside the bishop's office while he met one-on-one with various ward members.

[2] While most OCD rituals (or compulsions) center around what you do, they can also center around what you do *not* do. Avoiding what you're afraid of is just as obsessively carried out and cumbersomely maintained as other rituals. One example of this is someone waiting awkwardly in a public restroom for minutes on end until someone else either enters or leaves the restroom so he or she doesn't have to touch the doorknob for fear of 'catching' Hepatitis C. Another example is someone taking minutes to go around a grassy field when he or she could have simply spent seconds crossing the field directly in order to avoid walking on grass for fear of 'legions' of ants, ticks, and spiders 'charging' up his or her legs.

186

[3] Another common ritual, generally performed when you can't avoid your fear, is seeking reassurance from others. This compulsion is rather insidious because most people would never consider it to be such. Most kindheartedly go out of their way to answer an individual's questions and provide them with a sense of security. Indeed this ritual is extremely counter-intuitive since those without OCD, when given the simple reassurance that they need, are able to then dismiss the notion or fear and move on with their lives. Individuals with OCD, however, have a brain that does not follow conventional logic and, as such, fails to produce the same response and feeling of relief. Rather the affected person's brain generates the message that safety and calmness of mind can only come through asking someone the same question in multiple ways over and over again. For the patient and the friend, reassurance-seeking is an enormous challenge as the line distinguishing between giving and asking for reassurance and acquiring new, empowering data necessary to help the patient establish a correct and rational view of his or her world is extremely blurred. As such, it is critical for both the person with and the person without OCD to, when appropriate, seek out and maintain open lines of communication with the patient's doctor, so they can best help each other to recognize this line of distinction.

EpiLogue – Apr 7, 2013

"So whatever happened to this Gregory Gene Conrad that I've been reading about?" As I am preparing this book for publication (finally), this is the question that I've been told repeatedly that you, the reader, would want an answer to. While I understand this question in one sense, it seems strange and comes as a surprise on the other.

You see, this book was never really about me. If it had been, I never would have started this project to begin with. This book has always been about OCD—what it is, what it feels like, what drives a person to act so irrationally and so destructively. (At this point, I hope you understand that it's not a chosen preference or desired lifestyle.) What I have written is an insider's view—a glimpse into the mind of OCD and what drives a person who is unlucky enough to be attached to it. Think of it as a literary version of that perfectly tied set of shoes custom-made for someone with OCD and then altered just enough so that you (a person without OCD) can walk in them, at least for a little while.

My life and I only really serve as the backdrop to this story.

But that doesn't really answer your question.

Inasmuch as I have been very candid thus far, I will continue with that same open frankness. Life is still very much the same as it was when I finished writing this eight years ago. Every day is still a battle with OCD...and I'm not really sure if that will ever change. Sometimes I win more than I lose, and sometimes I lose more than I win.

My life is far different than I ever thought it would be growing up. I thought I'd have a college degree. I thought I'd have a career. I thought I'd be married and have a family. But none of those things are true. And I find this to be enormously distressing.

One of the most frustrating things I face is the question "What do you do?" It should be normal, routine, and innocuous. It's the most natural question in a world where we're almost always either introducing ourselves to someone new or giving status updates of one kind or

another to people we already know. The only real, honest answer that I have found so far is "I survive." I do my best to get from one moment to the next with as much sanity as I can possibly muster.

Having said that, though, I have been richly blessed with many wonderful friends, a healed relationship with a loving family, the strength of a firm knowledge of the gospel, a deep witness of the reality of my Lord and my God, and no shortage of miracles therefrom.

The most notable miracle has to do with babies. I can hold them. It took me roughly 27 years to do it, but I did it. More importantly, though, I now have a niece and two nephews. When the first was born, I was scared to death. It took me three months to touch him—a single touch of his forehead with the very tip of my right index finger. For Christmas that year, I gave him the only gift that I thought could possibly mean something to such a tiny creature. I gave him a real, honest-to-goodness, full hug.

Shortly thereafter the greatest miracle happened. I learned to love that baby. Now I can hold him, kiss him, play with him, crawl with him, hold his hand as he crosses the street, help him put on his shoes, and almost unreservedly love him with all my heart and soul. I can even hold and play with him when he has a dirty diaper, though my unabated preference still involves the lack of such pollutants attached to his body.

It astounds me that the brightest hope and the sweetest joy I feel today is when I am with those babies.

Guide to Log Topics (Index)

S

School
  Classes
      Dance, 43, 45
      English, 107-108, 121, 127,
          143, 156
      Religion, 31, 107-108
      Science, 107, 109, 122,
          127, 143, 169-170, 175,
          181
  Faculty, 11, 43, 45-46,
      155-156, 167, 170, 177
  Grading, 5, 43-44, 108-109,
      121, 131, 170
  Homework, 24, 31, 43,
      108-109, 122, 127-128,
      156, 169, 181
  K-12 (Public School), 6, 63,
      114, 131, 175
  Majors, 45, 108, 121, 127,
      155-159, 190
  Testing, 5, 43-44, 127, 143,
      170
  Transfer, 157-158
Searching (Lost Items), 44
Self-Harm, 1, 5, 41, 46, 63-64,
    104, 107, 134, 149-152, 156,
    162-163

Suicide, 70

T

Tardiness, 45-46, 147-148, 184
Technology
      Computers, 10, 12-13, 15,
          27-28, 56, 58, 84, 122,
          169
      Data Collection (Lists), 12, 16,
          101, 122
      File Management, 16, 27-28,
          32
      Media Collection (Hoarding),
          11, 84-85, 102
      Telephones, 46, 55, 101, 129,
          147, 181-183, 185
Terrorism (Analogy), 65-66
Tormentor (Analogy), 2-3, 5, 15,
    27, 62, 102, 111, 150

W

War (Analogy), 5, 15-16, 27
Weather, 1, 53-54, 173, 182-183
Writing, 31, 43, 61, 84, 108-109,
    122, 128, 155-157, 189-190

Made in the USA
Columbia, SC
01 November 2024

45495148R00115